ART NOUVEAU AND ART DECO
SILVER

ART NOUVEAU AND ART DECO
SILVER

ANNELIES KREKEL-AALBERSE

with 330 illustrations, 25 in colour

THAMES AND HUDSON

Main text and notes
translated from the Dutch
by Patricia Wardle

Printed and bound in Singapore by
C.S. Graphics

CONTENTS

Though this book is the result of almost a decade of research about ACKNOWLEDGMENTS
modern silver from 1880 to 1940, its complicated but fascinating
subject matter ensures that no study can ever be final. Many new
discoveries about designers, silversmiths and their international
contacts and influences can be expected following further research.
Indeed, I hope that any lacunae in my own publication will encourage
others to attempt more investigation.

Certainly, any imperfection that remains in the present book is due
to my own shortcomings and not to the many friends, collectors and
museum curators who provided me with valuable suggestions and
information. R. Baarsen, Amsterdam; J. ter Molen and I. Tirion,
Rotterdam; S. Barten, Zurich; L. Daenens, Ghent; P. Glanville,
E. Turner, R. Edgecombe, S. Hare and D. Beasley, London;
G. Dietrich, Cologne; K.B. Heppe, Düsseldorf; R. Joppien, Hamburg;
R. Sänger and P. Schmitt, Karlsruhe; E. Schmuttermeier, Vienna –
all have contributed in various ways to the book.

Tom Haartsen skilfully tackled the difficult task of providing
photographs from private collections.

Lastly, I am particularly grateful to two friends in the Dutch
'Zilverclub': Mr K.A. Citroen, the first to collect Art Nouveau silver,
was in the beginning my guide to the complicated field of artists' and
makers' marks; and Mr W.A. Hofman carefully read my manuscript,
making valuable constructive criticisms, which helped to eliminate
ambiguities in the original.

INTRODUCTION
SILVER AND THE MODERN MOVEMENT
1880-1940

I N 1929 an article in *The Studio* declared, 'Ever since the silver industries and their associates in the fields of similar metals and merchandise have developed their mediums for production, to meet the standards for mass production, their only aim has been to copy the looks and finesse of the hand-made pieces with one of their machines.'[1] These lines were written after almost fifty years of struggle against the production of badly executed machine-made silver objects in historical styles. Ornament that had been done by hand in previous centuries was copied and applied to machine-made objects in imitation of traditional forms.

In the last decades of the nineteenth century idealistic individuals, such as William Morris in Britain, Siegfried Bing in France and Henry van de Velde in Belgium, reacted against the low standards of cheap, mass-produced imitations and aimed to improve their quality. For Morris it was partly a question of reviving the old crafts. Bing, on the other hand, first cultivated a broad interest in the new art from Japan and later sold high-quality goods in a new style. Van de Velde's contribution was to design furniture and other domestic items to be produced in small series. As is well known, these initiatives helped to create a movement for the renewal of ornament and forms in the applied arts, the results of which are of great interest to collectors and design historians today.

This movement, however, itself exhibited two seemingly opposite styles until well into the 1930s, one of which is called 'decorative', the other 'geometrical'. The advocates of the decorative style rejected the use of machines, because the division of labour inherent in machine-production was liable to result in the loss of traditional craft skills. New art schools were established and workshops were founded to

Silversmiths at work *c.* 1895 in J.M.
van Kempen's factory in Voorschoten,
the Netherlands.

improve designs and revive the old crafts. Modern-looking, asymmetrical, naturalistic ornament was introduced as an appropriate decoration. At first this ornament was applied to traditional shapes, in   II
continuation of the nineteenth-century idea that this enhanced the
aesthetic value of an object. As naturalistic ornament became more
and more stylized, it developed into a strong curvilinear style, away
from the imitation of nature. The two trends in the decorative style,
the naturalistic and the curvilinear, are the first phases of what is
generally known as Art Nouveau.

In countries where art education played a major role, a new
generation of craftsmen emerged, leading after 1905 to a second
phase of Art Nouveau, in which the curvilinear style developed into a
plastic, abstract, individualistic style. The marvellous hand-made
objects to which this gave rise – few compared with the vast quantity
of factory-made goods – were to have no impact on silver production
and faded away during the thirties. The newly founded workshops,
such as Charles Robert Ashbee's Guild of Handicraft in England,
Bing's Maison de l'Art Nouveau in France and Osthaus's Hagener
Silberschmiede in Germany, were all short-lived experiments, lasting
for only a few years. They could not survive, because they lacked
continuing support from idealistic financiers. With their carefully
hand-made objects they could not compete with the quantities of
serially produced silverware. Only Jensen's in Denmark, one of the
last of these workshops to be founded, survived the difficult starting
period. This firm managed to keep going during the crisis of the
thirties and is still in existence.

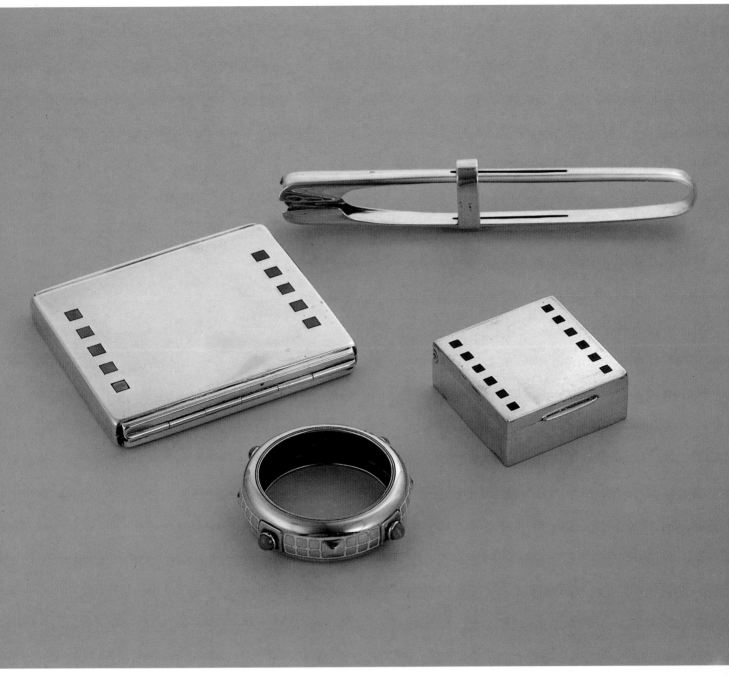

I Background: green enamelled cigarette-case and sealing-wax holder. Maker's mark: Georg Adam Scheid, Vienna. Imported into the Netherlands *c.* 1906. Width of cigarette-case: 8 cm (3¼ in.). Length of sealing-wax holder: 12.5 cm (5 in.). Foreground: napkin-ring set with amethysts and enamelled pillbox to match cigarette-case. Maker's mark: C.J. Begeer, Utrecht, *c.* 1906 and 1909. Diameter of napkin-ring: 5.7 cm (2¼ in.). Width of pillbox: 4.4 cm (1¾ in.). All items in private collection.

II Example of the naturalistic style of around 1900. Tea caddy. Maker's mark: C.J. Begeer, Utrecht, 1895. Height: 11 cm (4¼ in.). Private collection.

III The geometrical style of around 1900, exemplified by a tea caddy with brown, yellow and cream enamel, designed by Jan Eisenloeffel. Maker's mark: C.J. Begeer, Utrecht, 1906. Height: 9 cm (3½ in.). Private collection.

III

IV The Japanese influence, 1900–25.
An *inro* made into a vanity case.
Maker's mark: Louis Kuppenheim,
Pforzheim, *c.* 1925. Length: 8.5 cm
($3\frac{1}{4}$ in.). A belt buckle in the shape of
a sword guard. Maker's mark: E.
Cardeilhac, Paris, *c.* 1900. Height:
6.5 cm ($2\frac{1}{2}$ in.). The use of different
metals in one object: a gunmetal box
incorporating silver. Diameter: 5 cm
(2 in.). A cloak clasp with a
grasshopper with gold-encrusted
wings, designed and made by Henri
Husson and sold by H. Hébrard,
Paris, *c.* 1900. Width: 16 cm ($6\frac{1}{4}$ in.).
Cigarette-case. Maker's mark: Johann
Rothbauer, Vienna, *c.* 1900. Width:
11 cm ($4\frac{1}{4}$ in.). Private collection.

V 'Magnolia' vase with *plique à jour*
enamel border. Maker's mark:
Philippe Wolfers, Brussels, 1905.
Signed 'P. Wolfers. Ex. unique'.
Height (without pedestal): 12.5 cm
(5 in.). Museum voor Sierkunst,
Ghent.

V

The other style reflecting a renewal of the applied arts, the geometrical, shows a different development. Its advocates accepted as a fact of life the use of machines to produce whatever people wanted them to make. They were of the opinion that independent artists with an understanding of the workings of the machines to be used should be asked to design plain forms appropriate to modern production methods. Simple, inconspicuous ornament, emphasizing I,III geometric forms, was to be the key. The style that developed from this thinking was the precursor of the geometrical style of the twenties, based on cubes, cylinders, rectangular prisms and spheres, and of the modernism of the thirties.

In some European countries, particularly in Germany, developments in both the decorative and the geometrical style were interrupted by the First World War. In neutral countries, such as Denmark and the Netherlands, the economy was unaffected and silversmiths executed some of their most elaborate and expensive pieces during and shortly after the war.

INFLUENCES Japanese art strongly influenced both styles. The decorative style was IV influenced by the choice, application and arrangement of naturalistic

The curvilinear style of around 1900. Silver-gilt sugar sifter designed by Edward Colonna and executed in Siegfried Bing's workshop. Maker's mark: S. Bing Art Nouveau, Paris, 1900. Length: 14.5 cm (5¾ in.). Museum für angewandte Kunst, Cologne. Photograph: Rheinisches Bildarchiv, Cologne.

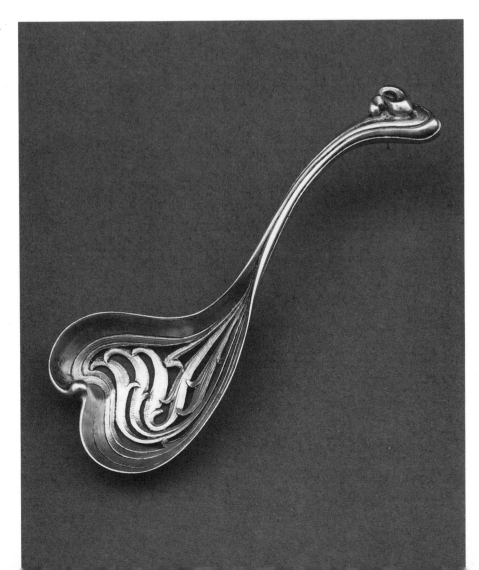

motifs, such as flowers or birds. The combination of different materials such as gold or silver encrusted on to other metals, which originated in Japan, was also taken up. Even some characteristically Japanese objects, such as *inros*, were 'translated' into the fashionable vanity-cases of the twenties. Designers in the geometrical style adopted the simple forms and wicker-covered handles.

Apart from these Japanese influences, the decorative style in each country showed characteristics of more local cultural traditions: Indian ornament in America, Celtic in Britain and Viking in Scandinavia. In addition, more geometric forms and ornament were inspired by Egyptian and Greek art of the kind that could be seen in all the important archaeological museums. In the twenties, moreover, ornament was influenced by Eastern European folk art and African art.

If the sources of inspiration were diverse, there was also another development that helped to display them. For the first time, from the end of the nineteenth century, printed reproductions of photographs could be widely disseminated. Art magazines were founded in all

Tea service. Design attributed to Christopher Dresser. The shapes are based on those of Japanese wine jars. Maker's mark: Hukin & Heath. Tea-kettle and stand marked 'Birmingham 1895', the other pieces marked 'London 1894 and 1891'. Height of kettle (with stand): 23.5 cm (9¼ in.). Private collection.

Western countries. The first and most influential was *The Studio*. It was first published in 1893 in London and was soon to be followed by Austrian, French and German equivalents. Readers all over the world could be informed about exhibitions and artists and their work.

EXHIBITIONS Just over a hundred years ago, in 1888, the first Arts and Crafts Exhibition took place in London, showing new craft products. Many exhibitions followed, in a variety of countries, until the outbreak of the Second World War, the most important being the World's Columbian Exposition in Chicago in 1893, the Exposition Internationale in Paris in 1900, the Esposizione Internazionale in Turin in 1902, the Louisiana Purchase Exhibition in St Louis in 1904, the Exposition Internationale des Arts Décoratifs et Industriels Modernes in Paris in 1925 and the Exposition Internationale des Arts et Techniques in Paris in 1937. The development in both the decorative and the geometrical style in silver can be followed clearly in these exhibitions.

82,83   Europeans visiting the Chicago exhibition of 1893 were surprised
85,89   by the originality of the naturalistic ornament on American silverwork and bought examples to show to their fellows in the Old World. Many visitors from outside the United States were expecting that the new decorative style, characterizing the beginning of the twentieth century, would come from America, whose inhabitants – so it was said at the time – 'have nothing behind them, have no models to copy'.[2]

Examples of the decorative style in silver in the twenties. From Tony Bouilhet's *L'Orfèvrerie française au 20ème siècle*.

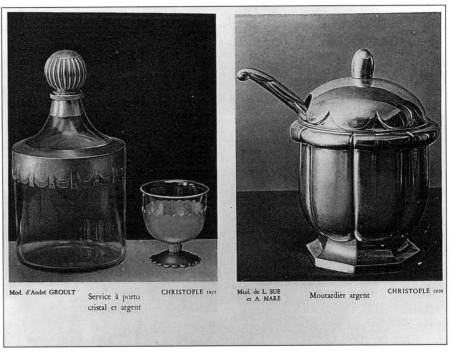

Mod. d'André GROULT   Service à porto cristal et argent   CHRISTOFLE 1925   Mod. de L. SUE et A. MARE   Moutardier argent   CHRISTOFLE 1920

In the silverwork shown in Paris in 1900 the different trends could
already be distinguished: the decorative style, both naturalistic and
curvilinear, and the geometrical. The naturalistic style went into
decline shortly after 1900, because the market became flooded with
mass-produced objects with naturalistic ornament imitating the
costly, early hand-made examples. More promising for the future,
however, was the geometrical style found in a small group of silver
objects designed by Jan Eisenloeffel and made by the firm of Hoeker
in Amsterdam. These exhibits showed simple forms decorated with
straight lines and enamelled chequered borders.

At the exhibition in Turin two years later, more countries showed
objects in the geometrical style, with its plain, logical forms, which
were so suitable for mechanical production. While these were the
precursors of the modernistic designs of the late twenties and the
thirties, in the early twentieth century the idea of designing objects in
simple forms with modest decoration that could be made by machines
still seemed innovative, despite the fact that more than twenty years
earlier Christopher Dresser had made the first simple, geometrical
industrial designs in Britain.

The Louisiana Purchase Exhibition in St Louis in 1904 offered
Americans an opportunity to compare the various trends in the
applied arts from European countries such as France, Germany and
the Netherlands with those of the United States.

Just as Art Nouveau, which was originally only one of many names
varying from country to country or even region to region, is the
general name later applied to the pre-First World War styles, so Art
Deco, derived from the title of the Paris Exhibition of 1925, is the
equivalent term for those of the twenties and thirties. The Paris

The geometrical style of the twenties
exemplified by a coffee and tea
service. Maker's mark: Boulenger et
Cie, Paris, c. 1930. Height of coffee
pot: 20.5 cm (8 in.). Width of tray:
61.5 cm (24¼ in.). Sotheby's, Monaco,
5 April 1987, no. 218.

Exhibition showed a new approach by a new generation of artists. In the decorative style the old asymmetry was replaced by accentuated symmetrical ornament, such as bouquets of flowers, garlands of roses or fountains, applied to architectural forms. Much of the hand-made silver was executed in supple, round, flowing forms and had a hand-hammered finish as its sole decoration. The geometrical style comprised silverwork with heavy geometric forms in a well-balanced modern style. In these designs finding solutions to questions of basic form seemed more important than solving decorative problems.

The Paris Exhibition of 1937 showed that stylized ornament, straight lines and angular forms were now outdated. Fluent curves and plain forms predominated, with a hammered surface when hand-made. Some welcomed mechanical production and had sought to improve its efficiency by reducing the number of separate parts necessary to form hollow-ware (for example, a teapot assembled from

Advertisement for silver from the thirties.

four instead of twelve components, retaining its fine shape). In this steady progress towards efficient form and function the designer, working daily with machines, had 'the key to the language of machines, the language of the future', as an article in the *Nieuwe Rotterdamsche Courant* declared in 1927.[3] At last people had learned to work with machines and achieved a new art resulting from the harmony of technique and object.

In spite of this achievement, production of silver in the modern style remained a sideline for silver factories in the various countries. Christofle in France, Bruckmann, Koch & Bergfeld and Wilkens in Germany, Michelsen in Denmark, Elkington and Mappin & Webb in England, Gorham and Tiffany in the United States, Begeer and Van Kempen in the Netherlands all tried to sell modern designs, but found that it was impossible to survive commercially without traditional styles.

At last machines were able to turn out pieces of beauty, but such pieces were used only by the intellectual avant-garde. The introduction of this beauty into daily life was to be accomplished in the forties and fifties with a different metal, stainless steel. But if modernism was not a generally accepted style before 1945, today we can appreciate to the full its early achievements in silver, which are now avidly collected.

NOTES

1   Peter Müller-Munk, 'Machine-Hand', *The Studio*, October 1929, Vol. 98, p. 709.
2   See, for example, Diana Chalmers Johnson, *American Art Nouveau*, p. 36.
3   C.J.A. Begeer, *Nieuwe Rotterdamsche Courant*, 12 July 1927.

1

GREAT BRITAIN

ALTHOUGH the movement for a renewal in the applied arts originated in Britain, the continental European Art Nouveau, Jugendstil and Secession style of around 1900 never became popular there. Exuberant floral ornament and curvilinear abstract decoration were seldom used. Instead, surfaces were hammered and decorated with enamel and semi-precious stones, Celtic ornament or stylized leaf motifs. After 1905 Britain's leading role in the renewal of the applied arts was played out. Silversmiths devoted to their craft often found it difficult to take the step towards the modern, smooth, angular forms from France and Germany that conquered the world in the twenties.

THE AESTHETIC MOVEMENT

As the cradle of the industrial revolution, Britain was a prosperous nation in the nineteenth century. The middle classes were able earlier than those in other European countries to spend more money than ever before on luxury goods. However, the way in which such objects were made and the ornament used on them were a thorn in the flesh of a number of 'aesthetically-minded' artists. Their criticisms eventually led to their bringing some order into the 'High Victorian' interior of the last decades of the nineteenth century.

In Owen Jones's influential book *The Grammar of Ornament*, published in December 1856, examples were given in twenty chapters of the most widely divergent ornament, from those of 'Savage Tribes' to 'Leaves and Flowers from Nature', but as yet there was no mention of Japanese ornament. Interest in this arose only after the International Exhibition held in London in 1862, the first person in England to write about it being the architect William Burges, who was particularly struck by the daring asymmetrical ornament resulting from the 'Japanese horror of regularity'.[1]

Some of the objects at the exhibition were afterwards sold at Farmer & Rogers' Oriental Warehouse in London, of which Arthur Lasenby Liberty became the manager. In 1875 he opened his own shop, Liberty & Co., which is still to be found in London's Regent Street today. Many leading artists, such as William Morris, James Abbott McNeill Whistler and John Ruskin, were among his customers. Christopher Dresser, who was one of the few designers actually to visit Japan, also had a shop of his own at that time. Japanese influence is clearly visible in much of his metalwork, not only in the design itself, but also in the rational way in which the objects are made. In most of the silver factories in England, however, Japanese influence was confined to engraved motifs in the Japanese style: exotic plants, butterflies and other insects, cranes and peacocks, while finials and handles often took the form of bamboo canes.

The Aesthetic Movement, the contemporary catchword for all those who adhered to this new aesthetic in England, led to a deliberate revival in decorative art. What was wanted was a new art for the coming new century and an end to looking back to the past. Nature must be taken as the starting-point, not careful copies of nature, but nature seen from the point of view that 'the basis of all form is geometry . . . the result is symmetry and regularity'.[2]

THE ARTS AND CRAFTS MOVEMENT

The second movement that had its origin in nineteenth-century Britain was the Arts and Crafts Movement. The impulse behind this was the awareness of the often very bad working conditions of factory workers. Idealistic reformers such as John Ruskin and William Morris did not envisage that it might be possible to control technology, but hoped to be able to solve many of the social problems by bringing back good hand-work. A designer ought himself to know the possibilities and limitations of the material with which he was working and this, in Morris's view, could only be learned in practice. If factory production was unavoidable, then the factories must be sited in beautiful surroundings, so that people could enjoy working in them. In order to realize these ideals, education courses in the applied arts were organized in various cities.

The foundation of the Arts and Crafts Exhibition Society was also an important contribution to the dissemination of British ideas about design and decorative art. The exhibitions organized by the Society from 1888 onwards attracted attention both at home and abroad.

English artists who travelled to the United States, such as Charles Robert Ashbee, stimulated the foundation there of similar societies, which propagated the Arts and Crafts ideals in the New World. The German architect Hermann Muthesius, who lived in London for seven years, after being commissioned by the Prussian Government to report on developments in the fields of architecture and the applied arts, introduced the new ideas into Germany.

Although the modern applied art movement originated in the two above-mentioned movements, continental European Art Nouveau – if one defines this as a style based on supple, asymmetrical curving lines derived from more or less stylized naturalistic motifs – never became established in Britain. Art Nouveau or Jugendstil was regarded there as a 'strange decorative disease.'[3]

CHRISTOPHER DRESSER

The first person in England to design really new forms for the silver industry was Christopher Dresser (1834–1904). As early as 1873 he wrote, 'The first aim of the designer of any article must be to render the object which he produces useful.'[4] He was born in Glasgow, studied at the School of Design at Somerset House in London, took a course under the botanist Dr John Lindley and was appointed teacher of botany at the Department of Science and Art, South Kensington, in 1854. In 1876 he visited the International Exhibition at Philadelphia and delivered three different lectures, in which he put forward recommendations for improvements in American art industry. Then he went to Japan for a visit of three months. He returned to England via China with a large number of Japanese objects, which were sold at Tiffany's in New York and Londos & Co. in London.

Dresser's first silver designs were executed in 1878 by J.W. Hukin & J.T. Heath in Birmingham and London. Not only, however, did he supply designs to other well-known firms, such as James Dixon & Sons of Sheffield and F. Elkington & Co. of Birmingham, but also sold his designs to foreign firms, such as Boin-Taburet in Paris. In making designs for silver he took account of the fact that 'if the designer forms works which are expensive, he places them beyond the reach of those who might otherwise enjoy them'.[5] Costly materials must be worked in an economical way. Thus he used light, thin plates of silver for forms which were afterwards strengthened at salient points by a rim or an angle, so that they would keep their shape. Dresser was also one of the few at that time who was capable of designing three-dimensional objects in widely differing materials. 'He has proved that an artist may so master the materials and the processes of manufacture that he can project himself to the potter's wheel, the loom, the

1,2,3

metal-smith's forge, or the calico printer's and evolve beautiful and novel things in the most perfect accord with the process that is destined to translate them into being.'[6] He was for many years the only person in England to supply the silver manufacturers with designs for simple, undecorated useful objects. His designs based on stereometric forms, lozenges, triangles, cubes and spheres, anticipate the functional forms of the twenties and thirties.

LONDON SILVERSMITHS

The Arts and Crafts influence was particularly strong on silver. Gilbert Marks; Charles Robert Ashbee, the founder of the Guild of Handicraft; Nelson Dawson, the founder of the Artificers' Guild; Edward Spencer; John Paul Cooper; Alexander Fisher; Omar Ramsden and Alwyn Carr, all of London, each had his own recognizable style. What they all had in common was that they emphasized the craft aspect of their work by letting the hammer blows remain visible. These are unavoidable on pieces raised by hand, but are very easy to remove, as is obvious from smooth eighteenth-century silver. These London silversmiths enjoyed the financial support of wealthy patrons, but because their methods were expensive, they were not in a position to make good objects for a wide public. Under their influence the younger generation of silversmiths also continued to work in this manner into the thirties.

Gilbert Leigh Marks (1861–1905) was apprenticed at the firm of Johnson, Walker & Tolhurst. He set up on his own as a silversmith in 1885, but did not register a maker's mark at Goldsmiths' Hall until 1896. He was chiefly renowned for his tazzas and dishes with embossed naturalistic flowers, which seem strongly inspired by Baroque silver of the second half of the seventeenth century. The salmon on the rim of the dish illustrated are also borrowed from seventeenth-century models, but the open and closed tulips on the candlesticks of 1900, with the stylized leaves over the node, stem and foot, were clearly designed under the influence of his contemporaries.

4,5

In contrast to Marks, Charles Robert Ashbee (1863–1942) began as an architect. He had a good knowledge of the theoretical aspects of silversmithing and had translated Benvenuto Cellini's *Trattato del'Oreficeria* and *Trattato della Scultura* for the metalworkers of the Guild of Handicraft 'to bring home the methods and practice of the goldsmith of the Renaissance'. Ashbee was a gifted modeller and designer, but seldom finished anything himself. In *Modern English Silverwork* he wrote of his collaboration with William Hardiman: 'We often worked on the wax or the metal together, after I had completed the design, but his touch was more delicate and sure than mine.'

VII

The first silversmith Ashbee took on after founding the School of Handicraft in 1887 and the Guild a year later was John Pearson. He became the first teacher there of hammering, modelling and chasing, the most important techniques for a silversmith. In his above-mentioned book Ashbee named John Williams, W.A. White and William Hardiman as the first pupils. He considered the last of these to be a good modeller, as was Arthur Penny. Other silversmiths he mentioned are J.K. Bailey, G.H. Hart, W. Mark, G. Horwood and Alec Miller. Because (as Ashbee put it) 'the craftsman should continually check and control and answer to the designer', it is not possible, or scarcely so, to establish who was responsible for which design. Thus it is rightly stated in *The Studio* of November 1899 that 'the work to which the name of Mr Ashbee is attached ought to be regarded less as his individual work than as that of the Guild of Handicraft in its collective capacity'. After the Guild of Handicraft's silver had been discussed in *The Studio* for the first time in 1895, it won great renown both nationally and internationally. For example,

Sporting cup designed by Charles Robert Ashbee and executed by Arthur Cameron and J. Bailey. From *The Studio*, April 1900.

Selection of silverware from an advertisement in *The Studio*, September 1904. The tea caddy is illustrated on p. 208.

various silver objects decorated with marigolds were made for a Dr Mandello of Pressburg (now Bratislava).

In 1902 all the members of the Guild moved with their families to Chipping Campden, in Gloucestershire. This was the beginning of the end, even though their work was exhibited all over Europe and both their objects and their ideas were a source of inspiration to many in the rest of Europe and the United States. Because of increasing competition from firms which produced more cheaply, heavy financial losses were incurred and in 1907 the Guild was forced to go into liquidation. Thus Ashbee lamented in 1909, 'An artist under the conditions of Industrialism has no protection, any tradesman can steal his design.'[7] Under the influence of discussions with the American architect Frank Lloyd Wright, whom he had met several times, both in America and England, Ashbee wrote in 1910, 'Modern civilization rests on machinery, and no system for the encouragement or the endowment of the teaching of the arts can be found that does not recognize this.'[8] These thoughts are in accord with the ideas of the Deutscher Werkbund, which had been founded in 1907, and with them Ashbee adopted one of the basic rules of the modern movement, even though he himself never put them into practice.

Ashbee's interest in silverwork of past centuries comes out in prize cups with cast caryatids and carefully modelled figurative stems. His designs for flatware are also based on such seventeenth-century models as seal-top and rat-tail spoons. Characteristic of his designs is the use of bent silver wire for handles, finials and nodes. In these one finds something of the curved, elongated, whip-lash lines which were becoming popular in continental Europe under the influence of Henry van de Velde. Another conspicuous characteristic of Guild of Handicraft silver is the copious use of enamel, often by Arthur Cameron and Fleetwood C. Varley, cabochon-cut semi-precious stones and mother-of-pearl. These ideas were soon copied by other English silversmiths.

Like Ashbee, Nelson Dawson (1859–1942) trained as an architect, but felt more attracted to painting and silversmithing. After learning enamelling from Alexander Fisher, he set up his own workshop, in which his wife enamelled most of the objects he made. In 1901 he founded the Artificers' Guild, which was taken over only two years later by Montague Fordham, a successful businessman who had previously been director of the Birmingham Guild of Handicraft. After 1914 Dawson devoted himself entirely to painting.

Edward Spencer (1872–1938) succeeded Nelson Dawson as principal designer to the Artificers' Guild. He combined silver with all sorts of other materials, such as ivory, shagreen, wood, mother-of-pearl and coconut. The Artificers' Guild, one of the few guilds to be a

11

Bonbonnière. Maker's mark: Artificers' Guild, London, 1936. Height: 8 cm (3¼ in.). Private collection.

commercial success, survived until 1942. In contrast to the work of, for example, Omar Ramsden, Edward Spencer's designs for the Guild moved with the times. The work of John Paul Cooper and Henry Wilson, both of whom worked at J.D. Sedding's architectural practice in London, was also sold there.

14   John Paul Cooper (1869–1933) began silversmithing in 1897 under the influence of Henry Wilson. He was taught by one of the latter's assistants, so that his work is often difficult to distinguish from Wilson's. It is strongly architectural in form. In 1900 *The Studio* was already waxing enthusiastic about his 'refined work in shagreen'.[9] He taught at the Birmingham School of Art from 1904 to 1907, but afterwards devoted himself entirely to silversmithing.

Alexander Fisher (1864–1936) was originally a sculptor, but made his name principally as an enameller. He had studied enamelling techniques during a visit to France and it was already acknowledged in 1899 that much was owed to him for his initiative in promoting the art.[10] Many silversmiths, from other countries as well, learned enamelling from him and no other silversmith contributed so much to its development, both as teacher and author.

Henry Wilson (1864–1934) embarked on silversmithing after 1890. Around 1895 he set up a workshop of his own and taught at the

Central School of Arts and Crafts in London. There he met Alexander Fisher, with whom he collaborated for a short time. He also taught at the Royal College of Art. In 1903 he published *Silverwork and Jewellery*, which is still regarded as one of the best handbooks on the subject. The work he sent in to the Paris Exhibition of 1925 was among the most important in the English Pavilion.

Omar Ramsden (1873–1939) and Alwyn C.E. Carr (1872–1940) were fellow-students at the School of Art in Sheffield. Together they travelled through Belgium, France, Italy, Switzerland and Germany and in 1898 had a joint maker's mark officially registered in London. They continued to work together until the outbreak of the First World War. After Carr's return in 1919, however, he set up on his own as a silversmith.

Although many of their objects are inscribed OMAR RAMSDEN & ALWYN C.E. CARR MADE ME or OMAR RAMSDEN ME FECIT, it is certain that Ramsden soon stopped making anything himself.[11] He was everywhere recognized in his day as an important silversmith and praised for his rich forms and ornament, yet most of the objects of before the First World War appear to have been made after designs by Alwyn Carr, who also had an important share in the financing of the workshop, which they named after St Dunstan, the patron saint of silversmiths. The various outstanding chasers, engravers and designers who worked there had all been trained in the workshop.

Inkpot with embossed masks of comedy and tragedy between oval plaques of mother-of-pearl. Maker's mark: Omar Ramsden & Alwyn Carr, London, 1912. Height: 7 cm (2¾ in.). Private collection.

Ramsden himself was not willing to admit it, but only a few of the objects were made entirely by hand, despite the 'hand-made look'. For instance, in an advertisement in *The Studio* of January 1929 he recommended his 'Silver of Distinction for Gifts and Presentation' with the words 'Specially designed and well-made original work at much the same cost as multiple reproduction.' His customers were not allowed to get the impression that labour-saving moulding techniques were used. The objects are often decorated with Tudor roses and chased texts, which constitute a highly decorative element. Both in the choice of the type of object, mazer bowls, for example, and that of ornament, they hark back to fifteenth- and sixteenth-century models. It is notable that the earliest objects for domestic use were sometimes

7   executed in the Art Nouveau style, but the later work is sometimes very stereotyped, with the same ornaments often being used in different combinations. Because Ramsden and Carr were able to make objects that appealed to the taste of the most widely differing customers, they were the most important exponents of the Arts and Crafts Movement in English silver.

H.G. Murphy (1884–1939) was trained by Henry Wilson at the Central School of Arts and Crafts in London. After having worked for some years in Emil Lettré's workshop in Berlin, he set up in London in 1913. His workshop was at 'The Sign of the Falcon', which is why his silver bears not only his maker's mark, but also that bird. His style developed out of the Arts and Crafts tradition, the objects being made

13   largely by hand in contemporary modern forms. He carried out not only his own designs, but also some by the sculptor and typographer Eric Gill and the designer R.M.Y Gleadowe. Some of his own designs, with wide S-shaped fluting or vertical folds are reminiscent of designs of the twenties from Germany and Austria.

Charles Boyton (1885–1958) applied himself from 1930 onwards to making contemporary objects, at first in his father's firm and from

12   1934 as an independent silversmith. Sometimes his work seems to have been inspired by silver by Georg Jensen of Copenhagen. For example, he designed a set of cutlery which is closely related to the famous and successful Pyramid pattern designed by Harald Nielsen for Jensen in 1926.

BIRMINGHAM SILVERSMITHS   Although Birmingham was more of a centre for the silver industry than for hand-work, the influence of the Arts and Crafts Movement was clearly visible there, through the Central School of Art in Margaret Street and the Vittoria Street School for Jewellers and Silversmiths, where one of Morris's assistants, Robert Catterson-

Smith, was director and both John Paul Cooper and Arthur Gaskin taught.

Bernard Cuzner (1877–1956) was a pupil of Arthur Gaskin. He worked as an independent silversmith in Birmingham, making some objects for Liberty's of London around 1900. From 1910 onwards he was head of the Department of Metalwork at the Central School of Art in Birmingham. He made fine one-off pieces to commission for churches, government bodies and private individuals and also produced simple designs for silver firms, setting high standards in decoration and finish.   16

A.E. Jones (1879–1954) studied at Birmingham's Central School of Art. In 1902 he set up a silver department at his father's smithy. Like that of the other Arts and Crafts silversmiths, his work had a lightly hammered surface, but this was combined with beautiful interlaced or pierced rims. Sometimes his designs are reminiscent of those of Liberty's, which were also executed in Birmingham.   15

A Guild of Handicraft was established in Birmingham in 1890, with Montague Fordham as its first director. Five years later it was compelled to expand. The architect and silversmith Arthur Dixon was its most important designer. This guild was more commercially-minded and despite its motto, 'By hammer and hand', the use of the lathe was not automatically ruled out. While the Guild of Handicraft in London concentrated on the production of luxury objects, simpler articles were made in Birmingham. A catalogue of 1910 states, 'In the purely ornamental part of the Guild's work machinery plays no part; but in the constructional parts the most perfect and scientific accuracy is guaranteed.'[12] In contrast to most of the objects made by the Guild, the muffin dish illustrated does not have a hammered surface. The   18 Birmingham Guild's silver is characterized by simple, honest forms, generally decorated with cabochon-cut semi-precious stones.

The designs of the Scottish architect Charles Rennie Mackintosh SCOTLAND (1868–1928) were quite different in character. The modern movement in Scotland was completely separate from the English Arts and Crafts Movement, and Mackintosh's contributions to exhibitions in England were regarded with a mixture of astonishment and distaste. Yet, along with Ashbee, he was the prime representative on the Continent of the modern applied arts movement. In Vienna in particular, but also in Germany, his work was widely admired. The Scottish contribution to the Turin Exhibition of 1902 was awarded various medals and belonged, with the German, Dutch and Austrian, among the most interesting to be seen there. No designs by

Christening set designed by Charles Rennie Mackintosh for his godchild Friedrich Eckart Muthesius. Maker's mark on spoon: David Hislop, Glasgow, 1904. Fork marked 'C. Hahn, Berlin'. Length of fork and spoon: 15.5 cm (6 in.). Museum für Kunst und Gewerbe, Hamburg. Photograph: Kiemer & Kiemer.

189,190

Mackintosh for hollow-ware are known, but he did design three models for flatware. In 1900 a set of electroplated cutlery was made for William Davidson, the owner of Windy Hill, a house designed by Mackintosh. In 1904 he gave a christening set of his own design to his godchild F.E. Muthesius, one of the sons of the German architect Hermann Muthesius. This is very similar to the cutlery Mackintosh designed for Francis H. Newberry, the director of the Glasgow School of Art. Both have extremely long stems and the breast of the fork is no wider than the stem. Also striking is the way in which Mackintosh worked the initials of his godchild into square decorations. This model is reminiscent of the first cutlery designed by Josef Hoffmann in Vienna around 1904, although Hoffmann's ends less austerely in a row of four beads. Mackintosh's design was certainly very far ahead of his time. The cutlery for the Cranston tea-rooms in Glasgow was less so, but it also has the long slender stems which characterize his other flatware. This was electroplated and probably made by Elkington's in Birmingham, although it sometimes bears the maker's mark of David Hislop. However, Hislop was registered at the Glasgow Assay Office as 'Watchmaker, jeweller and dealer in stones' and would certainly not have had the necessary equipment.

17

SILVER FACTORIES

Most of the Arts and Crafts silversmiths were chiefly renowned in their own country. The one who ensured that the English modern movement became widely known elsewhere was Arthur Lasenby Liberty (1843–1917). In 1875, at about the same time as Siegfried Bing in Paris, he opened a shop in London, where he sold oriental goods, from Japan and India in particular. As a good businessman with a nose for future developments he managed to realize the ideals of the proponents of the Arts and Crafts Movement in a way that was commercially successful.

The first silver mark, Ly & Co., was registered in London in 1894. It was initially used on silver imported from Japan, but from around 1898 onwards it also appears on silver made in London. It was employed up to 1901 and is now in use again on newly made spoons and jewelry sold in the Hera Collection. It is impossible to mistake this for earlier silver, however, since the outline of the maker's mark is different now and bears contemporary date letters.

LIBERTY & CO.

In May 1899 the first Liberty silver was introduced under the name 'Cymric' by means of a modest exhibition. In advertisements in *The Studio* in 1900 it was announced, 'Messrs Liberty claim the recognition of "Cymric" Silver as an innovation which may identify them with a new era of art silver-work.' This silver in the Arts and Crafts style, which was made in William H. Haseler's factory in Birmingham, proved a great commercial success right from the start. The new company was registered in Birmingham in 1899. The intention throughout was to sell products of good quality at reasonable prices as an alternative to the often expensive hand-made objects of the Arts and Crafts Movement. Since the objects were made of spun or pressed parts, which were then soldered together, the method normally used in silver factories, no expensive man-hours were lost in time-consuming hand techniques. In order to give the finished objects a craft appearance, they were often hammered afterwards, some-

21,22 thing that was also done on occasion at Jensen's in Copenhagen, for example.

If one surveys the enormous output up to 1910, in terms of numbers, types and decoration, one realizes how much has changed since then. A series nowadays comprises hundreds or thousands of identical objects, but around 1900 a small number of examples of each model was made and if there proved still to be a demand for such a series

Advertisement in *The Studio*, June 1900, for Liberty & Co.'s sporting and loving cups.

once it had sold out, it was put into production again, sometimes with minor variations in the stamped ornament.

In fact designs were by no means always used in their original form. This is one of the reasons why it is often impossible to attribute a design to a given artist. However, the main reason is the fact that Liberty's designers were required to remain anonymous. Only if an object was exhibited at the Arts and Crafts Society or illustrated in, for example, *The Studio*, did they emerge from this anonymity. Thus objects are illustrated after designs by Oliver Baker and Bernard Cuzner, well-known Birmingham silversmiths, as well as by others, such as Miss Maud Coggin and the enameller Cecil Aldin, who have now passed into oblivion. Harry Craythorn was head of the design department at Haseler's and a gifted chaser. Other silversmiths there were Jessie Jones, Thomas Hodgetts and Charles Povey.[13] Rex Silver and his brother Harry of London also supplied Liberty's with silver designs.

The firm's most important designer, however, was Archibald Knox   VIII (1864–1933). The environs of his birthplace, the Isle of Man, and the world-famous Irish manuscript the *Book of Kells* were the sources of inspiration for the countless Celtic interlacing motifs he used in his designs. Since these were always meant for serial production, they have smooth surfaces, but as Liberty's ideas about designs for the 'new era in art silver-work' often demanded a hand-made look, the objects were finished off by hammering. The enamelled decorations and semi-precious stones also served to emphasize the craft aspect.

Just how much trouble Ashbee must have had with Liberty's from the very beginning can clearly be seen from the fact that when a number of designs for modern prize cups by the Guild of Handicraft were described in *The Studio*, Liberty's advertised 'Sporting and Loving Cups in "Cymric" Silver' on the back cover of that journal only a month later. This silver remained much in demand up to about 1910. After that, interest gradually declined and few new designs were executed. The Cymric company was dissolved in 1927, but Haseler continued to supply Liberty's with silver.

Many factories in Birmingham, including large ones like Elkington & Co. and small ones like Jones & Crompton, were influenced both by the Liberty silver and the flowing lines of Continental Art Nouveau. Elsewhere in England too, factories such as James Dixon & Sons, Mappin & Webb, Walker & Hall and William Hutton & Sons in Sheffield and Connell and Wakely & Wheeler Ltd in London produced some silver in the Art Nouveau and Arts and Crafts styles out of sheer necessity. But in all these factories production of this   VI modern silver was marginal by comparison with the unimaginably   19,20 large numbers of objects in extremely cheap imitations of old styles –

'of very little value . . . the trade shops stand for nothing at all except volume'.[14]

INDUSTRIAL DESIGNERS

In 1915 the Design and Industries Association was founded. It aimed 'to harmonize right design and manufacturing efficiency, accepting the machine in its proper place, as a device to be guided and controlled, not merely boycotted'.[15] For some time these good intentions came to nothing, owing to the indifference of the buying public. Only around 1930, when outsiders such as the sculptor and typographer Eric Gill, designers such as R.M.Y. Gleadowe and Harold Stabler and architects such as A.E. Harvey and Keith Murray began supplying designs for modern silver suitable for factory production, was the collaboration between independent artists and industrialists resumed, nearly fifty years after Dresser's activities.

Thus in 1936 H.G. Murphy was able to state with satisfaction that 'the craft of the silversmith is very much alive, and when machinery is used to produce masses of silver in a machine-like manner, it will have entered on a new phase'.[16] Stepped rims and bases, rectangular, octagonal and square forms determined the contours of the objects, while horizontal, vertical and zigzag lines were copiously engraved as ornaments on English Art Deco silver.

From 1926 onwards the Worshipful Company of Goldsmiths tried to promote the design of modern silverwork by means of competitions and exhibitions. The then Prince of Wales (the late Duke of Windsor) also took great pains to further the contribution of artists to the industry, seeing this as an essential means of selling British products successfully.[17] Yet modern English silverwork did not please everyone. In a review of an exhibition organized by the Goldsmiths' Company in 1938 an anonymous critic wrote, 'Timidity in design, lack of invention, make modern silver commonplace. A higher calibre of artistic craftmanship is required. Where is the modern Cellini, the modern Dürer?'[18]

The first design in which the trend towards, simple, smooth, angular forms found expression is a teapot designed in 1916, in which the spout and handle form part of a cube. In order not to break this form the lid is sunk into the smooth top. This is a very early modern object, and that not only for England. It was made in both silver and electroplate by various factories. 25

R.M.Y. Gleadowe (1888–1944) worked from 1929 for the silver factories Edward Barnard & Sons and Wakely & Wheeler in London. Under his influence there was a growing interest in engraving. His 27

Cover of one of the many books on cocktails, the new and fashionable drink of the twenties and thirties. London, 1922.

designs for this were always executed by G.T. Friend, who taught engraving at the Central School of Arts and Crafts in London.

A.E. Harvey was an architect and head of the Department of Industrial Design at the Central School in Birmingham. He made various designs for objects in both silver and electroplate, which could be produced simply by machines, for factories like Hukin & Heath and Deakin & Francis in Birmingham, Mappin & Webb in Sheffield and the Goldsmiths' and Silversmiths' Company in London (not to be confused with the Worshipful Company of Goldsmiths).

Cocktail set designed by Keith Murray for Mappin & Webb, *c.* 1935. Worshipful Company of Goldsmiths, London.

33

The best-known designer of this period was New Zealand-born Keith Murray (1892–1981), who was also an architect. In the thirties he designed earthenware for Wedgwood's, glass for Steven & Williams' Glassworks and silver for Mappin & Webb. A brochure with designs for modern silverwork put out by Mappin & Webb in 1935 gives an idea of his modern forms, which are architectural in structure and undecorated.

Harold Stabler (1872–1945) was one of the founders of the Design and Industries Association. He trained at the Keswick School of Industrial Art and taught at the Royal College of Art in London from 1912 to 1926. He was a highly versatile artist, being a potter, silversmith and enameller. He also designed for factories such as Wakely & Wheeler and the Goldsmiths' and Silversmiths' Company in London and Adie Bros in Birmingham.

Many of Stabler's designs are decorated with unpretentious angular stamped ornament. They have neither the pronounced mechanical character of modern German and Dutch functional forms nor the luxuriousness of the heavy, undecorated forms of the silver of French contemporaries like Jean Puiforcat or Tétard. The covered bowl Stabler designed in 1929 for an exhibition in Buenos Aires would not, however, look out of place beside the work of French competitors.

26 The stepped silver supports under the amber handles are characteristic of his style. His best-known silver design is a tea-set, which he designed in 1935 for Adie Bros. The forms here are smooth and rectangular, with rectangular wooden handles and flat rectangular hinged lids with semicircular disk finials.

A number of able silversmiths such as F.S. Beck and W.E. King worked for the London firm of Wakely & Wheeler. In addition to work by freelance designers such as Harold Stabler, R.M.Y. Gleadowe and Cyril Shiner, designs by Kenneth Mosley and Arthur

28 Wakely himself were also executed there.

Around 1930 Jane Barnard (b. 1902), who had trained at the Central School in London, designed smooth, round objects decorated

31 with blue enamelled lines and edges. These were made at her father's factory, Edward Barnard & Sons Ltd, in London. Some designs by R.M.Y. Gleadowe were also executed there.

A year after Mappin & Webb had produced the striking designs by Keith Murray, Elkington's of Birmingham advertised 'modern teasets, recently produced by Elkington craftsmen, embodying all the latest improvements and maintaining their recognised quality'.[19]

35 Among the designers here were Bernard Cuzner, Reginald Hill and Frank Nevile.

A survey of factory production of modern silverwork in Britain forces one to conclude with H.G. Murphy that the 'pitchforking of artists into factories with the idea that design will arise' was a mistake.[20] His hope that the silver industry would start producing 'masses of silver in a machine-like manner' remained unfulfilled. The country was too conservative in the applied art field to make a success of industrial design. That honour was reserved for the Scandinavian countries and the Bauhaus in Germany.

NOTES

1   Elizabeth Aslin, *The Aesthetic Movement*, New York 1969, p. 81.
2   Owen Jones, *The Grammar of Ornament*, London 1856, p. 157.
3   Gillian Naylor, *The Arts and Crafts Movement*, London 1971, p. 115.
4   Christopher Dresser, *Principles of Decorative Design*, London 1973, p. 136.
5   ibid., p. 136.
6   *The Studio*, November 1898, p. 113.
7   C.R. Ashbee, *Modern English Silverwork*, p. 3.
8   Gillian Naylor, op. cit., p. 172.
9   *The Studio*, June 1900, p. 48.
10   *The Studio*, November 1899, p. 107.
11   Peter Cannon-Brooks, exhibition catalogue *Omar Ramsden 1873–1939*, City Museum & Art Gallery, Birmingham 1973.
12   Exhibition catalogue *Birmingham Gold and Silver 1773–1973*, Section F, City Museum and Art Gallery, Birmingham 1973.
13   Shirley Bury, 'New light on the Liberty metalwork venture', *Bulletin of the Decorative Arts Society*, no. 1, p. 14.
14   ibid., p. 10.
15   Patrick Nuttgens, 'The Renaissance in British Design', in *Eye for Industry*, London 1986, p. 14.
16   *The Studio*, October 1938, p. 212.
17   *The Studio*, January 1934, pp. 3, 4.
18   *The Studio*, January 1936, p. 42.
19   *The Studio*, July 1936, p. AD.1.
20   H.G. Murphy, 'British Silver To-day', *The Studio*, January 1936, pp. 36–42.

VI Salt cellars and mustard pot with matching spoons and pepper pot, enamelled in the style of Liberty's. Maker's mark: B.T.C., Birmingham, 1905. Height of pepper pot: 8 cm (3¼ in.). Length of spoons: 6.8 cm (2¾ in.). Enamelled belt buckle. Maker's mark: Liberty & Co., Birmingham, 1904, 'Cymric'. Width: 7.8 cm (3 in.). Private collection.

VII Enamelled box. Maker's mark: Guild of Handicraft Ltd, London, 1903. Height: 4.5 cm (1¾ in.). Diameter: 8.8 cm (3½ in.). Private collection.

VIII Enamelled vase of a design attributed to Archibald Knox. Maker's mark: Liberty & Co., Birmingham, 1902, 'Cymric'. The vase is set with turquoise cabochons and mother-of-pearl. Height: 19.2 cm ($7\frac{1}{2}$ in.). Sotheby's, London, 13 April 1984, no. 50.

1 Egg coddler designed by Christopher Dresser. Maker's mark: H. Stratford, 1884. Height: 20 cm (7¾ in.). Claret jug with silver mounts. No hallmarks. Made by Hukin & Heath and stamped beneath the lip with 'Designed by Christopher Dresser' and the Patent Office registration mark for 26 March 1879. Height: 24.2 cm (9½ in.). Victoria & Albert Museum, London.

1

2 Picnic tea-set designed by Christopher Dresser. The milk jug and sugar bowl fit inside the teapot. Maker's mark: Hukin & Heath, London, 1880. Patent Office registration mark for 18 October 1879. Height of teapot: 8.7 cm (3½ in.). Private collection.

3 Two cruets from a set of four designed by Christopher Dresser. Maker's mark: Hukin & Heath, Birmingham, 1881. The design was registered on 11 May 1878. Height of cruet: 9 cm (3½ in.). Length of salt spoons: 5.7 cm (2¼ in.). Length of mustard spoons: 6.3 cm (2¼ in.). Private collection.

2

3

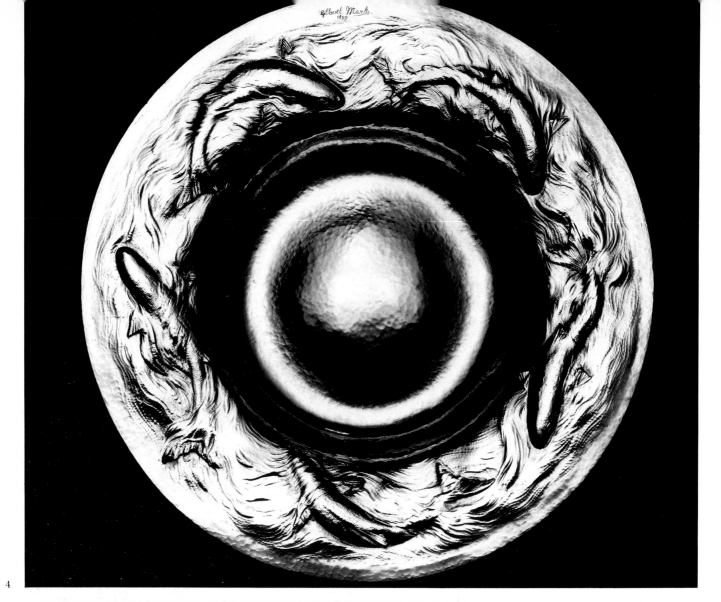

4

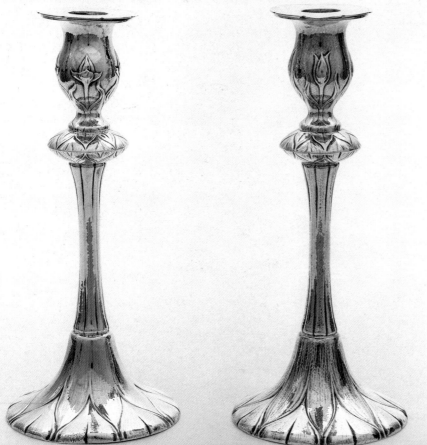

5

4 Plate with leaping salmon.
Signature and maker's mark of Gilbert
Marks, London, 1899. Diameter:
42.2 cm (16½ in.). Worshipful
Company of Goldsmiths, London.

5 Candlesticks designed by Gilbert
Marks, London, 1900. Height:
23.2 cm (9¼ in.). Private collection.

6 Spoon. Maker's mark: Omar Ramsden & Alwyn Carr, London, 1906. Length: 15.5 cm (6 in.). Mustard pot. Maker's mark: Omar Ramsden & Alwyn Carr, London, 1910. Height: 7.5 cm (3 in.). Private collection.

7 Vase. Maker's mark: Omar Ramsden & Alwyn Carr, London, 1902. Height: 13 cm (5 in.). Worshipful Company of Goldsmiths, London.

8

9

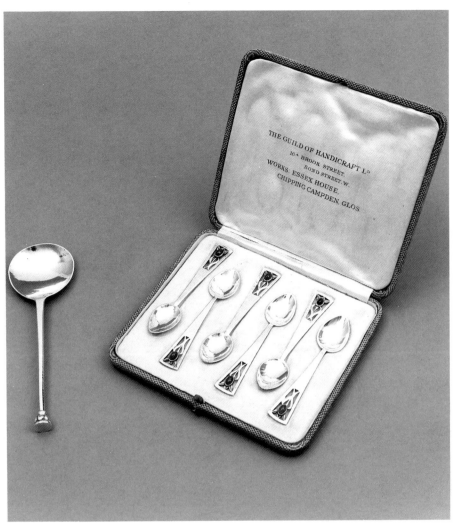

11

10 Inkpot designed by Charles Robert Ashbee. Maker's mark: C.R. Ashbee, London, 1900. Height: 11.5 cm (4½ in.). Private collection.

8 Syphon-stand set with citrine cabochons. Maker's mark: Guild of Handicraft Ltd, London, 1905. Height: 13.5 cm (5¼ in.). Private collection.

9 Silver-gilt fruit bowl. Maker's mark: Guild of Handicraft, London 1896. A similar bowl, with flowers instead of berries, appears in plate 97 of Charles Robert Ashbee's *English Silverwork*. Diameter: 19.6 cm (7¾ in.). Sotheby's, Belgravia, London, 9 September 1976, no. 206.

11 Spoon in seventeenth-century style with fig-shaped bowl and seal top. Illustrated in Charles Robert Ashbee's *English Silverwork*, plate 19. Maker's mark: Guild of Handicraft, London, 1905. Length: 15.5 cm (6 in.). Set of teaspoons with chrysoprase cabochons. Maker's mark: Guild of Handicraft, London, 1903. Length: 10 cm (4 in.). Private collection.

12

13

14

12 Sweetmeat dish with ivory stem. Signature and maker's mark: Charles Boyton, London, 1934. Height: 7 cm (2¾ in.). Private collection.

13 Cigar box with ivory knob. Designed and made by H.G. Murphy, London, 1935. Height: 15.2 cm (6 in.). Private collection.

14 Shagreen and silver cigar box. Maker's mark: Paul Cooper, London, 1927. Width: 27 cm (10¾ in.). Worshipful Company of Goldsmiths, London.

15 Fruit stand. Maker's mark: A.E. Jones, Birmingham, 1919. Height: 12.5 cm (5 in.). Private collection.

16 Bowl with niello ornament. Maker's mark: Bernard Cuzner, Birmingham, 1933. Height: 5.7 cm (2¼ in.). Worshipful Company of Goldsmiths, London.

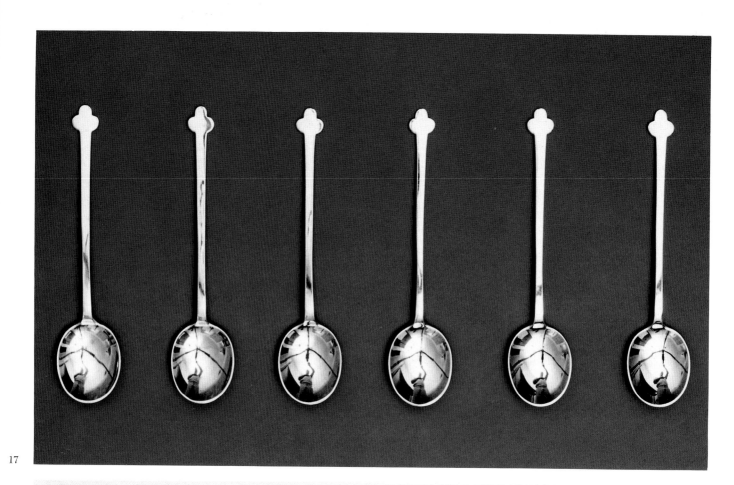

17

18

17 Six teaspoons from a set of twelve,
after a design of Charles Rennie
Mackintosh of 1903 for Miss
Cranston's tea-rooms in Glasgow.
Maker's mark: Elkington & Co.,
Glasgow, 1907. Length: 13.5 cm
(5¼ in.). Private collection.

18 Muffin dish with pale-green jade
finial. Maker's mark: Birmingham
Guild of Handicraft, Birmingham,
1901. Height: 10 cm (4 in.). Diameter
of dish: 19 cm (7½ in.). Private
collection.

19 Candlesticks. Maker's mark:
William Hutton & Sons, Sheffield,
1905. Height: 18 cm (7 in.). Private
collection.

20 Biscuit box. Maker's mark:
Mappin & Webb, Sheffield, 1903.
Height: 15 cm (6 in.). Private
collection.

21 Candlesticks. Maker's mark: Liberty & Co., Birmingham, 1903, 'Cymric'. Height: 17.5 cm (7 in.). Private collection.

22 Teapot. Maker's mark: Liberty & Co., Birmingham, 1901, 'Cymric'. Height: 14.5 cm (5¾ in.). Sugar bowl and milk jug. Maker's mark: Liberty & Co., Birmingham, 1903, 'Cymric'. Height of bowl: 5 cm (2 in.). Height of jug: 5.5 cm (2¼ in.). Private collection.

23 Milk jug. Maker's mark: Liberty & Co., Birmingham, 1900. Height: 11.5 cm (4½ in.). Private collection.

24 Rose-bowl and photograph-frame set with turquoises. Maker's mark: Liberty & Co., Birmingham, 1904, 'Cymric'. Height of bowl: 12.5 cm (5 in.). Diameter of frame: 13.5 cm (5¼ in.). Napkin-ring set with lapis lazuli. Maker's mark: Liberty & Co. struck over that of W.H. Haseler, Birmingham, 1934. Width: 6.2 cm (2½ in.). Private collection.

23

25 Teapot 'The Cube'. Maker's mark: Napper & Davenport, Birmingham, 1922. Height: 13.2 cm (5¼ in.). A three-piece tea service, of a smaller size, was made by T.W. & S., Birmingham in 1925. Sotheby's, London, 30 September 1983, no. 79.

26 Covered bowl with amber grips, designed by Harold Stabler. Maker's mark: Wakely & Wheeler Ltd, London. Shown in Buenos Aires in 1930. Diameter: 22.5 cm (8¾ in.). Worshipful Company of Goldsmiths, London.

26

27 Covered beaker designed by
R.M.Y. Gleadowe. Maker's mark:
Wakely & Wheeler, London, 1938 for
Goldsmiths and Silversmiths Co. Ltd.
Height: 28 cm (11 in.). Worshipful
Company of Goldsmiths, London.

28 Flower vase designed by Kenneth
Mosley. Maker's mark: Wakely &
Wheeler, London, 1932. Height:
25 cm (9¾ in.).

27

31 Fruit bowl with blue enamelled rim and three lines of different widths around the foot, designed by Jane Barnard. Maker's mark: Edward Barnard & Sons, London 1932. Diameter: 28.5 cm ($11\frac{1}{4}$ in.). Worshipful Company of Goldsmiths, London.

29 Tea caddy designed in 1932 by C.W. Gilbert and J. Sparrow, students of the Central School of Arts and Crafts, London. Height: 14.3 cm ($5\frac{3}{4}$ in.). Worshipful Company of Goldsmiths, London.

30 Box with lock of ivory and jet. Maker's mark: C.J. Shiner, Birmingham, 1933. Width: 8.5 cm ($3\frac{1}{4}$ in.). Worshipful Company of Goldsmiths, London.

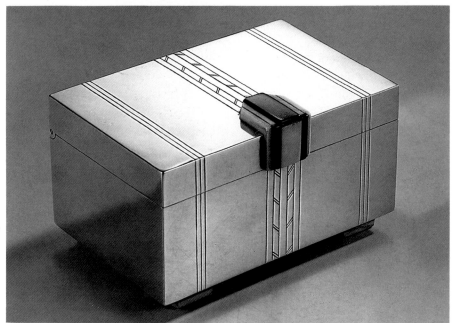

32 Cigarette box. The lid bears *cloisonné* enamelled symbols for the four elements: a fish for water (*aqua*) a hare for earth (*terra*), a bird for air (*aer*) and a salamander for fire (*ignis*). Maker's mark: Joyce Himsworth, Sheffield, 1934. Height: 10.2 cm (4 in.). Worshipful Company of Goldsmiths, London.

33 Glass jam pot with silver lid and spoon, designed by A.E. Harvey. Maker's mark: Mappin & Webb, Sheffield, 1929. Height: 7.6 cm (3 in.). Worshipful Company of Goldsmiths, London.

32

33

34

35

34 Fruit stand. Maker's mark: R.E. Stone for Hamilton & Inches, Edinburgh, 1938. The stem shows the influence of Georg Jensen and Johan Rohde. Height: 20.5 cm (8 in.). Sotheby's, Belgravia, London, 29 September 1977, no. 205.

35 Sugar caster. Maker's mark: Elkington & Co., Birmingham, 1938. Height: 9 cm ($3\frac{1}{2}$ in.). Private collection.

IX Gilt-silver and enamelled vase by Eugène Feuillâtre, Paris, 1900–02. Height: 15.5 cm (6 in.). Museum Bellerive, Zurich.

X

X Cigarette-case. Maker's mark: Jean
Dunand, Paris, *c.* 1930. 12.8 cm ×
8.5 cm (5 in. × 3¼ in.). Musée des Arts
Décoratifs, Paris.

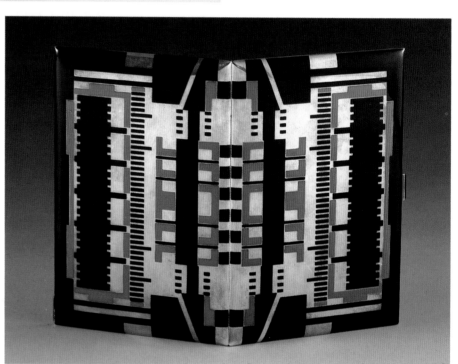

XI

XI Cigarette-case. Signed 'Raymond
Templier', *c.* 1925–30. 12.8 cm ×
8.5 cm (5 in. × 3¼ in.). Musée des Arts
Décoratifs, Paris.

XII Enamelled box by Camille Fauré,
Limoges. Diameter: 15 cm (6 in.).
Museum für Kunsthandwerk,
Frankfurt am Main.

XII

2

FRANCE

1890–1914

FROM the end of the seventeenth century, France, and Paris in particular, had led the way in Europe in changes of style in the applied arts. The Rococo, the elegant French style of the middle of the eighteenth century, governed form and ornament once again in the second half of the nineteenth. There was a strong influence from Japanese art too, both in the composition of naturalistic, two-dimensional ornament and the choice of decorative motifs, such as cranes and irises. This decorative, naturalistic Art Nouveau style found its first expression in Lorraine.

The glass-maker Émile Gallé exhibited his earliest objects with naturalistic decoration at the International Exhibition held in Paris in 1889. In the years preceding the Paris Exhibition of 1900 this new style blossomed mightily in Paris and Nancy. In contrast to Nancy, where the emphasis continued to be on a strong naturalism, the designers in the capital were more inclined to stylize these motifs after 1895. Around 1900, under the influence of the artists of Siegfried Bing's Maison de l'Art Nouveau, abstract ornament in flowing, curvilinear lines gained the upper hand. Art Nouveau reached its peak in France around that time.

At the Paris Exhibition of 1900 the displays of numerous large and small silversmiths' workshops were highly lauded. These can be divided into three groups. To the first belong those silversmiths who used modern floral ornament on traditional forms, such as E. Lefèbvre and, sometimes, Maison Christofle. To the second belong those who arrived at new forms via the traditional chasing technique. The most important representatives of this group were E. Cardeilhac and G. Keller Frères. To the third group belong those silversmiths who had the new modern forms and ornaments cast. This was the general rule in the case of mounts for glass and stoneware and also that of small objects such as heads for parasol handles and belt buckles. Since these forms and decoration were clung to in France, in contrast to Denmark, Germany, the Netherlands and Austria, the public tired of them and returned once again to the current copies of eighteenth-century styles.

The French were always highly individualistic in their approach. Luxury objects made by artist-craftsmen (*artistes artisans*) were always greatly valued in France, while the Socialist ideals behind the Arts and Crafts Movement in England and Belgium were unimportant there. Hence both the Art Nouveau style of around 1900 and the Art Deco style of the twenties were typical luxury styles, certainly as far as silver was concerned. France, unlike Germany, was no place for mass production.

France had for centuries been the pre-eminent country for costly MOUNTS *objets d'art* mounted in precious metals and this tradition was certainly not abandoned around 1900. Nowhere else were so many costly mounts made for ceramics and glass. Sometimes a mount was necessary to hide damage or because an object was not stable enough, owing to a mishap during firing or blowing, but equally often mounting served to accentuate the beautiful form or the colour and structure of the glaze. Nor was it just French glass and ceramics that were mounted in this way. Siegfried Bing sold glass by L.C. Tiffany with a mount attributed to E. Colonna[1] and a vase by Gallé was shown at an exhibition in St Petersburg with a mount by Fabergé.[2]

At the Salon des Artistes Français of 1896 at least thirty objects by Gallé were exhibited with mounts by Lucien Falize.[3] Falize (1839–1897) derived all his ornament from the plant world, which he rendered in great detail. He had even conceived the plan of devoting an exhibition to the importance of plants in the new style of ornament. A broth cup and saucer, on which he worked various soup vegetables 38 into a highly appropriate and decorative design, demonstrates the way in which he used naturalistic motifs for contemporary ornament. The jug by Gallé illustrated has a silver-gilt mount which, if one 36 overlooks the naturalistic additions, is reminiscent of models of the mid-eighteenth century.

A mount by Lucien Gaillard (b. 1861) is also naturalistic in character, with pendant plane-tree fruits. The way in which the mount enhances the modern aspect of the vase makes it a fine example of how Japanese influence was incorporated into French Art 37 Nouveau. The combination of patinated bronze with silver, as in the

43   vase illustrated, is likewise a product of Japanese influence. Lucien Gaillard, a brother of the furniture designer Eugène Gaillard, worked in his father's workshop from 1878 onwards. He was a silversmith who knew how to give metals various colours, a technique of which he made copious use in his silverwork.

       Mounts of quite a different character are those by Lucien Bonvallet and the firms of G. Keller Frères and R. Linzeler. For the concave bowl by Auguste Delaherche, Bonvallet designed a base of similar form. The bowl is held in four abstract volutes and the base rests on trefoil feet. Both the volutes and trefoils frequently appear on objects

41   made by Maison Cardeilhac after Bonvallet's designs. Keller's mount for the jug by Bigot is in a highly individual style, an undecorated, asymmetrical, fluent form with a superb line. Here the mount enhances the simple form and fine proportions, adding no superfluous ornament. It is vastly different from the heavy mounts used by

39   Linzeler for the jug and beakers illustrated. Here the large, stiff volutes are too dominant, so that they fail to support the curving form of the oval jug as intended.

ENAMELS   Another characteristic aspect of de luxe French silverwork is the use of enamel. One generally thinks of jewelry here, but this colourful decorative technique was also used on countless small objects, such as boxes, bowls, hand mirrors and vases. Fernand Thesmar (1843–1912) was the first artist to succeed in making small objects in *plique à jour* enamel. He had learned the technique of *cloisonné* enamelling, which was much in vogue in Paris as a result of Japanese influence, in the 1870s at Barbedienne's, where he was apprenticed in 1872. After some years he settled in Neuilly and it was in 1888 that he first used

42   *plique à jour* enamel for small objects. The forms of these remained virtually unchanged thereafter, so that it is understandable that a critic of the Salon of 1902, where bowls of this type were to be seen yet again, should have wondered why Thesmar did not vary them more.[4] For the mounts of these little *objets d'art* he collaborated with Hirné.

       What the collaboration between various artists could lead to is

46   illustrated by a gold hand mirror, which was part of a toilet set designed by Félix Bracquemond (1833–1914) for Baron Vitta in 1900. The plaquette with a figure of Venus Astarte made by sculptor Auguste Rodin is surrounded by a wide border of turquoise enamel by Alexandre Riquet and the mirror was mounted by André Falize, who had succeeded his father in 1897.

IX   Eugène Feuillâtre (1870–1916) scored a great success with his enamelled silver objects in 1898, when he participated in the Salon of the Société des Artistes Français for the first time under his own name. Before he set up on his own as a silversmith, he had been employed in the workshop of René Lalique, the most famous of all silversmiths around the turn of the century. Feuillâtre used various enamelling techniques in his work, translucent, *cloisonné* and *plique à jour*. His objects in translucent enamel, in various colours overlapping each other on an engraved ground, are particularly beautiful. In contrast to Thesmar's decoration, he used imaginative naturalistic motifs like fish or blackberries in the *plique à jour* enamel of bowls and little boxes with lids. He also experimented with glass in combination with enamelled silver.

    Like the Belgian artist Philippe Wolfers, Étienne Tourrette was a pupil of L. Houillon. From 1878 onwards he and Houillon exhibited jointly, but after 1893 he exhibited under his own name. He is known to have made jewelry for Georges Fouquet and other Paris jewellers. Characteristic of his work after 1900 is the use of *paillons* in the enamel to give it a livelier, more brilliant appearance. He used this technique not only on jewelry, but also on boxes and vases.[5]

48

49

The most famous artist in France was René Lalique (1860–1945). He was apprenticed to Louis Aucoc at the age of sixteen and then spent two years studying in London before returning to Paris, where he produced designs for various jewellers. In 1885 he was able to take over the workshop of one of his clients, but he was twice forced to move because the premises had become too small, and around 1890 he employed thirty people. He became engrossed in enamelling and had a complete glass-blowing installation in his workshop in rue Thérèse.[6] Here were created his first sensational, imaginative, sculptural jewels and objects, which represented a real revival of the art of the silversmith.

    Lalique made fascinating jewels in gold, silver and precious stones combined with glass, enamel or horn. That he also made ornamental objects in which he combined various materials is less well known. For example, in response to the Japanese influence he made a bowl in which he combined silver with enamel and bronze. The chalices in which he combined glass and silver are seen more often. He also made small silver objects such as heads for walking-sticks and scent bottles. The motifs, derived from nature, are always executed in relief. Lalique was so successful that his designs were bought by museums and collectors all over the world. He even considered making table silver, jardinières, candlesticks, tureens and cutlery , but lack of time and the fact that he would have had to install a new workshop,

LALIQUE

equipped with the special tools used by silversmiths, prevented him from doing so.[7]

<table>
<tr>
<td>

SIEGFRIED BING AND HIS
MAISON DE L'ART
NOUVEAU

</td>
<td>

Art Nouveau, one of the many names later given to the applied arts revival of around 1900, was originally the name of a shop in Paris, which was opened at the end of December 1895. The owner was Siegfried Bing (1838–1905), a German born in Hamburg, who had come to Paris in 1854.[8] He already had a great interest in Japanese art at an early age and in 1878 he opened a shop called Le Japon Artistique. Like Christopher Dresser of London, he himself went to the Far East, not to seek inspiration for designs, but to make business contacts.

</td>
</tr>
</table>

Bing sold Japanese art to collectors and museums in Europe and the United States, and by organizing exhibitions tried to arouse an interest everywhere in this 'new art', which he regarded as highly important for the development of creativity in Europe. What he hoped to achieve was a climate in which Japanese applied art would inspire European artists to design and have produced well-made objects for daily use. In 1895 he established a new exhibition gallery, La Maison de l'Art Nouveau, in which contemporary fine and applied art were sold under the same roof. Among the things on sale were stained-glass windows designed by the American Louis Comfort Tiffany and some French painters, furniture by Henry van de Velde of Belgium, who later became very well known, ceramics by Alexandre Bigot and Auguste Delaherche, jewelry by Lalique, metalwork by W.A.S Benson of London, Japanese prints, lithographs by Toulouse-Lautrec and much besides. It proved impossible to display well such a mass of disparate objects, so the critics were not kind. The chauvinistic French had little appreciation of the work of foreign artists in particular.

Despite the critics, Bing's Maison de l'Art Nouveau developed into an international meeting place. There, Frenchmen, and visitors from England, the United States, Belgium, the Netherlands, Germany and Scandinavia could see the best work of both sides of the Atlantic. But to bring a genuinely new decorative style into being it was not enough to sell work by others. Objects would have to be made under Bing's personal supervision by his own designers and artists. Thus he set up various workshops for designers, modellers, goldsmiths and cabinetmakers. In the goldsmith's shop, designs by Edouard Colonna and Georges de Feure, among others, were executed, not only for jewelry, but also for mounts for purses, glass and ceramics, and even a flatware design.

In designs by Edouard Colonna (1862–1948), the ornament always consisted of abstract, curvilinear whip-lash lines, which Henry van de Velde had first introduced at Bing's. Colonna, who was born in Cologne, studied architecture in Brussels and in 1882 went to New York, where he worked for some years for Tiffany's Associated Artists. In 1887 he published a small book entitled *Essay on Broom-Corn*, in which motifs with intertwined curvilinear lines first appeared. This did not create much of a stir at the time, but it must have had an unconscious influence on the work of other designers after 1890.

In 1893 Colonna returned to Europe and in 1898 Bing took him on as a designer, seeing him as a talented successor to Henry van de Velde. In all Colonna's metalwork designs, just as in his jewelry, there can be found abstract decorations which are 'simply happy combinations of lines and curves and reliefs'.[9] In 1909 he went to Toronto, and later to New York, but he designed no more silver there.

44

In contrast to the abstract designs of Colonna, those of Bing's son Marcel (1875–1921) were always based on naturalistic models, as can be seen in the mount for a vase illustrated. Another of Bing's designers was Georges de Feure (1868–1928), a painter from the Netherlands, whose real surname was Van Sluyters.[10] From 1899 onwards this versatile artist worked mainly for Bing, designing furniture, glass, ceramics, and carpets.

50

At the Paris Exhibition of 1900 Bing had a pavilion of his own, 'Art Nouveau Bing'. Everything sold there had been made in his own workshops and illustrated his ideas about harmonious interior decoration. The central characteristics of the entire display were the abstract, flowing, curvilinear, decorative lines, pale colours and elegant contours of all the component parts. In Turin two years later Bing's Art Nouveau, with its inevitable curvilinear lines, was already somewhat dated. In contrast to those from Germany, the Netherlands, Austria and Scotland, the French participants showed no further development, whereas elsewhere the new movement was tending more and more towards functional interiors and geometric ornament. In 1903 both Colonna and de Feure went their own ways. The turnover of Bing's shop declined and in 1904 he sold his premises to Majorelle Frères of Nancy. His pioneering work had brought about a revolution in the applied arts. He was one of the first to engage artists to design interiors complete with everything. He was not interested in serial production, his *objets d'art* being intended, virtually without exception, as one-off pieces for a limited, wealthy clientele.

Bing's story does not stand alone. In 1895 Julius Meier-Graefe (1867–1935), the art critic and co-founder of the German periodical

Pan, came to Paris. He was a friend of Bing and Henry van de Velde. The latter designed the interior of his shop, La Maison Moderne, which was opened in 1898. Van de Velde designed for La Maison Moderne mounts for glass and ceramics, which were executed by the silversmith A. Debain.[11] The objects sold here were less exclusive and thus cheaper than those at Bing's shop, but even Meier-Graefe was forced to close his in 1904. Neither he nor Bing was capable of providing the new art, in which they had played a leading part, with further artistic impulses to meet the demands of a public specific in its requirements. This public, for preference, wanted something new, but if that were not forthcoming, turned back to familiar eighteenth-century models.

Liberty's of London sold a wider range and was not bound to any one style, so that it was always able to survive, while the Wiener Werkstätte (Vienna Workshop), which was established in 1903, was able to call on a large number of designers capable of giving shape to the most divergent modern ideas. It thus remained attuned to changing taste, so that, despite all its great financial difficulties, it was able to continue in existence until 1932.

LARGE WORKSHOPS AND FACTORIES

The *objets d'art* described above were, almost without exception, made in the workshops of goldsmiths and makers of small silver objects. For the making of large pieces of silver, different equipment and more workshop space were needed. The output of these larger workshops did not differ from that in other countries. Account was taken of the taste of the customers and there was certainly no attempt to play a pioneering role in the field of modern silverwork. After all, unlike jewelry, there was no need for silver utensils to fit in with the mode of the moment.

For special occasions, such as participation in the Salons of the Société des Artistes Français, where applied art had also been shown since 1895, recourse was had to independent artists. For example the sculptor Edouard Becker made beautifully carved bas-reliefs in ivory and exotic woods, which were afterwards mounted in gold or silver at the firms of Aucoc, Boucheron and the Société Parisienne d'Orfèvrerie. Another artist who made many designs for hollow-ware was Maurice Giot. These were executed by A. Debain, one of the most gifted silversmiths in Paris at that time. He also executed designs by various other artists and his work was to be seen at all the Salons and international exhibitions of around 1900.

At that period Aucoc, Boucheron, Cardeilhac, Christofle and Keller were important Paris factories, where modern silver was also made.

In the workshops of Louis Aucoc (where, as we have already seen, Lalique began his training) and Frédéric Boucheron the production of jewelry played a more important part than that of silver. Lucien Hirtz (b. 1864), a former assistant of Lucien Falize, designed a great deal of silver and *objets d'art*, such as vases, cups and clocks, for Boucheron. The ashtray illustrated was also modelled on a design by him and   52
made at Boucheron's. It has a highly unusual decoration: a profile of a young man smoking.

The most important designer for Maison Cardeilhac was Lucien Bonvallet (1861–1919). For the Paris Exhibition of 1900 he designed one of the most successful objects to be seen there: a chocolate pot with an ivory handle and swizzle-stick. This was made in various sizes and with a variety of chased decorations, such as stylized poppies or thistles. The preference for coloured ivory finials and ornament was   55
also found in other silver items that formed part of Cardeilhac's display at the exhibition. These included covered bowls, coffee pots, sugar bowls and toilet sets.

The contribution of G. Keller Frères was well received too, the beautiful hand-raised jugs with supple curved contours attracting particular attention. The one illustrated is a contemporary version of   53
the elegant French silver of the mid-eighteenth century, although the raffia-covered handle is strongly inspired by Japanese and English models, those of Liberty's in particular. Even the way the handle is set on the jug is based on English models. Smooth, undecorated forms were highly unusual in France at this time, so that it is understandable why Keller Frères was praised as one of the pioneers of modern design. The firm's display at the Paris Exhibition of 1900 also included a 45-piece silver 'Five o'clock Service for excursions by motor car in a small, conveniently portable case', but unfortunately this is now untraceable.[12]

Naturally, the biggest factory in France, Maison Christofle, had taken the trouble to show a number of special objects at the 1900 exhibition. This firm had been the first in France to succeed with the electroplating process and after achieving this in 1842 it had grown into the largest. The Japanese mode, which played such an important part in France from the early 1870s onwards, did not go unnoticed by Maison Christofle either. Indeed, the factory led the way in the use of *cloisonné* enamel on large objects.

For twenty years the sculptor Arnoux supplied designs which were shown at all the exhibitions in which Maison Christofle participated in the decades either side of the turn of the century. The decorations consisted mainly of naturalistic flower motifs combined with slender leaves and curving lines and were meant to lend a modern accent to the generally traditional forms. Objects such as a lamp modelled on a   60 design by Arnoux, as well as plates, coffee pots, vases and bowls 'made for the delicate and with a universal appeal',[13] formed only a limited part of the display at the exhibition. The *pièce de résistance* was an enormous centrepiece, 'Air and Water', in the tried and tested nineteenth-century style, with allegorical figures representing the four continents, bathed by the oceans. The customers of conventional tastes were not forgotten either.

In the smaller silver factories, such as Lefèbvre, Linzeler, Olier et Caron and Tirbour, few large silver objects were made in the modern style. These firms could not afford to take financial risks as long as the

57,58 preference for eighteenth-century styles remained so strong.

A special place in silverwork is occupied by the designs of Henri Husson (1852–1914) from Alsace, who settled in Paris in his youth. His experiments with gold and silver incrustations and the painterly effects he achieved with combinations of different alloys were discovered around 1900 by the Paris gallery owner Hébrard. Various

IV of Husson's vases, boxes and jewels with cast and chased plant and animal ornament were a great success from 1902 onwards.

The centre of French glass and furniture production at that time was Nancy, in the north-east. Alsace and part of Lorraine had been incorporated into the German Empire in 1871, which is why various silversmiths and designers with German-sounding names, such as Becker, Erhart, Hirtz, Keller, Linzeler and Risler, had moved to Paris from these contested regions or maintained close contacts with those who had settled in the capital. Even the well-known Paris jeweller and author Henri Vever of Metz had settled in Paris in 1871.

Nancy played no significant role in the production of table silver. The objects made there were mainly small, simple items, which were generally cast. A very common motif was the thistle, which figures in the arms of Nancy and is thus regarded as a symbol of the region, but other naturalistic motifs were used as well. Two important designers who worked in Nancy were Henri Bergé and Victor Prouvé. Jules Déon, Daubrée et Kauffer, Lexellent, Ronga and Séverin Rongy were the most important silversmiths. Various small silver objects, such as napkin rings with the usual naturalistic ornament of the region, were also made by Dériot, who appears to have worked at Sarreguemines.

Around 1900 many in France hoped that the new style would be that of the future: 'This style which everyone essays, which each one creates according to his own ideas and of which no-one has yet tried to define the principles and establish the basic lines'.[14] The ineradicable nineteenth-century idea that styles must be firmly defined, if it were to be possible to use them for different purposes, hampered further development in France. Thus in 1908 it had to be admitted that the French silversmiths were still using naturalistic plant ornament with a certain elegance, but that this was in the long run becoming monotonous.[15]

Some were well aware of this monotony and tried to force an acceptable solution. The result of these attempts is illustrated by a mocha pot made by Boucheron around 1910, which was described by   61 Tony Bouilhet as 'a sagely balanced piece with wide inverted facets, which combine perfectly with floral ornament of an admirable finesse'.[16] The form with its wide facets is new, but the applied ornament old-fashioned. Clearly, the development of the applied arts had reached an impasse in France around 1910.

After the First World War two opposing trends can be distinguished   1918–40 in the applied arts in France, an eclectic, decorative one and a modern, geometrical one. Designers who worked in the eclectic manner modernized forms and ornament derived from the last, traditional, typically French style, that of the reign of Louis Philippe (1830–48), with stylized roses, fountains, baskets of flowers and garlands as the most common decorative motifs.[17] Designers who aimed for renewal were inspired by the way in which Cubist painters analysed form.

Some French silversmiths occasioned a real revolution in French silverwork by making objects with substantial, angular forms and smooth, undecorated, shiny surfaces in mathematically calculated proportions. This innovative tendency came to govern French silverwork in the twenties, with a newcomer, Jean Émile Puiforcat, as the undisputed leader. The development of French silver can be followed closely on the basis of the exhibitions held in Paris in the twenties and thirties: the annual Salons, the Paris Exhibition of 1925, the exhibition 'Décor de la Table' in 1930 and the Exposition Internationale des Arts et Techniques in 1937.

Visitors to the Paris Exhibition of 1925 could observe both trends, the eclectic decorative and the modern geometrical. The exhibition had a lengthy genesis. In 1906 some members of the Société des Artistes Décorateurs had already conceived the plan of organizing an exhibition exclusively devoted to the modern applied arts, in emulation of the Turin Exhibition of 1902. It was to have been held in 1915, but because of the outbreak of war was first postponed for a year, then put off until 1922, and later to 1924, to open finally in 1925. All the well-known French silver factories took part in it: Aucoc, Boulenger, Cardeilhac, Christofle, Lapparra, Ravinet d'Enfert, Tétard and finally – and most interesting – Puiforcat.

Saucière with ebony handle by Carl Christian Fjerdingstad, Paris, *c.* 1925. Height: 11 cm (4¼ in.). Private collection.

In a separate pavilion Maison Christofle, along with the Baccarat glass factory, showed designs by leading designers, such as André Groult, the architect Louis Süe and the painter André Mare. The forms and ornament in their designs are characteristic of the decorative trend in French Art Deco. Those of Christian Fjerdingstad and Luc Lanel were in the geometrical style. The work of the Dane Fjerdingstad (1891–1968) in particular displays great expertise. He had a command of all aspects of silversmithing and sometimes executed his own designs. He was a highly valued designer at Maison Christofle.

The saucière illustrated shows the way in which Fjerdingstad managed to combine geometric French ornament with the hammered surface and the simple round forms which are so characteristic of Danish silver. There is no 'beautiful polished metal'[18] here, as in purely French silver of this period. Not only did Henry van de Velde, who had met Fjerdingstad in the Netherlands in 1921, before going to Paris, regard him as one of the best silversmiths of his day, but the directors of Christofle and countless art critics also shared that opinion.

The silverwork shown by Maison Tétard was made after designs by Valéry Bizouard and Louis Tardy. Bizouard did pioneering work as a designer of modern silver. His first designs date from 1902, after which he participated in all the stages of development of French silver up to 1937. In 1925 he attracted much attention with a monumental ten-sided vase a metre (39 in.) high, sober in form and simply decorated with vertical, wedge-shaped grooves.

The contribution that most surprised everyone was that of Puiforcat. Even Tony Bouilhet, the director of Maison Christofle, thought it the most interesting, along with that of Georg Jensen of Denmark. Thanks to the subtle way in which they were shown, all the objects were seen to their best advantage.

After the First World War was over, Jean Émile Puiforcat (1897–1945) joined his father's workshop in order to train as a silversmith. At the same time he took a course under the sculptor Lejeune. He sent some designs to the Salons des Artistes Décorateurs for the first time in 1920. These were conspicuous for their new forms and ornament, although they still exhibit reminiscences of the Baroque decoration that had come into fashion around 1910. Before 1925 the last ornaments had disappeared from Puiforcat's work and smooth surfaces had gained the upper hand. Straight horizontal, vertical and diagonal lines accentuated the faceted or rounded forms. To some critics who accused him of a 'mechanical beauty', Puiforcat answered, 'It is only logical that we should involuntarily unite with the machine: the same material, the same concern for utility. In the machine there is nothing superfluous, in silverwork nothing useless . . . Silverwork has beautiful polished metal in common with the machine.'[18]

Like the designers of the Bauhaus in Germany, Puiforcat based his new forms on the sphere, the cone and the cylinder, but the results are very different. Despite the similarities he posited between machines and silver, these objects with large, undecorated surfaces and sharp angles could scarcely be made by machinery, but only by skilled craftsmen. They were perfectly made de luxe objects, in accordance with the high standards set for such by the French. Puiforcat's silver has an extremely luxurious character, which is enhanced by its combination with costly materials like ivory, lapis lazuli, jade, rock crystal and exotic woods. Nor was it only the outward appearance that was important, for great attention was also paid to the making of essential technical details such as hinges.

The forms and structure of Puiforcat's objects reveal his leaning towards sculpture, something he shared with his colleagues the silversmiths Georg Jensen of Copenhagen and Philippe Wolfers of Brussels. He defined his idea of design as follows: 'What we need today are utilitarian objects without ornamentation, that are not disguised as something else, although this does not prevent their being refined pieces of great value. The form imposed by its ultimate function is the object's permanent element. The desire to create a form of expression out of that form is what gives the object its constantly changing character.'[19]

In the years after his success at the 1925 Paris Exhibition the cube took an ever more important place as the basic form for Puiforcat's

Coffee pot with lapis lazuli handle and finial, designed by Jean E. Puiforcat in 1923. Maker's mark: E. Puiforcat, Paris. Height: 15 cm (6 in.). Musée des Arts Décoratifs, Paris.

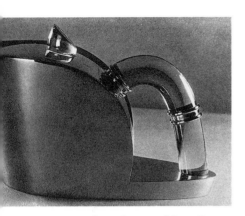

Teapot with rock-crystal handle, designed in 1937 by Jean E. Puiforcat. Photograph from *L'Orfèvrerie française au 20ème siècle*, by Tony Bouilhet.

designs. Later, mathematically calculated curved lines came to predominate in his work. Sometimes they determine the whole form, as in the teapot illustrated. The function, pouring, is strongly accentuated. However, in most cases Puiforcat combined curved lines with other forms. This development in his work can clearly be followed in his contributions to the 'Décor de la Table' exhibition of 1930 and the Paris Exhibition of 1937.

Puiforcat even gave flatware a modern appearance, although it had previously been thought that there was little room for experiment here. The shape of the bowl of the spoon, the position of the prongs of the fork and the curvature and length of the stem together determine the balanced form of good cutlery and the same form had already served perfectly well for two centuries.

Like Josef Hoffmann in Vienna and Harald Nielsen for Georg Jensen in Copenhagen, Puiforcat shortened and widened the stems into flat, straight forms with horizontal and vertical grooves. The bowls of the spoons became shorter and took on an oval form, while the prongs of the fork were also shortened and the breast made slightly concave, so that 'eating peas ceases to be a problem'.[20] The traditional heel was adapted to the motif at the end of the stem. The unexpectedly great acclaim received by these new designs, with undecorated forms and large, shiny surfaces, was a clear indication to other famous silver manufacturers that this modern style certainly offered sound prospects of commercial success.

In 1930 the exhibition 'Décor de la Table' was held at the Musée Galliera. Everything used in a dining-room was displayed, giving a clear picture of modern applied art. Such a collaboration between various contributors to achieve a unified whole would have been unthinkable in France before 1925. Henri Clouzot wrote of the work of Puiforcat, Hénin, Lapparra, Tétard, Cardeilhac and Bloch-Eschevêque that no other branch of industry gave such clear evidence of good taste and originality. 'The pieces derive their beauty from frankness of execution, concise form and plain polished surfaces which reflect as in a mirror the light of day or the brilliance of electricity.'[21]

From 1930 onwards Jean Tétard (b. 1907) also made various designs for his father's firm. These objects were to be seen for the first time at the Musée Galliera exhibition. Like Bizouard, who had such an important share in Tétard's display in 1925, Jean Tétard was a master of the structural combination of geometric forms. A good example of this is a tea caddy in which a narrow triangular notch in the plain wall, which is carried through to the edge of the lid, constitutes the only decoration. This decoration is at the same time extremely functional, since it makes it easier to hold and open the tea caddy.

The contributions to the 1930 exhibition of Boulenger, Cardeilhac, Aucoc and Hénin were also lauded for their good design and execution. Maison Lapparra, which had previously specialized in flatware, sent in for the first time hollow-ware designed by Paul Follot.

In 1937 another exhibition was held in Paris, the Exposition Internationale des Arts et Techniques. The timing was not very favourable because of the economic climate; nevertheless thirty French silversmiths took part. From Puiforcat's work it can be seen that rounded forms and flowing lines were gaining ground over the strict rectilinearity of the previous decade and he was not alone in this. Over the preceding ten years a definitive break had been made with old-fashioned ornament and the way was now clear for modest new decorations which simply underlined the form and function, like the silver-gilt rings round the handle of Puiforcat's teapot.

In contrast to the artists mentioned above who worked in the leading ateliers or as freelance designers, Jean Després (1889–1980) executed his designs for jewelry and silver himself. He had started work in a silversmith's workshop at an early age, taking drawing lessons in the evenings. As an aeroplane pilot and then a technical draughtsman for aircraft during the First World War, he became fascinated by the shapes of machine parts. After the war he set up on his own as a silversmith. Many of his designs exhibit technical-looking ornament applied as a decorative contrast around a smooth, shiny surface.

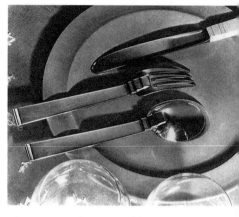

Flatware with stepped heels, made by Lapparra, Paris, 1935. Photograph from *L'Orfèvrerie française au 20ième siècle*, by Tony Bouilhet.

70

In addition to the large workshops already discussed there were also at this time small ones belonging to independent silversmiths. They experimented with enamel, lacquer and other decorative techniques, often achieving surprising results. Jean Dunand (1877–1942), sculptor and silversmith, is chiefly known for his lacquerwork on both wood and metal. After his training at the École des Arts Décoratifs in Geneva, he worked in the studio of the sculptor Jean Dampt in Paris. He then turned to making silver. At first his pieces bore ornament in the current Art Nouveau style, but then simple forms took over and in place of chased decoration geometric motifs were encrusted in various metals on the smooth surfaces.

Dunand's preference for plain, simply decorated forms led him to study the techniques of Japanese lacquerwork and after the First World War he applied these in a highly personal way to metal and wood. Although lacquer and opaque enamel look almost the same, they are two completely different materials. Lacquer comes from

LACQUER AND ENAMEL

X

68 plants, whereas enamel is a vitreous paste. The erratic zigzag motif on the lacquered matchbox holder illustrated is characteristic of Dunand's work of the thirties.

XI Another artist who decorated various, mostly small, objects with lacquer at this period was Raymond Templier (1891–1968). After studying at the École des Beaux Arts in Paris, he went to work for his father, the jeweller Paul Templier. From 1911 onwards he took part in all the important exhibitions. In his designs for de luxe functional objects he sometimes combined widely differing materials such as silver, lacquer and eggshells.

XII Enamel was still greatly loved in the twenties and there were various good enamellers at that time. The best known were Camille Fauré, Jean Goulden and Gérard Sandoz. Fauré (1872–1956) worked in Limoges, long a traditional centre for enamelwork. His forms were simple and generally with geometric motifs. For his floral decoration he used soft pastel tints with a metallic sheen.

67 Jean Goulden (1878–1947) worked as a doctor in Macedonia during the First World War. In the Greek Orthodox monasteries on Mount Athos he discovered the beauty of Byzantine enamels. After his return to Paris he learned the technique of *champlevé* enamel from Jean Dunand. His objects, which are decorated with modernistic enamel ornament, sometimes resemble Cubist sculptures.

The idea that it should be possible for everyone to buy well-designed objects at a reasonable price was far less prevalent in France than in Germany. A price has to be paid for good quality and it is a high one, but the French did not begrudge it. Around both 1900 and 1925 French silversmiths were in the lead in the field of de luxe objects, but as soon as inexpensive serial production was in question, they lost ground, to the Germans in particular. Serial production was irrelevant to the French, especially for a costly material like silver. French silver objects were and still are of a high standard, both literally and figuratively (0.950 as opposed to the English 0.925). Modernistic objects meant for serial production in silver, such as those in the Netherlands around 1930, are found only in electroplate in France.

NOTES
1 Gabriel P. Weisberg, *Art Nouveau Bing: Paris Style 1900*, New York 1986, p. 155.
2 'Exposition d'orfèvrerie et bijouterie à Petersbourg', *Revue des Arts Décoratifs*, 1902.
3 Henri Vever, *La Bijouterie Française au XIXe siècle*, Vol. III, Paris 1908, p. 517.
4 Léonard Penicaud, 'L'émail aux Salons de 1902', *Revue de la Bijouterie, Joaillerie et Orfèvrerie*, 1902, p. 165.
5 ibid., p. 164.
6 Henri Vever, op. cit., p. 711.

7 ibid., p. 741.

8 Gabriel P. Weisberg, op. cit., p. 9.

9 Gabriel Mourey, 'Modern French Jewellery & Fans', supplement to *The Studio*, London 1901–2, p. 3

10 Gabriel P. Weisberg, op. cit., p. 241.

11 Wolfgang Ketterer, Munich, Sale 100, no. 720, Sale 107, no. 630.

12 *Kunst und Kunsthandwerk*, 1901, p. 120.

13 Paul Vitry, 'L'Orfèvrerie à l'Exposition', *Art et Décoration*, Paris 1900, p. 173.

14 *Revue de la Bijouterie, Joaillerie et Orfèvrerie*, 1900, p. 27.

15 R. Rücklin, 'Die franko-britische Ausstellung in London', *Deutsche Goldschmiede-Zeitung*, 1908, p. 301.

16 Tony Bouilhet, *L'orfèvrerie française au 20ème siècle*, Paris 1941, p. 25.

17 Yvonne Brunhammer, *Cinquantenaire de l'Exposition de 1925*, Paris 1976–7, p. 29.

18 Tony Bouilhet, op. cit., p. 55.

19 Françoise de Bonneville, *Jean Puiforcat*, Paris 1986, p. 64.

20 ibid., p. 242.

21 Henri Clouzot, 'Décor de la table', *The Studio*, October 1930, p. 288.

36 Glass water jug by Émile Gallé, with a gilt-silver mount by Joindy and Peureux. Maker's mark: Joseph Joindy and Francis Peureux, Paris, c. 1893. Height: 22 cm (8½ in.). Musée des Arts Décoratifs, Paris.

38

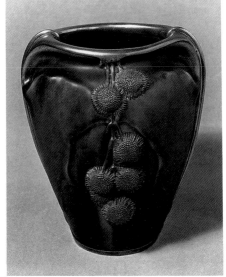

37 Ceramic vase by Eugène Baudin, with a silver mount by Gaillard. Maker's mark: Lucien Gaillard. Bought at the Paris Exhibition of 1900. Height: 14.6 cm (5¾ in.). Museum für Kunst und Gewerbe, Hamburg. Photograph: Kiemer & Kiemer.

38 Broth cup, saucer and spoon, decorated with soup herbs, designed by Lucien Falize. Maker's mark: Falize Ainé et Fils, Paris. Dated '15 Août 1895'. Height of cup: 7.8 cm (3 in.). Diameter of saucer: 16.6 cm (6½ in.). Length of spoon: 18 cm (7 in.). Private collection.

40

39 Pitcher and two matching beakers with silver mounts. Maker's mark: Société Robert Linzeler; stamped 'PIAULT-LINZELER'. Paris, c. 1901. Height of pitcher: 26.5 cm (10½ in.). Height of beakers: 11 cm (4¼ in.). Rijksmuseum, Amsterdam.

40 Ceramic pitcher by Alexandre Bigot, with a silver mount by G. Keller. Maker's mark: G. Keller, Paris, c. 1900. Musée des Arts Décoratifs, Paris.

41 Bowl by Auguste Delaherche with a silver mount designed by Lucien Bonvallet. Maker's mark: E. Cardeilhac. Bought at the Paris Exhibition of 1900. Height: 9.3 cm (3¾ in.). Kunstgewerbemuseum, Staatliche Museen Preussischer Kulturbesitz, West Berlin.

42 Small bowl with *plique à jour* enamel by André Thesmar, Paris, c. 1895. Height: 3.5 cm (1½ in.). Museum für Kunst und Gewerbe, Hamburg. Photograph: Kiemer & Kiemer.

43 Triangular, patinated bronze vase with a silver mount. Maker's mark: Lucien Gaillard, Paris, c. 1900. Height: 28.5 cm (11¼ in.). Sotheby's, Monaco, 7 December 1981, no. 344.

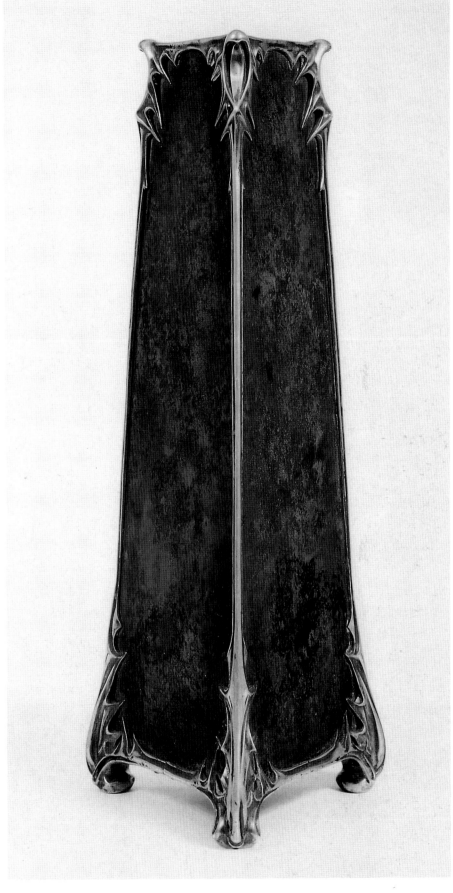

43

46 Hand mirror designed by Félix Braquemond with ivory relief carved by Auguste Rodin. Enamelled by Alexandre Riquet and mounted by Alexis Falize. Height: 32.2 cm (12¾ in.). Cleveland Museum of Art. Gift of Ralph King by exchange.

47 Silver-mounted hand mirror, the back with pale-blue wistaria and the colourless handle set with an enamelled beetle. Maker's mark: René Lalique, Paris, *c.* 1900. Length: 23 cm (9 in.). Museum für Kunsthandwerk, Frankfurt am Main.

48 Pale-green enamelled box, signed 'Eugène Feuillâtre', Paris, *c.* 1898. Height: 6.3 cm (2½ in.). Museum für Kunst und Gewerbe, Hamburg. Photograph: Kiemer & Kiemer.

49 Small gold box with an enamelled lid set with a chalcedony. Signed 'Étienne Tourrette' and dated '1913'. 6 cm × 5.5 cm (2¼ in. × approx. 2¼ in.). Musée des Arts Décoratifs, Paris.

50 Vase by Pierre Adrien Dalprayat with silver mount by Marcel Bing. Maker's mark: Siegfried Bing Art Nouveau, Paris, *c.* 1898. Bought at the Paris Exhibition of 1900. Height: 9.9 cm (4 in.). Museum für Kunst und Gewerbe, Hamburg. Photograph: Kiemer & Kiemer.

44 Water jug designed by Alexandre Bigot with silver mount designed by Edouard Colonna. Maker's mark: Siegfried Bing Art Nouveau, Paris, *c.* 1899. Musée des Arts Décoratifs, Paris.

45 Plate with enamelled purple clematis. Maker's mark: René Lalique, Paris, 1896. Diameter: 21 cm (8¼ in.). Musée des Arts Décoratifs, Paris.

45

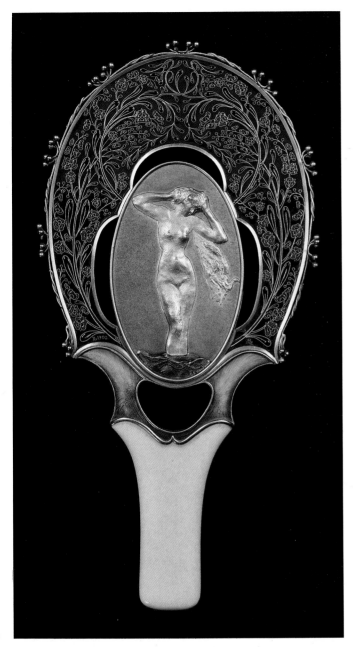

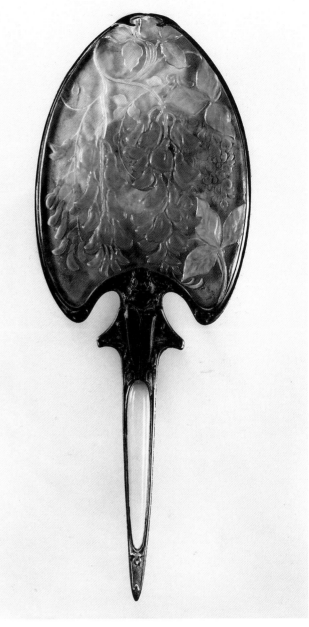

47

49

50

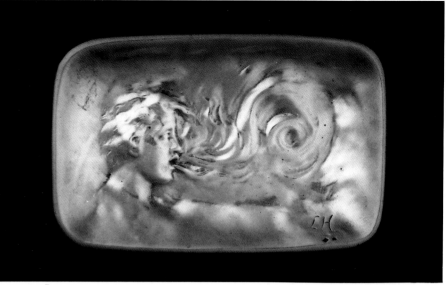

51 **Umbrella handle.** Maker's mark: Lucien Gaillard. Bought at the Paris Exhibition of 1900. Length 6.5 cm (2½ in.). Kunstgewerbemuseum, Staatliche Museen Preussischer Kulturbesitz, West Berlin.

52 **Ashtray** designed by Lucien Hirtz. Maker's mark: Frédéric Boucheron, Paris, *c.* 1900. Width: 9 cm (3½ in.). Collection of Inez Stodel, Amsterdam.

53 **Jug.** Maker's mark: G. Keller, Paris, *c.* 1900. Height: 20 cm (8 in.). Private collection.

54 **Jewelry box.** Ivory plaques carved by Edmond Becker. Maker's mark on the silver mount: Société Parisienne d'Orfèvrerie, Paris, *c.* 1900. Height: 7 cm (2¾ in.). Private collection.

55 Chocolate pot with stirring-rod
and handle in two-tone ivory,
designed by Lucien Bonvallet for the
Paris Exhibition of 1900. Maker's
mark: E. Cardeilhac. Height: 30 cm
(11¾ in.). Musée Bouilhet-Christofle,
Paris.

56

56 Bread basket. Maker's mark:
Orfèvrerie Christofle, Paris, *c.* 1900.
Width: 35 cm (13¾ in.). Private
collection.

57

57 Fruit stand. Maker's mark:
Tirbour, Paris, *c.* 1904. Diameter
22.5 cm (8¾ in.). Private collection.

58 Beaker, tea strainer and serving
spoon. Maker's mark: E. Lefèbvre,
Paris, *c.* 1900. Height of beaker:
8.5 cm (3¼ in.). Length of serving
spoon: 22.5 cm (8¾ in.). Private
collection.

58

59 Silver-gilt teapot designed by Edmond Becker. Maker's mark: H.H. Hébrard, Paris, *c.* 1907. Height: 12 cm (4¾ in.). Musée des Arts Décoratifs, Paris.

60 Silver-mounted glass lamp designed by Arnoux for Orfèvrerie Christofle for the Paris Exhibition of 1900. Musée Bouilhet-Christofle, Paris.

61 Mocha pot. Maker's mark: F. Boucheron, Paris, *c.* 1910. Height: 13 cm (5 in.). Private collection.

59

60

62

62 Vegetable dish designed by Jean E. Puiforcat in 1926. Maker's mark: E. Puiforcat, Paris. Diameter: 24.5 cm (9¾ in.). Musée des Arts Décoratifs, Paris.

63 Christening set designed by Jean E. Puiforcat. Beaker designed in 1925. Flatware design named 'Beaulieu'. Maker's mark on all pieces: E. Puiforcat, Paris. Height of beaker: 7.3 cm (2¾ in.). Length of spoon: 12 cm (4¾ in.). Private collection.

63

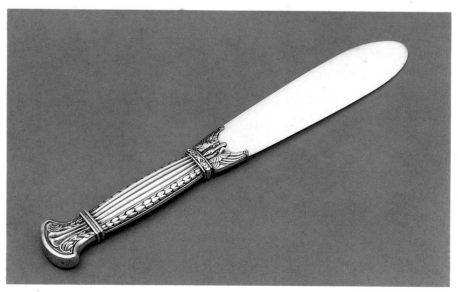

64 Ivory letter opener with silver-gilt handle. Maker's mark: Risler et Carré, Paris, c. 1920. Length: 27 cm (10¾ in.). Private collection.

64

65 Five-piece coffee and tea service
designed by Jean E. Puiforcat in 1923.
Maker's mark: E. Puiforcat, Paris.
Height of hot-water jug: 17 cm
(6¾ in.). Private collection.

66 Tea service designed by Henry
van de Velde. Maker's mark:
Christian Fjerdingstad, Paris, 1922.
Height of teapot: 15 cm (6 in.).
Museum Bellerive, Zurich.
Photograph: Marlen Perez.

66

67 Fruit stand. Signed 'Jean Goulden' and dated '29, nr XCV'. Stem decorated with white and green enamel, round foot with green and brown-red enamel. Diameter: 24.5 cm (9¾ in.). Sotheby's, Monaco, 25 June 1981, no. 302.

68 Lacquered matchbox holder. Maker's mark: Jean Dunand, Paris, c. 1930. Width: 6.8 cm (2¾ in.). Collection of Inez Stodel, Amsterdam.

67

6

69

70

right71

69 Tea caddy designed by Jean
Tétard in 1931. Maker's mark:
Maison Tétard, Paris. Height: 13.5 cm
(5¼ in.). Badisches Landesmuseum,
Karlsruhe.

70 Bowl. Signature and maker's
mark: Jean Després, Paris, c. 1930.
Diameter: 11 cm (4¼ in.). Private
collection.

71 Vegetable dish. Maker's mark:
André Aucoc, Paris, c. 1925. Musée
des Arts Décoratifs, Paris.

72 Cake plate. Maker's mark: J. et P.
Cardeilhac, Paris, c. 1930. 20 cm ×
20 cm (7¾ in. × 7¾ in.). Private
collection.

72

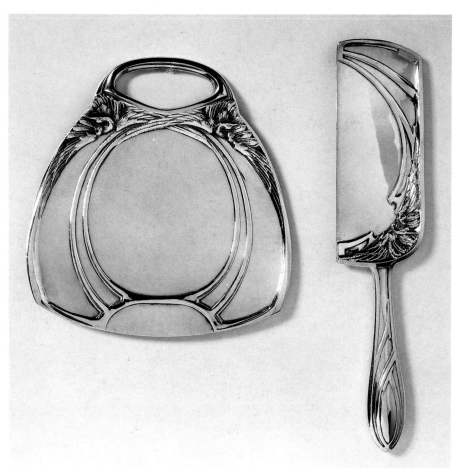

73 Crumb scoop and tray. Maker's mark: Wolfers Frères, Brussels, *c.* 1902 for As. Bonebakker, Amsterdam. Length of scoop: 29 cm (11½ in.). Rijksmuseum, Amsterdam.

74 Vegetable dish designed by R. Altenloh for the Paris Exhibition of 1925. Height: 12.4 cm (5 in.). Koninklijke Musea voor Kunst en Geschiedenis, Brussels. Photograph: Bernard Daubersy.

73

74

75 Plate. Maker's mark: Wolfers Frères, Brussels, *c.* 1885–90. Diameter: 23 cm (9in.). Private collection.

76 Tea service 'Gioconda', designed by Philippe Wolfers. Maker's mark: Wolfers Frères, Brussels. Made for the Paris Exhibition of 1925. Height of urn: 35.6 cm (14 in.). Width of tray: 68.5 cm (27 in.). Museum voor Sierkunst, Ghent.

75

77

77 Coffee and tea service. Maker's mark: Wolfers Frères, Brussels, *c*. 1930. Height of coffee pot: 17.5 cm (7 in.). Private collection.

78

78 Tray of amboina mahogany with silver rim and handles. Maker's mark: Delheid Frères, Brussels, *c*. 1930. Length: 59 cm (23¼ in.). Private collection.

79 Coffee and tea service with tray. Maker's mark: Delheid Frères, Brussels, *c*. 1930. Width of tray: 62.5 cm (24½ in.). Sotheby's, Monaco, 6 March 1983, no. 227.

79

3

BELGIUM

1880–1914

IN no other country in Europe was the link between changes in society and the applied arts so clear as in Belgium. William Morris's artistic and social ideas soon struck a responsive chord there, but the way in which people wanted to achieve a better and more honest society was conceived differently. Morris believed that workers had a right to decent, humane working conditions and that this would only be possible with a return to traditional crafts. In Belgium there was no opposition to machine production, but a desire to educate the workers and make them into fully-fledged citizens with the same rights as everyone else.

Art for the people through the creation of beauty in the everyday environment was the Socialist ideal. Thus in 1895 the Volkshuis was built in Brussels after a design by the architect Victor Horta. It was unprecedentedly modern in form and construction, the façades being built entirely of glass and iron. It housed a co-operative department store, offices, a bar, meeting rooms and a theatre. Concerts and exhibitions were held there and in the classrooms courses were given on a very wide range of subjects.

Naturally, these ideas had not come out of the blue. In 1881 the magazine *L'Art Moderne* had been founded by Octave Maus and Edmond Picard, two young liberal jurists with radical ideas about Socialist reform. In 1884 Maus had also founded the Société Les Vingt, of which twenty avant-garde artists were members and which regularly held exhibitions of contemporary art. The progressive bourgeoisie showed a great interest in modern art. For instance, some works by Vincent van Gogh were to be seen for the first time at Les Vingt in 1889. The first exhibition at which fine and applied art were shown together took place there in 1891. When this concept proved successful, the Société Les Vingt was dissolved and La Libre Esthétique founded. After that, countless English Arts and Crafts artists took part in exhibitions in Brussels. The influence of Morris, Ashbee, Voysey and Mackmurdo on Belgian applied art is clear, especially in furniture and graphic art. La Libre Esthétique continued to hold exhibitions until the beginning of the First World War in 1914, but after 1905 the pioneering role of the last decade of the nineteenth century was already a thing of the past.

Because great decorative value was attached in Belgian architecture to flowing, curvilinear lines in the construction, an organic whole was created. For this reason Brussels has been called the capital of curvilinear Art Nouveau. The architects Victor Horta (1861–1947), Paul Hankar (1861–1901) and Gustave Serrurier-Bovy (1856–1910) were the leaders of the Art Nouveau movement in Belgium.

In contrast to England and Germany, where many architects and painters made designs for silver, the members of Les Vingt stuck to what they did best. Nor did the architects Hankar, Horta and Serrurier-Bovy venture on this course either, although they did design various interiors. The only architect by whom designs for silver have survived is Antoine Pompe (1873–1980), but these were probably never executed. The Belgian curvilinear forms and ornament are very emphatically present in these drawings.[1]

Henry van de Velde (1863–1957) was originally a painter. Not until 1895 did he take his first steps along the path of architecture and applied art. In all his designs he showed himself to be a champion of the abstract, curvilinear version of the modern style, which was far removed from the naturalistic ornament generally found in France and Germany. It was through Van de Velde that this abstract, dynamic design spread to those two countries. The major part of his work, particularly his designs for silver, was done in Germany, where he worked from 1900 onwards, and will be discussed in that chapter. In his workshop, Société van de Velde, at Ixelles, a suburb of Brussels, a few pieces of jewelry and silvered bronze objects were made, as was furniture, but these fall outside the scope of this book. The mounts he designed for La Maison Moderne, the shop in Paris owned by Julius Meier-Graefe and opened in 1898, were not made in Belgium, but by the Paris silversmith A. Debain.

It is striking that in a prosperous country with a flourishing industry so little innovation should have occurred in the field of silverwork. Only the names of a firm called Debous, Fernand Dubois and Wolfers are known. Among the objects made by Fernand Dubois was a chalice with a beautifully modelled stem and a simple, smooth bowl with engraved linear decoration free from 'excess of ingenuity'.[2]

The Wolfers factory in Brussels was much bigger. Here modern silver was made on a large scale alongside the current classic models. Initially Wolfers was only a factory and it was not until later that the firm acquired its own shops in the most important cities in Belgium. It also exported a great deal to Germany, France and the Netherlands. It had its own outlet on Königsallee in Düsseldorf (J. Krischer Nachfolger), but a great deal of its silver was also sold by others, such as E. Goldschmidt of Cologne. The plate by Maison Wolfers

75 illustrated exhibits a combination of Rococo motifs and naturalistic ornament, which indicates that it was made before 1895.

Contrary to what one would expect in a country where curvilinear ornament played such a prominent role in architecture and furniture design, the ornament on the silver of Maison Wolfers is derived from nature and very realistically rendered. 'The workmanship is somewhat laboured, but the richness of the material used is strikingly displayed.'[3] The firm was very successful in Germany, in particular with these floral motifs.

In the Netherlands Wolfers's silver was sold by Begeer in Utrecht and

73 Bonebakker in Amsterdam. A crumb scoop and tray show an unusual motif for Wolfers: stylized cranes with abstract linear ornament which has links with the style which became fashionable in Germany after 1902.

The entire modern development at Maison Wolfers was due to Philippe Wolfers (1858–1929), who from 1876 onwards was trained in the workshop of his father, a manufacturer of gold and silverwork in Brussels, in all aspects of silversmithing: modelling, casting, burnishing, chasing and stone-setting. He took courses in drawing and sculpture at the Academy in Brussels under Isidore de Rudder and learned enamelling in Paris from the best enameller of the day, Louis Houillon.[4] The silver designs of that time were made largely in the current Louis XV style, but around 1890 studies from nature, especially orchids, irises, wild flowers and lilies, began to occupy a more important place so that these are frequently found on Wolfers's silver. After his father's death in 1892, he became artistic director of the family firm, which, like others, worked in widely differing styles.

In addition to the family firm, Wolfers also had a workshop of his own, in which a modeller, ivory carver, chaser, enameller and diamond-setter worked under his personal direction. The designs for this were kept in a separate catalogue of *Exemplaires Uniques*. In all, 136 one-off pieces are illustrated there, mainly jewels in a style closely related to that of the great French artist René Lalique, but also some ten silver objects decorated with enamel and stones, plus a few ivory and crystal vases.[5] When the architect Paul Hankar designed and built a house with a workshop for Philippe Wolfers

Vase designed by Philippe Wolfers, Brussels, c. 1898. Height: 16.2 cm (6½ in.). Württembergisches Landesmuseum, Stuttgart.

at La Hulpe in 1899, the latter's close associates were also housed in the village.

Wolfers's work attracted much attention at international exhibitions and his absence from the Paris Exhibition of 1900 was widely regretted. His display at the Turin Exhibition of 1902 carried off the palm for both quantity and quality. The jewelry and silver he showed there evinced his growing interest in sculpture, which is seen even more clearly in the magnolia vase illustrated. The enamelled decoration is restrained and the ornament does not stray outside the simple, strong form. This vase also shows that floral Art Nouveau had passed its peak in Belgium. As in France, there was a lack of artists capable of genuine innovation.

It was for this reason that Adolphe Stoclet commissioned Josef Hoffmann of Vienna to build a house for him in Brussels, which was to be decorated and furnished throughout by the Wiener Werkstätte.

Carved ivory vase with lizards in pewter and bronze around the base, made by Philippe Wolfers, Brussels, 1894.

The finest monument created by the artists of the Wiener Werkstätte is thus not to be seen in their native land, and the same applies to the buildings in Germany which Henry van de Velde designed before 1914.

IVORY WITH MOUNTS A characteristic aspect of the silver of Maison Wolfers has not yet been discussed. This is ivory carving, which reached great heights in Belgium at the end of the nineteenth century, due to King Léopold II, who placed ivory from the Belgian Congo at the disposal of a number of Belgian artists. He did so because he wanted to convince his subjects that this vast region in Central Africa offered economic possibilities. Ivory was one of the materials he used as propaganda for the products of the colony. The artists eagerly seized on this unusual

opportunity and in no other country at that time does one find such a variety of ivory carvings. These were generally combined with precious or base metals, since according to the ideas of that period it was by the use of bases and mounts in other materials that works of art were integrated into their surroundings.[6]

Wolfers kept to the shape of the tusks, carving naturalistic ornament in the ivory in bas-relief. From the same material the sculptor Égide Rombaux made sensitive female figures, which seem to be entwined in the silver mounts of the candelabra made by Frans Hoosemans. These objects, with matching jardinières, formed part of the Belgian contribution to the Paris Exhibition of 1900[7] and must have evoked much admiration in Germany in particular, for they were immediately bought by museums in Berlin and Hamburg.

The artists of the Art Nouveau movement in Belgium were too individualistic to train a gifted second generation to whom the torch

Candelabrum with ivory carved by Égide Rombaux and silver executed by Frans Hoosemans, Brussels. Bought at the Paris Exhibition of 1900. Height: 36 cm (14¼ in.). Formerly in the Museum für Kunst und Gewerbe, Hamburg. Photograph: Kiemer & Kiemer.

Candelabrum with ivory carved by Égide Rombaux and silver executed by Frans Hoosemans, Brussels. Bought at the Paris Exhibition of 1900. Height: 45 cm (17¾ in.). Kunstgewerbemuseum, Staatliche Museen Preussischer Kulturbesitz, West Berlin.

could be handed on. Victor Horta, the only modern architect to have been in at the start who was still working after 1905, returned to conventional forms.

1918–40 The work submitted by Robert Altenloh of Brussels to the exhibition Arts Industriels et du Métier, held in that city in 1910, won an award, but unfortunately it is impossible to form any idea of it. However, by the time of the Paris Exhibition of 1925, the situation is rather better, for we at least know that, in addition to a tea-set, he exhibited the 74 vegetable dish illustrated.

Wolfers, who had devoted himself exclusively to sculpture after 1905, ventured on a modern design once again for this exhibition, introducing his Gioconda range, which included a tea-set, as well as furniture, table silver and everything else required for the complete furnishing of a dining room. All the objects, composed of ten-sided forms, showed links with the French geometrical style with 76 undecorated angular planes, which was becoming popular in Paris. This much-discussed tea-set, Wolfers's last striking design, shows that he invariably moved with the times, even though he had not designed any silver for twenty years. After his death, countless beautiful objects were produced by Wolfers Frères under the direction of his sons Marcel and Lucien.

Around 1930 the Brussels firm Delheid, which had never been noted for modern silver until the twenties, made a number of exceptionally fine objects, in which silver was often combined with wood or ivory from the Belgian Congo. The angular forms of the tray 78 illustrated are akin to the angular, geometric French forms of the twenties, whereas the undulating curves of the tea-set are closer to the streamlined forms of the thirties. After the First World War French design was the great model for the applied arts, but the Belgians were not able to imbue it with a character of their own, as an earlier generation had succeeded in doing with English ideas.

At the age of sixty-one and after an absence of twenty-five years, Henry van de Velde was brought back to his native land in the twenties. He was required to set the tone for modern Belgian architecture and was the only artist of the old guard who, apparently effortlessly, was able to adapt to the development towards Functionalism of that decade and the thirties. He was the architect of the modern Belgian Pavilion at the Paris Exhibition of 1937. Only a great artist can move with the times in this way.

1 Exhibition catalogue *Art Nouveau in België*, Brussels 1980–1, pp. 275, 276 and 287.

2 F. Khnopff, 'Modern Belgian Jewellery', special Supplement to *The Studio*, London 1901–2, p. 125.

3 *The Studio*, 15 November 1898, p. 135.

4 Exhibition catalogue *Die Fouquet, 1860–1960, Schmuckkünstler in Paris*, Museum Bellerive, Zurich 1984, p. 64.

5 M. Wolfers, *Philippe Wolfers, précurseur de l'art nouveau*, Brussels 1965, p. 13.

6 Exhibition catalogue, Brussels 1980–1 (see Note 1), p. 167.

7 'L'Orfèvrerie étrangère à l'Exposition de 1900', *Revue de la Bijouterie, Joaillerie et Orfèvrerie*, 1900, p. 195 ff.

4

UNITED STATES

1880–1918

I
N the last decades of the nineteenth century the United
States, a country in which a great variety of cultures had
merged together, was in search of an identity of its own.
In the prosperous industrial regions in particular there
was an openness to artistic innovation.

The influence of Japan on design and on the way ornament was
applied is even more clearly detectable in America than in Europe,
especially in the use of copper encrusted on silver. This was
permissible in the United States, where there were no stringent laws
regarding silver, as there were in various European countries.

The great distance between the United States and Europe proved
no hindrance to the maintenance of mutual contacts. For artists on
both sides of the Atlantic it took a week's journey to find out what was
going on artistically on the other side. In 1876 Christopher Dresser
travelled through America on his way to Japan, calling at Philadelphia, where he visited the Centennial Exhibition and gave three
lectures at the Pennsylvania School of Industrial Design. In Japan he
bought applied art objects not only for the London firm of Londos &
Co., but also for Tiffany & Co. of New York.

Siegfried Bing and André Bouilhet wrote about decorative art in
the New World after their visit to the World's Columbian Exhibition
in Chicago in 1893. Conversely, Elbert Hubbard, founder of the
artists' community known as the Roycrofters, Gustav Stickley,
publisher of the influential periodical *The Craftsman*, and Louis
Comfort Tiffany visited artists in Europe. Charles Robert Ashbee
visited the United States a number of times after 1896, giving lectures
in various cities and meeting the architect Frank Lloyd Wright. In
1898 Ashbee's work was exhibited in the United States for the first

time. Not only did his ideas about the guild system, as applied in his Guild of Handicraft, catch on there, but his designs did too, some even to the extent that they were directly imitated.

94

Not all European designers were as successful as Ashbee, however. Archibald Knox, the most important designer of the London firm of Liberty & Co., who went to the New World to try his luck in 1912, returned to Britain empty-handed only a year later and settled on the Isle of Man. The best proof of the good transatlantic contact between artists was the Louisiana Purchase International Exhibition at St Louis in 1904, in which silversmiths and silver factories from a number of European countries successfully participated.

In 1897 the first American Arts and Crafts exhibition was held in Boston and an Arts and Crafts Society was established on the English model. Craft silversmithing burgeoned and 1901 saw the opening of the Handicraft Shop, where work was sold by various individual silversmiths who had workshop space there. The direction was in the hands of the Finnish silversmith Karl F. Leinonen, who was born in Turku and had arrived in Boston in 1893 after completing his training.

THE EAST COAST

Elizabeth Copeland (1866–1957) was born in Boston. She learned enamelling in England under Alexander Fisher and after her return to the United States worked for the Handicraft Shop. Up to 1937 she made a variety of objects, in particular silver coffers with naturalistic motifs in *cloisonné* enamel, which were deliberately made to look rather primitive, in order to emphasize the fact that they were hand crafted. George Gebelein (1878–1948) also worked as a member of the Handicraft Shop from 1903, but in 1909 set up on his own.

81

George E. Germer (1868–1936) trained as a silversmith in Berlin, before emigrating to the United States in 1893. In 1912, having worked for some years for various firms in New York and Providence, Rhode Island, he set up on his own in Boston, making mainly church silver.

The oldest silver factories in the United States were in the north-eastern part of the country, where the oldest cities were situated: Gorham at Providence (Rhode Island); Alvin Manufacturing Co., Black, Starr & Frost, Theodore B. Starr, Tiffany & Co. and Whiting in New York (New York); William B. Kerr and Unger Bros. in Newark (New Jersey); Reed and Barton in Taunton (Massachusetts); Bailey, Banks & Biddle Co., J.E. Caldwell & Co. and Simons Bros. Co. in Philadelphia (Pennsylvania).

In 1909 Ashbee wrote, 'In America the aesthetic revival is not nearly so developed and has not struck such roots as it has in England, but characteristically the industrial development is much more highly and intelligently worked out. Great houses like those of Gorham and Tiffany have been quick to realize, what the English firms have not yet discovered, that in order to march with the times they must at least make show of employing the artist and designer to help them in their industry.'[1] The effective co-operation between artists and manufacturers, which Ashbee noted in the United States, resembled that in Germany, where the Deutscher Werkbund had been founded in 1907.

The firm of Tiffany & Co., established in New York in 1837, enjoyed great international renown. It not only sold jewelry and silver, but also dealt in Japanese art, which was why Christopher Dresser bought objects for it during his visit to Japan in 1876. Conversely, in the 1870s and 1880s Japanese craftsmen went to America to introduce new techniques, forms and ornament into silverwork at Tiffany's. On the Japanese model, various materials were used in combination in a single object, while a motif of Japanese origin, such as the chrysanthemum, is frequently found after the 1880s as an ornament on silver candelabra, vases and even a 165-piece dinner service.

Edward C. Moore, the artistic director of Tiffany & Co., was in charge of the silver department. He was succeeded in 1891 by John Curran. The objects made there were in some cases extremely costly in execution – for example, a coffee pot set with Baroque pearls and a bowl set with aquamarines. The magnolia vase, Tiffany's showpiece at the Chicago Exhibition of 1893, was designed by John Curran. It is decorated with various flowers native to America. The naturalistic chased and partly enamelled motifs are very busy and dominant, certainly by comparison with Philippe Wolfers's magnolia vase of 1905. However, this is not solely the product of American taste, since it also reflects the *horror vacui* characteristic of many applied art objects of that period and certainly not only those of the United States. André Bouilhet, the then director of Maison Christofle in Paris, wrote in the *Revue des Arts Décoratifs* in 1893 that Tiffany's work was the only true art industry worthy of that name. The execution of the magnolia vase displayed great craftsmanship, but in his opinion the final result was disappointing.[2]

Louis Comfort Tiffany (1848–1933), the son of the founder of Tiffany & Co., is the best known and most versatile of all the American Art Nouveau artists. In 1879 he had set up a firm of his own, Associated Artists. The company was disbanded in 1885, but in those few years it had carried out a number of interior decorating commissions, including one for some rooms in the White House, in Washington. Tiffany next founded the independent Tiffany Glass Company, for which a workshop was set up in his father's firm. The

80,83
86

V

experiments he carried out there resulted in the famous lamps with shades in stained glass and Favrile glass.

Since the younger Tiffany had a great interest in Japanese art, he got to know Siegfried Bing on his visit to Paris in 1889. Bing was the largest dealer in Japanese art in continental Europe. He admired Tiffany's glass designs and sold his work to various museums and collectors in Europe.

Sometimes Tiffany himself designed silver mounts for his glassware. At the Paris Exhibition of 1900, for example, a punch-bowl with four ladles in Favrile glass was shown, in which all the parts had silver mounts. Other silversmiths also designed mounts for Tiffany glass. The famous Russian firm of Fabergé designed a silver base with three peacocks for a Favrile vase with a design of peacock feathers.

As Tiffany & Co. also sold in New York objects by others, such as glass by Émile Gallé of Nancy and Royal Copenhagen porcelain, it is not surprising that Tiffany acquired objects for American clients at the Paris Exhibition of 1900. He is known, for example, to have bought a number of objects designed by Jan Eisenloeffel, which were exhibited there by the Amsterdam firm of Hoeker & Zoon.[3] This silver had caught the attention of many, since smooth simple forms like this, which were decorated only sparsely with *champlevé* enamel, filigree ornament or cabochon-cut semi-precious stones, were still highly unusual at that time. After his father's death in 1902, the younger Tiffany succeeded him as director of Tiffany & Co.

In contrast to Tiffany's, which made silver for sale in its own shop, Gorham Corporation Inc. of Providence (Rhode Island), was a true silver factory, the biggest in the country. It was one of the first firms in the United States to make silver with the aid of machinery. Gorham supplied jewellers and small firms throughout the country, such as Spaulding & Co. in Chicago, Black, Starr & Frost in New York, and Shreve & Co. in San Francisco. In a Gorham sales catalogue of 1888 silver is illustrated that seems to foreshadow the Art Nouveau silver of 85,91 the 1890s in its use of naturalistic ornament, even though it still lacks the supple, flowing lines so characteristic of the silver of around 1900. That these objects were regarded as important in Europe is evident from the fact that the museum in Berlin bought some of them at Chicago in 1893 to serve as examples of good design with appropriate modern ornament.

In 1891 William C. Codman, a London silversmith, went to the United States at the request of the then director of Gorham's, Edward Holbrook. There Codman established a workshop devoted exclusively to hand-made silver in the Art Nouveau style. In silver objects sold under the name Athenic, silver was combined with other metals. As the name indicates, the forms were inspired by Greek models. In contrast to the normal sterling silver (0.925), the Martelé objects were in 0.950 silver, which was known as the Britannia Standard in England. Initially only vases, bowls and beakers were made in it, but it was soon possible to order complete tea-sets and even dinner services.

87,90

From a catalogue in French, which Gorham's published in 1900 through its Paris representative Spaulding & Co., it appears that not only hand-made silver in the Art Nouveau style was sold under the name Martelé, but also silver in the Louis XV style of the eighteenth century. Also illustrated in this catalogue is a liqueur set of Favrile glasses and decanters in Martelé mounts. Gorham's Martelé silver is characterized by both naturalistic and more abstract ornament, a lightly hammered surface and flowing, wavy contours. It ceased to be produced around 1910, when interest in it had declined. In addition to this expensive hand-made silver, countless cheap objects were also wholly or partly machine-made, with only the ornament embossed or chased by hand.

88,91

A firm which produced much Art Nouveau silver from 1900 onwards was Unger Brothers of Newark (New Jersey). An important part of its very large output consisted of toilet sets, in which, in the case of some models, it was possible to make a choice from over fifty pieces, with motifs ranging from Indians to poetic subjects like 'Love's Dream' or 'Reine des Fleurs'. Women in fluttering garments and flowers in long, wavy hair were the favourites.

97

How strongly the factories were influenced by everything to be seen at the Paris Exhibition of 1900 is clear from the extensive production of small objects like sweetmeat dishes, vases, and desk and toilet sets. There was a large clientele for articles in the fashionable Art Nouveau style with stamped whip-lash lines, plant motifs or heads of girls gazing dreamily into the distance, their faces framed by long, wavy hair. Even after 1905, when interest in this decorative Art Nouveau style declined rapidly in Europe, objects with these motifs embossed in high relief continued to be made in the United States for years. By contrast, the geometrical style, which played an important part after 1902 in Germany, the Netherlands and Austria in particular, found little or no favour in America, as is evident, for example, from the flatware model illustrated which was designed at Gorham's only in 1913.

100

THE MIDWEST

In the last decades of the nineteenth century there was a rapid growth in prosperity in the Midwest. There were only a few silver factories of any size and the interest in hand-made silver was great. This may have been the reason why Edward (Edouard) Colonna felt attracted to this prosperous region. After completing his architectural training in Brussels, he had gone to New York in 1882 and worked for some time for Louis Comfort Tiffany's Associated Artists. When the company closed down, he settled in Dayton, Ohio, where in 1887 he published a little book entitled *Essay on Broom-Corn*.[4]

The book was, as Martin Eidelberg writes, 'an essay not of words but of images'. It was the earliest publication in which motifs derived from nature, in this case a kind of cultivated grass used for making brooms and brushes, were given as models for curvilinear ornament in architecture and applied art. These rhythmically arranged, undulating abstract lines are also seen on a pitcher of the same period made by Tiffany & Co. of New York and on the base of the above-mentioned magnolia vase of 1893 designed by John Curran. Around 1900 these ornaments turn up again as supple curvilinear forms in Colonna's designs for Siegfried Bing's Maison de l'Art Nouveau in Paris.

84

44

Chicago grew rapidly in importance, both economically and culturally at this period. By the time the World's Columbian Exhibition was held there in 1893, it had eclipsed the older East Coast cities like Philadelphia and Boston and had become the second city in the country. The silver at the Chicago Exhibition was a revelation to the numerous European visitors. The Paris jeweller Henri Vever thought that the experiments of the Americans at that point revealed interesting attempts at innovation. André Bouilhet, too, concluded that the ideas current in France on the use of floral motifs were already being applied in the United States.[5]

Julius Lessing, at that time the director of the Kunstgewerbemuseum in Berlin, found the unique and surprising character of the American silver exhibited at Chicago so interesting that he bought a number of pieces to serve as models for students at applied art schools and artists in Germany. The heavy forms and the motifs of fish, seaweed and shellfish may have inspired Danish, as well as German, artists. There is a striking similarity between the heavy ornament on the American bowls and some of Thorvald Bindesbøll's designs with powerful abstract ornament for the firms of Michelsen and Mogens Ballin in Copenhagen. Cornelis Begeer of the Netherlands introduced into the Utrechtsche Fabriek van Zilverwerk the modern spoons with flower motifs, which were to be seen all over the exhibition.

83,89

205,206

The influence of the English Arts and Crafts Movement was stronger in the big cities of the Midwest, such as Chicago, Dayton, Cincinnati and St Louis, than on the East Coast. In 1897, the same year as in Boston, an Arts and Crafts Society was founded in Chicago. Within a few months it already had 128 members, including the architect Frank Lloyd Wright. The Art Institute of Chicago also endeavoured to raise the standard of craft work, organizing applied art exhibitions annually between 1902 and 1921.

There was an Art School at the Institute, where day and evening courses were given in, among other things, decorative design, pottery and ornamental metalwork. One of the students was Frank Hazenplug, a capable silversmith, who from 1903 to 1911 supplied designs for the metal workshop at Hull-House. This institution had been founded at the end of the 1880s by Jane Adams, after she had visited Ashbee's Guild and School of Handicraft in London. The metal workshop was directed by A. Fogliati, a silversmith and enameller, and Isadore Friedman. However, most of the objects made there were of copper, not silver.

There were a strikingly large number of women designers and silversmiths in Chicago, some of them professionals, but most of them active as highly-skilled amateurs. The best known and most influential was Clara Barck Welles (1868–1965), a student of the School of the Art Institute. In 1900 she opened the Kalo Shop (*Kalo* is Greek for 'beautiful'), the first of a whole series of arts and crafts studios in Chicago. After 1905 it developed into a workshop with twenty-five silversmiths. These she had trained herself, demanding a high degree of expertise. A remarkably large number of them had Scandinavian names – for example, Arne Myhre, Yngve Olsson, Einar Johansen, Bjorne O. Axness, Daniel Pederson and Julius Randahl.[6] Some of them later started workshops of their own.

98,102,111   The work of the Kalo Shop is characterized by fine craftsmanship and classic round and curving forms, often with initials or monograms as the only decoration. At first all the models were designed by Clara Barck Welles, but later designs were also supplied by Yngve Olsson, who had already come to Chicago before the First World War. The engraving and chasing on the Kalo silver was generally done by Olsson too.

Robert E. Jarvie (1865–1941) from New York, was registered as a silversmith in Chicago from 1893 to 1917. A number of objects for domestic use, which were given as prizes in competitions, such as the annual International Live Stock Exposition, were made in his workshop, the Jarvie Shop. His designs for punch-bowls with

101   matching ladles are particularly famous. The one illustrated, although not intended as a prize, gives a good idea of the monumentality and carefully calculated proportions that characterize Jarvie's work. The only decoration is the chased text and the monogram JJH below a border of rectangles around the rim. Jarvie derived geometrical

103   ornament of this type from Indian motifs. It is also found around the monogram CAH on a water pitcher.

In 1914 Kristopher Haga from Norway set up a studio with Grant Wood, which they called Wolund after the Norse god of smiths. It was not a success and in 1916 Haga had already returned to the Kalo Shop. Emery Todd, who had also worked there, did better with his studio, the T.C. Shop, which remained in existence until 1928. In contrast to Clara Barck Welles, Madeline Yale Wynne (1847–1918) and her pupil Frances M. Glessner (1848–1922) engaged in silversmithing as a hobby.

The success of these small studios led some of the big shops to establish workshops in order to be able to meet the great demand. The firm of Marshall Field & Company, for example, commissioned a silversmith named Dufford to start a silver department in 1904. The objects produced there were only partly hand-made, despite the conspicuous hammering with which they were finished.

Lebolt & Company, founded in 1912 by the jeweller J. Myer Lebolt (1868–1944), also offered its silverware to a wide clientele, enabling them to buy modern silver at competitive prices. The repoussé work **104** with floral Art Nouveau ornament sometimes found on Lebolt's silver of between 1912 and 1917 was the work of Edmund Boker (b. 1868). Boker was a Hungarian silversmith who had come to Chicago in 1907 with his compatriot Ernest Gould (1884–1954), and both had trained at the firm of A. Bachruch in Budapest. In 1912 they founded the Chicago Art Silver Shop, which remained in existence until 1934. Boker was responsible for the design of, and chasing on, the forms, which were hand-raised by Gould.

THE WEST COAST

One of the oldest firms in San Francisco was Shreve & Company. Here was made the mount for the bluish-green earthenware vase illustrated. In contrast to France, where numerous mounts were **106** made for ceramics, scarcely any such mounts are found in the United States. What was made in quantity there was silver deposit ware, in which motifs on glass were silver-plated by electrolysis.

As in England, so too in the United States interest in the Arts and Crafts Movement gradually waned. Naturally, hand-made silver continued to be sold after the First World War, but seldom in new modern forms like those which became popular in continental Europe.

1918–40

Neither the heavy, angular forms of de luxe hand-made French silver of the twenties, nor the machine forms of the modernistic silver of the

80 After-dinner coffee pot, set with baroque pearls. Maker's mark: Tiffany & Co., New York, 1880–90. Height: 17.7 cm (7 in.). The Art Institute of Chicago. Anonymous donor, Mr and Mrs James W. Alsdorf, Mrs Lester Armour and Mrs George Young. 1978.142.

80

81 Coffer with *cloisonné* enamelled panel. Maker's mark: Elizabeth E. Copeland, Boston. 1900–25. Height: 7 cm (2¾ in.). The Art Institute of Chicago. Laura S. Matthews Fund. 1982.1291.

82

82 Pitcher. Maker's mark: Gorham Mfg. Co., Providence, 1893. Bought at the World's Columbian Exposition in 1893. Height: 22 cm (8½ in.). Kunstgewerbemuseum, Staatliche Museen Preussischer Kulturbesitz, West Berlin.

83 Bowl set with aquamarines between seaweed motifs above fishes. Maker's mark: Tiffany & Co., New York. Bought at the World's Columbian Exposition in 1893. Height: 6.5 cm (2½ in.). Kunstgewerbemuseum, Staatliche Museen Preussischer Kulturbesitz, West Berlin.

84 Pitcher. Maker's mark: Tiffany & Co., New York, c. 1887. Height: 19.5 cm (7¾ in.). Sotheby's, Belgravia, London, 22 July 1976, no. 262.

84

85 Flask. Maker's mark: Gorham Mfg. Co., Providence, 1893. Bought at the World's Columbian Exposition in 1893. Height: 15.5 cm (6 in.). Kunstgewerbemuseum, Staatliche Museen Preussischer Kulturbesitz, West Berlin.

86 Silver and gold enamelled 'Magnolia Vase', designed by John Curran for the World's Columbian Exposition of 1893. Tiffany & Co., New York. Height: 77.5 cm (30½ in.). The Metropolitan Museum of Art, New York. Gift of Mrs Winthrop Atwell. 1899 (99.2).

85

87

88

87 Sauce boat and stand. Maker's mark: Gorham Mfg. Co. Martelé, Providence, *c.* 1900. Width of stand: 24 cm ($9\frac{1}{2}$ in.). Sotheby's Inc., New York, 20 November 1976, no. 561.

88 Umbrella handle. Maker's mark: Gorham Mfg. Co., Providence, 1905. Length: 19 cm ($7\frac{1}{2}$ in.). Private collection.

89 Bowl. Maker's mark: Whiting Mfg. Co., New York, 1893. Bought at the World's Columbian Exposition in 1893. Height: 10 cm (4 in.). Kunstgewerbemuseum, Staatliche Museen Preussischer Kulturbesitz, West Berlin.

89

90 Six-piece coffee and tea service.
Maker's mark: Gorham Mfg. Co.
Martelé, Providence, 1900. The Art
Institute of Chicago. Gift of Mrs
Thaddeus Dwight Hare in memory of
her father and mother, Charles Henry
Aldrich and Helen Urania Roberts.
1973. 769a–f.

91 Shaving cup and sweetmeat
dishes. Maker's mark: Gorham Mfg.
Co., Providence, 1892 and 1903.
Height of cup: 7.2 cm (2¾ in.). Width
of dishes: 13.8 cm (5½ in.). Private
collection.

91

92 Desk set comprising ink stand, letter stand, calendar, seal, paper knife and letter opener. Maker's mark: Whiting Mfg. Co., New York, *c.* 1900. Width of ink stand: 45.7 cm (18 in.). Sotheby's Inc., New York, 19 June 1977, no. 107.

93 Coffee service. Simpson, Hall, Miller & Company, Wallingford, Connecticut, *c.* 1900. Sotheby's Inc., New York, May 1983, no. 18.

94 Dish after a design by Charles Robert Ashbee. Maker's mark of the Arts and Crafts shop of Shreve, Crump & Low department store, Boston, 1902–14. Width: 29.2 cm (11½ in.). The Art Institute of Chicago. Gift of Mr and Mrs Kubicek. 1981.206.

95 Vase. Maker's mark: Black, Starr & Frost, New York, *c.* 1900. Height: 43.8 cm (17¼ in.). Sotheby's Inc. New York, 12 June 1981, no. 190.

95

96

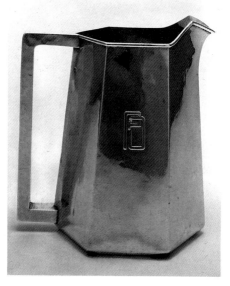

96 Coffee service. Maker's mark:
William B. Kerr, Newark, New
Jersey, c. 1900. Height of pot: 21.6 cm
(8½ in.). Diameter of tray: 28 cm
(11 in.). Sotheby's Inc., New York,
17 November 1984, no. 15.

97 Hand mirror 'Reine des Fleurs'.
Maker's mark: Unger Bros., Newark,
New Jersey, c. 1904. Museum voor
Sierkunst, Ghent.

98 Pitcher. Maker's mark: Kalo Shop,
Ridge Park, Illinois, 1910. Height:
19.1 cm (7½ in.). The Art Institute of
Chicago. Gift of Mrs Eugene A.
Davidson. 1973.345.

97

98

99 Bowl. Maker's mark: Simons Bro. & Company, Philadelphia, *c*. 1900. Diameter: 26 cm (10¼ in.). Private collection.

100 Cake server and serving fork. Maker's mark: Gorham Mfg. Co., Providence and Pat. 1913. Length of cake server: 22 cm (8½ in.). Matchbox holder with enamelled application. Maker's mark: Tiffany & Co., New York. Width: 4.2 cm (1½ in.). Private collection.

100

101

101 Punch-bowl, ladle and tray. Maker's mark: Robert Jarvie, Chicago, 1911. Diameter of bowl: 25.7 cm (10 in.). Diameter of tray: 52.7 cm (20¾ in.). Length of ladle: 45.7 cm (18 in.). The Art Institute of Chicago. Gift of Mr and Mrs John R. Hattstaedt in memory of his father. 1974.293.

102 Goblet. Maker's mark: The Kalo Shop, Chicago and New York, 1914–18. Height: 14.6 cm (5¾ in.). The Art Institute of Chicago. Gift of the Antiquarian Society through Mrs George B. Young in memory of her mother. 1987.125.

103 Pitcher. Maker's mark: Robert Jarvie, Chicago, 1911. Height: 26 cm (12½ in.). The Art Institute of Chicago. Gift of Raymond W. Sheets. 1973.357.

104 Loving cup. Maker's mark: Lebolt & Co., Chicago, 1912–17. Height: 23.9 cm (9½ in.). The Art Institute of Chicago. Restricted gift of Mr and Mrs William Steen, Dr Julian Archie Fund. 1987.123.

103

104

105 Coffee service with gilt and oxidized facets, 'The Lights and Shadows of Manhattan'. Designed and executed by Erik Magnussen in 1927. Maker's mark: Gorham Mfg. Co., Providence. Height of coffee pot: 24.1 cm ($9\frac{1}{2}$ in.). Collection of Charles H. Carpenter Jr.

106 Vase with silver mount. Maker's mark: Shreve & Co., San Francisco, 1900–17. Height: 21.9 cm ($8\frac{1}{2}$ in.). The Art Institute of Chicago. Gift of the Antiquarian Society through Mrs Robert Hixon Glore. 1984.1172.

107 Fruit stand. Maker's mark: Peer
Smed, New York, 1933. Height:
15.8 cm ($6\frac{1}{4}$ in.). The Art Institute of
Chicago. Gift of the Antiquarian
Society through the Mr and Mrs
James W. Alsdorf Fund. 1986.1061.

108 Standing covered bowl designed
by Erik Magnussen. Maker's mark:
Gorham Mfg. Co., 1926. Height:
31.1 cm ($12\frac{1}{4}$ in.). The Art Institute of
Chicago. Gift of the Antiquarian
Society. 1984.1172.

107

10

109

110

109 Urn and tray designed by Eliel Saarinen. Maker's mark: International Silver Co., Meriden, Connecticut, 1934. Height of urn: 45.7 cm (18 in.). Diameter of tray: 36.2 cm (14¼ in.). Cranbrook Academy of Art Museum, no. 1935.8a,b.

110 Box with enamelled lid. Maker's mark: Margaret Craver, Boston, 1938. Diameter: 14.7 cm (5¾ in.). The Art Institute of Chicago, Americana Fund. 1985.516.

111 Coffee pot, marked N. Post,
  c. 1932. Height: 19 cm (7½ in.).
Pitcher, Maker's mark: Kalo Shop,
Chicago, *c.* 1930–40. Sotheby's Inc.,
New York, 7 December 1985, no. 11.

112 Cigarette box designed by Eliel
Saarinen and made by Arthur Nevill
Kirk, Cranbrook, *c.* 1930. Height:
13.7 cm (5½ in.). Cranbrook Academy
of Art Museum, no. 1933.50.

112

113

114

113 Sweetmeat bowl. Maker's mark: Hallmark Silversmiths Inc., New York, *c.* 1930. Height: 7 cm (2¾ in.). Private collection.

114 Cigarette box. Maker's mark unknown, *c.* 1930. Height: 5.9 cm (2¼ in.). Kunstgewerbemuseum, Cologne.

thirties found much of a following in the United States. The round, hammered forms of Georg Jensen were much more successful there. Shown in America for the first time in 1915, they were awarded a Grand Prix.[7] After the newspaper magnate William Randolph Hearst bought virtually the entire collection on that occasion, Jensen silver rapidly became popular in the United States. In contrast to the Wiener Werkstätte of America Inc., which had opened a sales outlet on Fifth Avenue, New York, in 1922, after a successful exhibition, but was forced to close it again early in 1924,[8] the shop opened by Jensen in 1924 did very well indeed.

Although the United States did not take part in the Paris Exhibition of 1925, because American designers were said not to meet the requirements,[9] good modern silver was certainly made in that country.

THE EAST COAST

Peter Müller-Munk (b. 1904), a pupil of Bruno Paul in Berlin, went to New York in 1926. After having worked for a year for Tiffany & Co., he opened a workshop of his own in 1927. The first exhibition in which he took part in New York was held in the Chase Bank Building in 1928. As he himself wrote, the objects he made had 'the virtues of the slow and calculating process of design and execution with which they grew'.[10] After a significant part of the market for this hand-made silver disappeared as a result of the economic crisis, he accepted the post of associate professor at the Carnegie Institute in Pittsburgh. In contrast to much of the hand-made silver in the United States, which is influenced by Danish work, particularly that of Jensen, his pieces have angular forms with accentuated horizontal and vertical lines. They clearly reveal that he was trained in Germany.

The Dane Peer Smed (1878–1943) had a workshop in New York. Both the hand-made silver he produced there and the designs he made for Tiffany's in 1937 have the familiar characteristics of Danish silver: round, hammered forms and fluent, unobtrusive ornament. 107

After a seven-year apprenticeship, Arthur J. Stone (1847–1938) became a silversmith in his birthplace, Sheffield in England, where he worked for ten years as a chaser before emigrating to the United States in 1884. He set up a workshop of his own for hand-made silver in Gardner, Massachusetts, in 1901. His silver designs were widely admired and his work won many awards. He made it a point that each of the silversmiths in his workshop should set his own initials on the objects he made. (See the illustration on p. 124.)

In common with individual silversmiths, industry too tried to move in new directions at the end of the twenties, and some firms began

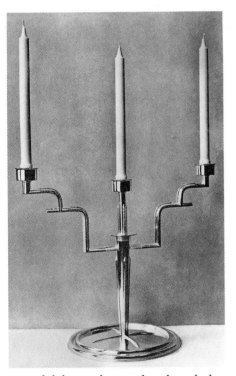

Candelabrum designed and made by Peter Müller-Munk, New York. Shown in *The Studio*, October 1928.

again to commission freelance artists to design silver for serial production. As it had done at the end of the nineteenth century, Gorham's once more appointed a European artist to produce modern hand-raised silver, but this time not an Englishman. In view of the great interest in Danish silver, the obvious response was to invite a designer from Copenhagen, so in 1925 Erik Magnussen (1884–1961) arrived in the United States. Most of his designs are characterized by soft curves, a hammered surface and restrained ornament in the   108
true modern Danish style. However, having a European view of the American phenomenon of cities bristling with skyscrapers, Magnussen also designed a very striking coffee service called 'Lights   105
and Shadows of Manhattan'. This is composed of triangular facets, which were burnished, gilded and oxidized by turns. In 1932 he opened a workshop of his own in Chicago and from 1933 to 1938 had one in Los Angeles.

Among the designers with whom the International Silver Company at Meriden, Connecticut, worked was the famous Finnish architect Eliel Saarinen (1873–1950), who went to the United States in 1923. For this large company he designed flatware, which was shown for the first time at the exhibition 'The Architect and the Industrial Arts', held in the Metropolitan Museum of Art in New York in 1929. In these models the handles and stems are long by comparison with the classic models then current. A bowl with a fluted base, after a design by Saarinen, was also put into production at that time. In 1934, he designed the most spectacular functional object to be made in silver in the United States at that period, a spherical coffee urn on a pierced cylindrical base.   109

At Simpson, Hall, Miller & Co., a subsidiary of the International Silver Company, silver was made after designs by Alfred G. Kintz from 1928 onwards. The moderately modern forms of these bread dishes, bowls, flower bowls and sweetmeat dishes, of which the models had picturesque names like 'Tropical Sunrise', 'Northern Lights' and 'Ebb Tide', proved a success.

It was not until around 1935 that silver was made by Tiffany & Co. again in contemporary modern forms with sharp angles and stepped edges. Some of these objects were highly de luxe in their execution. At the World's Fair in New York in 1939, for instance, Tiffany's showed a cocktail set adorned with emerald cabochons.

The Kalo Shop continued to be the most important producer of hand-made silver in Chicago after the First World War. Its designs, with   THE MIDWEST their beautiful rounded forms and hammered surfaces, remained in production unaltered for years.

After completing his training as a silversmith, Julius Randahl (1880–1972) left Sweden for the United States in 1901. He joined the Kalo Shop in 1907, after working for some years for Tiffany's and Gorham's in New York. Around 1914 he opened his Randahl Shop, which grew into a firm with about twenty employees. He himself sold the silver produced there, but he also sold hollow-ware to Marshall Field & Co. and other leading department stores. Production was partly mechanized, but the objects were always finished by hand. Randahl's earliest silver shows how great the Kalo Shop's influence was on many of those who had worked there, while his contribution to the Paris Exhibition of 1937 further illustrates Jensen's influence on other silversmiths. The fruit stand and candlestick he showed were awarded a silver medal.

Knut L. Gustafson (1885–1976), also from Sweden, went to Chicago in 1910. After working for Robert Jarvie, Lebolt & Company and the Randahl Shop, he founded the Chicago Silver Company in 1923. Initially he made spun hollow-ware, but later concentrated mainly on the production of flatware, most of it decorated with an unobtrusive leaf motif.

John P. Petterson (1884–1949) emigrated to the United States in 1905. He worked for Tiffany & Co. until 1911 and then went to Chicago, where he worked for Robert Jarvie for some years. In 1914 he opened his Petterson Studio, where, just as in the Kalo and Jarvie Shops, only hand-raised silver was made.

At Bloomfield Hills, near Detroit, Michigan, George C. Booth laid in the twenties the foundations for the Cranbrook Academy of Art. The American counterpart of the Bauhaus was at that time one of the few educational institutions for art, architecture and design in the United States. Booth had met Saarinen in 1924 and asked him to work out the architectural plans for the academy. One of the workshops at Cranbrook was for metalwork and here Booth's aim was twofold: the production of good hand-made silver and the supply of good designs for industrial production.[11] In 1927 he invited the silversmith Arthur Nevill Kirk (1881–1958) to work at Cranbrook and in 1929 Kirk was made director of the metal workshop, with Charles Price and Margaret Biggar as his assistants. Most of his work consists of costly objects set with precious stones and richly enamelled, and shows the influence of English silversmiths such as Alexander Fisher and Omar Ramsden. The tea-set illustrated on p. 125, with faceted sides, is one of the few objects that belongs to the geometrical Art Deco style. Kirk's designs were always worked out with great care down to the smallest details, as is evident from the finely carved ebony handles and finial.

Saarinen, as has already been seen, was interested in designing flatware for the silver industry, but also designed one-off pieces for the hand-work studio. Margaret Biggar, who collaborated on the cigarette box as Kirk's assistant, remarked that the way in which it had to be made was far from simple, because 'Mr Saarinen . . . was a marvellous architect, but he didn't know anything about silver to be handmade.'[12] Charles Price also executed some designs by Saarinen. Unfortunately, the Cranbrook workshop was forced to close in 1933, owing to the adverse economic situation, but Price taught at the Academy for two more years.

Margaret Craver (b. 1907) studied at the Art School of the University of Kansas City, Missouri, her birthplace. She then went to Sweden for further training and worked for some years under Baron Erik Fleming at the Atelier Borgila. She returned to the United States in 1938, set up as silversmith and became a teacher. Initially she made hollow-ware, sometimes decorated with enamel, but later concentrated on jewelry.

112

Bowl. Maker's mark: Arthur J. Stone, Gardner, Massachusetts, 1930. Height: 10.4 cm (4 in.). Cranbrook Academy of Art Museum. Gift of George G. Booth, 1931.26.

Standing fruit dish designed by Eliel Saarinen and made by Charles Price, Cranbrook, 1930. Height: 21 cm (8¼ in.). Cranbrook Academy of Art Museum, 1933.47.

110

THE WEST COAST

'Kem' (Karl Emanuel Martin) Weber (b. 1889) of Los Angeles, a pupil of Bruno Paul in Berlin, was in San Francisco when the First World

Tea service with carved finial and handles, designed by Arthur Nevill Kirk, Cranbrook, *c.* 1933. Height of teapot: 14.4 cm (5¾ in.). Cranbrook Academy of Art Museum, 1933.33a-c.

War broke out in 1914. In 1927 he started to work as an industrial designer and a year later designed two cocktail-shakers with ebony handles for the Friedman Silver Co. of New York. The silversmith Porter Blanchard of Pacioma, California, may have made some tea-sets after designs by him. Weber's designs for vases, dishes and bowls are mainly simple in form and undecorated. They are obviously intended for industrial production, like all his designs for other, less costly materials.

Modern silver was even more of a rarity in the United States than in Europe. For completely new objects, such as cars, refrigerators or radios, which came into general use earlier in America than in Europe, modern forms were self-evident, but the most modern buildings in the world, the skyscrapers, were furnished in copies of eighteenth-century styles. The silversmiths and silver manufacturers accommodated the conservative taste of a wealthy clientele. Fairly classic forms with a contemporary 'hand-made' look pleased the customers most. The heavy forms and angular contours of French Art Deco silver were too eccentric for most Americans. André Bouilhet was right when he wrote in 1893 that the new style which 'will characterize the beginning of the twentieth century' would come from America,[13] but as far as silver was concerned this hopeful beginning had scarcely a sequel.

113

1 Charles Robert Ashbee, *Modern English Silverwork*, London 1909, p. 10.
2 Diana Chalmers Johnson, *American Art Nouveau*, New York 1979, p. 37.
3 Jacobine E. Huisken and Friso Lammertse, *Koninklijke Geschenken, traditie en vernieuwing rond de eeuwwisseling*, Amsterdam 1988, p. 32.
4 Martin Eidelberg, 'Edward Colonna's "Essay on Broom-Corn": a forgotten book of early Art Nouveau', *The Connoisseur*, February 1971, pp. 123–30.
5 Johnson, op. cit., p. 36.
6 Sharon S. Darling, *Chicago Metalsmiths*, Chicago 1977, pp. 49 and 53.
7 Jørgen Møller, *Georg Jensen, The Danish Silversmith*, Copenhagen 1985, p. 71.
8 Werner J. Schweiger, *Wiener Werkstätte. Kunst und Handwerk*, Vienna 1982, p. 116.
9 Alistair Duncan, *American Art Deco*, London 1986, p. 20.
10 Peter Müller-Munk, 'Machine-Hand', *The Studio*, October 1929, p. 711.
11 J. David Farmer, 'Metalwork and Bookbinding', in *Design in America, The Cranbrook Vision 1925–1950*, New York 1983, p. 154.
12 ibid., p. 161.
13 Johnson, op. cit., p. 36.

5

GERMANY

1890–1914

GERMANY was for centuries divided into a large number of principalities and it was not until these had all been united, forcibly or otherwise, during the nineteenth century that the economy could take a favourable turn. After 1871, when the King of Prussia was proclaimed German Emperor, the country rapidly developed into one of the leading industrial powers of Europe. Economic growth brought unprecedented prosperity to a section of the bourgeoisie and this led to a great demand for silver objects, preferably in 'Altdeutsche Stil' – that is, Renaissance style – and the Neo-Rococo style, generally with very ostentatious ornament.

In the design offices of the silver factories grateful use was made of various reprints of old pattern-books with engraved ornament. The application of motifs from these to mass-produced objects made it possible to gratify the longings of the well-to-do bourgeoisie, who could now afford to set themselves up with family plate, just as noble and patrician families had done in the past. Around 1900 there were more than 160 silver factories in Germany and nowhere was the demand for a constant supply of new objects and models as great as in that country.

Close ties existed between the imperial family in Berlin, the grand-ducal family at Darmstadt and the English royal house. As a result, the ideals of those British artists, who, in emulation of William Morris, wanted to return to the era before the Industrial Revolution, when hand-work was still highly regarded, soon filtered through to Germany. From 1896 to 1903 the architect Hermann Muthesius, as technical attaché at the German embassy in London, was in close contact with various leading British artists. However, he did not share the British aversion to mechanical production, for he saw machines as the very means of improving the living conditions of workers, since they could be used to bring simple but good mass-produced, and thus cheap, objects within reach of the masses.

In numerous publications and through his lectures in Germany. Muthesius did his utmost to promote ideas for improving the applied arts. It was not the machines that were responsible for the poor quality of mass-produced articles, but the manufacturers. They must wake up to the fact that the industrial production of quality items was of great importance to their firms. On the advice of Muthesius, new art schools were established all over the country and great attention was paid in them to training in craft skills. In 1907 the Deutscher Werkbund was founded with the aim of promoting co-operation between designers and industry. The first president was Peter Bruckmann, director of the factory in Heilbronn that bore his name.

As a result of its former fragmented character, Germany possessed several cultural centres. While Berlin was now the capital of the empire as a whole, the cradle of the renewal of the applied arts was Munich, where, in 1896, the periodical *Jugend* was published for the first time. This became so influential that it lent its name to the modern movement in Germany, Jugendstil. Other centres which played a part in this revival around 1900 were Darmstadt, Weimar and Hagen. These came to prominence thanks to the initiative of the princeling of the region or leading local industrialists. These, like Hermann Muthesius, were inspired by the idea that progressive designs would revive the applied arts and related industry. They saw the bringing together of artists and industry as a means of furthering the development of their state or town. The artists who designed silver, or made it themselves, in these cultural centres are discussed below under each city.

In addition to these centres, factories in all parts of the country tried to lend forms and ornament a contemporary Jugendstil appearance, with or without the aid of designs by more or less well-known artists. The market for these factories was the whole of Germany. As they produced for jewellers all over the country, they linked up more with the general development in Germany during the imperial period than with the centres already mentioned, which were geared to regional development. Therefore they are treated below as a separate group.

In the movement for the revival of the applied arts in Germany, four styles can be distinguished in silver up to 1914: the naturalistic style, Jugendstil, the Secession style (Sezessionstil, as it is called in Germany) and the Munich style. In the first of these, flowers with long leaves were used for preference: irises, orchids, lilies of the valley, tulips and daffodils. The Jugendstil was influenced by Belgian and French curvilinear Art Nouveau with asymmetrical whip-lash lines. The term Secession style denotes the geometrical manner, with simple symmetrical lines and decoration. The silversmiths of Munich had a style of form and decoration entirely their own. It was based on the possibilities of the material, which seems to spring into life when light is reflected from its undulating surfaces.

Even more than in other countries, the First World War caused in Germany an obvious break in the development of the applied arts. Rather than continue the renewal movement along pre-war lines, the new generation felt that it had to begin anew. On the one hand this meant that potentially fruitful developments were broken off, but on the other it cleared the way for the new Art Deco movement and, in Germany in particular, for modernism.

MUNICH UP TO 1914   In 1897 the Vereinigte Werkstätten für Kunst im Handwerk (United Workshops for Art in Hand-Work) were founded in Munich on the model of the Guild of Handicraft in London and La Maison de l'Art Nouveau in Paris. Among the founders were the painters Peter Behrens, Richard Riemerschmid and Bernhard Pankok, who also won their spurs in the fields of architecture and the applied arts. Their aim was to sell objects for everyday use designed by modern artists. A proportion of these items were made in their own workshops, which included one for chasing and enamelling. Not only was the name of the association based on English models, but the forms used were sometimes similarly inspired. The influence of Charles Robert Ashbee for example, is clearly to be seen in a caviar dish by Bernhard Pankok (1872–1943).

117

Richard Riemerschmid (1868–1957), who was born and brought up in Munich, was one of the leaders of the new movement in Germany. He became famous mainly as an architect and designer of furniture, textiles, ceramics, glass and metalwork. He designed very little silver, but he was the first artist in Germany to create a completely new, functional model for flatware. In designing the shape of the knife handle Riemerschmid took account of the fact that one cuts with the index finger extended, while he enlarged the fork's breast and shortened its prongs, to make it easier to eat the sauce accompanying a dish. In 1911 he designed a set of cutlery for the Munich firm of Carl Weishaupt. This has a modern, slender version of the classic spatula stem.[1] Riemerschmid was an admirer of the work of the Dutch silversmith Jan Eisenloeffel; various of the latter's copper sets can be seen in photographs of interiors he designed.

In 1902 the artists Wilhelm von Debschitz (1871–1948) and Hermann Obrist (1862–1927) founded the Lehr- und Versuchs-

Ateliers für angewandte und freie Kunst, subsequently known as the Debschitz-Schule, a private art school for training applied artists and craftsmen on completely new lines. The accent was not on copying models, but on guiding and developing the students' powers of observation. Only after general formative courses with this aim could they choose the subject in which they planned to specialize. The first, surprising results of this training were to be seen at the exhibition held by the school in 1903. Forms and ornament were characterized as showing a 'remarkable talent for abstraction'.[2] These designs were sometimes executed in the workshops of Eduard Steinicken or M.T. Wetzlar.[3] Some years later this abstract geometrical ornament had become common property. The school produced versatile designers like Karl Johann Bauer, Fritz Schmoll von Eisenwerth, Friedrich Adler, Gertraud von Schnellenbühel, Marga Jess and Josef Urban, who are discussed later.

The trend towards abstract, geometric ornament is to be found in the work of the silversmith Karl Johann Bauer (1877–1914), who studied at the school and taught there from 1905 onwards. In addition to jewelry, he made a great many small silver objects, such as cigarette-cases, parasol handles and napkin rings.

Interior designed by Richard Riemerschmid, Munich. Tea service designed by Jan Eisenloeffel, Amsterdam. Illustrated in *Dekorative Kunst*, 1904.

Electric kettle designed by Fritz Schmoll von Eisenwerth for M.T. Wetzlar, Munich, *c.* 1914. From *Dekorative Kunst*, 1915.

Fritz Schmoll von Eisenwerth (1883–1963) was likewise first a student and then a teacher at the Debschitz-Schule, of which he was director from 1914 to 1920. During his time there he supplied silver designs to the firm of M.T. Wetzlar in Munich and the P. Bruckmann & Söhne silver factory at Heilbronn. His design for Wetzlar is simple and practical and thus meets the requirements of serial production. That the elaborate service for Bruckmann was also intended for such is more difficult to imagine, although a description survives of how the designer himself carved the decorative plates in plaster and afterwards carefully corrected the steel dies made at the factory with his own hand.[4]   120

Not all the Munich workshops collaborated with the Debschitz-Schule. The court silversmith Carl Weishaupt made silver after designs by Richard Riemerschmid as well as his own, but he also used   124
ornament from other sources. The angular spirals of a box for example, were borrowed from designs by Patriz Huber of Darmstadt.

Adolf von Mayrhofer (1864–1929) was one of the few surviving   XIV
craftsman silversmiths around the turn of the century. He had learned the craft in the traditional way as an apprentice in the workshop of F. Harrach, one of the most important firms in Munich. Afterwards he had worked for twelve years as an assistant to E. Wollenweber, silversmith to the Bavarian court, and he kept in close touch with the latter after setting up on his own in 1903. His work gradually took on a personal character: hand-raised beakers and boxes with slight curves, sometimes with spiral motifs soldered on to them, and tea-sets of a rather squat form, with broad, undecorated facets and carefully carved ebony or ivory finials and handles. He also made objects with *cloisonné* enamel and spiral ornament.

The collective display put on by the Munich silversmiths at the International Exhibition of 1910 in Brussels was awarded a gold medal.[5] In general Munich silversmiths emphasized their craft skills by applying rich ornament, piercing, foliate scrolls of a Gothic cast and soldered-on motifs. Copious use was also made of bosses on prize cups, as a modern variant of the columbine cup that had had to be made by craftsmen in the sixteenth and seventeenth centuries as a masterpiece.

DARMSTADT The young Grand Duke of Hesse, Ernst Ludwig, a grandson of Queen Victoria, was well informed about the English Arts and Crafts ideals through his contact with the artist H.M. Baillie Scott, who refurnished two rooms for him in the palace at Darmstadt. The furniture was made by Charles Robert Ashbee's Guild of Handicraft in London. In

1899, in order to promote the cultural and economic prosperity of his domain, the Grand Duke offered a number of young artists three-year contracts. It was his intention that Peter Behrens, Rudolf Bosselt, Paul Bürck, Hans Christiansen, Ludwig Habich, Patriz Huber and Josef Maria Olbrich should produce models which would be made available to various firms in Hesse. Alexander Koch, the publisher of the magazines *Innen-Dekoration* and *Deutsche Kunst und Dekoration* continually did all he could to publicize the best results achieved by these artists and the objects they made.

The artists remained active up to the outbreak of the First World War, the colony varying in size and composition during those fifteen years, but in all twenty-three artists worked there for varying lengths of time. Only two, Ernst Riegel and Theodor Wende, were silversmiths. Behrens, Christiansen, Huber and Olbrich, and later Paul Haustein and Albin Müller as well, made many designs for silver, which were executed by large and small factories, thus contributing to the Grand Duke's ideal of 'the prosperity of my Hesse'.

In 1900 the artists' colony took part in the Paris Exhibition, but it was not until the following year that it won great renown. In the summer of 1901 the exhibition 'A Document of German Art' opened in Darmstadt. Its plan was a novel one: for the first time objects were shown in a normal domestic setting, instead of a large exhibition hall. Houses had to be specially built for the occasion, all but one of them designed by Olbrich, who had trained as an architect in Vienna. The other house was designed, decorated and furnished throughout by Peter Behrens. Up to that point he had gained a reputation for himself in a completely different field, but this made his name as an architect.

Although Peter Behrens (1868–1940) was one of the founders of Munich's Vereinigte Werkstätten für Kunst im Handwerk, he worked solely as a painter and graphic designer there. Only in Darmstadt did he gain the opportunity to display his wide range of abilities, winning renown in that city in numerous fields: architecture, furniture, glass, porcelain, silver and jewelry. In Darmstadt he designed two different flatware models in the Secession style, which were made by the silver factory of M.J. Rückert in Mainz. The cutlery he designed for his own house had a motif with curved, intersecting lines and sharp angles, through which ellipses and triangles were created.

The same motifs are found on the parts of a desk set which was 121 made after his designs by Martin Mayer, likewise of Mainz.[6] The other cutlery has geometric motifs. In both models the ornament is very dominant and it is obvious why Behrens has been described as 'the leading representative of linear principles'.[7] In his later designs for the Franz Bahner silver factory at Düsseldorf this is certainly no longer the case. During his time in Darmstadt he gave a four-week

'Applied Art Master Course' in Nuremberg in the autumn of 1901 and the spring of 1902. After his departure in 1903 for Düsseldorf, where he was appointed director of the applied art school, the courses in Nuremberg were given in succession by the Munich artists referred to above, Richard Riemerschmid, Paul Haustein and Friedrich Adler.

In the three years of his participation in the artists' colony at Darmstadt (1899–1902) the painter and graphic artist Hans Christiansen (1866–1945) made a large number of designs for silver, glass, porcelain, textiles and stained-glass windows. In contrast to the other artists there he showed a preference for colourful naturalistic motifs, as seen in various designs for cigarette boxes and cases with enamelled lids. These were made at Louis Kuppenheim's enamel workshop in Pforzheim, by far the best in Germany. Christiansen's graphic work is characterized by profiles of girls with flowers in their long, wavy hair and these motifs are found on a parasol handle, which was made at Martin Mayer's in Mainz. E.L. Viëtor, the court silver factory in Darmstadt, also executed some of his designs. The fact that some objects bear a Vienna import mark indicates that there was also an interest in Christiansen's work in Austria.

126

The artist's flatware design for the firm of Bruckmann at Heilbronn, with abstract, symmetrical, linear ornament, is modern in form. The forks have shorter prongs and a larger breast than the traditional models, while the narrow shape of the bowls of the spoons matches the elegant, slender stems. Both Christiansen's naturalistic motifs and his abstract, curvilinear decorations were heavily influenced by French Art Nouveau. He lived in Paris and Darmstadt alternately until 1911, but was no longer a member of the artists' colony.

128,12

The architect and furniture designer Patriz Huber (1878–1902) likewise went to Darmstadt in 1899. For the exhibition there in 1901 he designed furniture and a number of small silver objects (parasol handles, boxes and stoppers) with simple geometrical ornament and angular spirals.

122

Josef Maria Olbrich (1867–1908), from Vienna, had been an assistant to the architect Otto Wagner, one of the founders of the Vienna Secession and the architect of the exhibition building for this group of avant-garde artists. Olbrich, like Huber, arrived in Darmstadt in 1899, designing the houses for the 1901 exhibition, together with a large part of their interior decoration. His designs for silver were not a success. Only a candelabrum and some objects for the tea table, a tea caddy, sugar bowl and biscuit barrel, have survived. All these pieces were made at the factory of P. Bruckmann & Söhne at Heilbronn. The time was not yet ripe for these severe architectural forms. Olbrich designed some electroplate flatware, but none in

118
XV

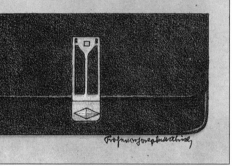

Designs for purses illustrated in *Ideen von Josef M. Olbrich* (2nd edn, Leipzig 1904).

silver. He was very domineering and this was presumably the reason why various of the original artists left Darmstadt in 1902 and 1903.

Paul Haustein (1880–1944) was one of the artists who came to Darmstadt in 1903 to swell the thinning ranks. His designs from his time there cover the whole spectrum of the applied arts, but even before he arrived in Darmstadt, he had a leaning towards silver and copper. He combined these materials in a highly original way in his enamelled-copper inkwell with a silver mount. This dates from 1901, when he was still working for the Vereinigte Werkstätten für Kunst im Handwerk in Munich. The silver he designed in Darmstadt was, like that of Hans Christiansen, made at E.L. Viëtor's. His work, not only metalwork, but also ceramics, furniture and graphic design, was shown at exhibitions in Darmstadt and St Louis in 1904 and was even awarded a prize at the latter. In 1905 Haustein became a teacher at the Königliche Lehr- und Versuchswerkstätte (Royal Teaching and Research Workshop) in Stuttgart, of which Bernhard Pankok, one of the founders of the Vereinigte Werkstätten für Kunst im Handwerk in Munich, had meanwhile been made director.[8] From 1906 onwards Haustein designed silver for the firm of Bruckmann, which was simple in form, but richly decorated with abstract foliate scrolls.

Before Albin Müller (1871–1941) went to Darmstadt in 1906, he worked as a teacher and architect at Magdeburg. In 1908, after the death of Olbrich, he became the leading architect of the artists' colony, but by then its fame had already passed its peak. For the International Exhibition of 1910 in Brussels he designed two centrepieces and two different services, which were made by Koch & Bergfeld of Bremen. One of these, with vertical beaded ribs, shows Viennese influence. It was a successful design for serial production; several examples of it are known. The same cannot be said of the large centrepieces. Müller also designed at this time two sets of cutlery for the silver factory of M.H. Wilkens & Söhne.

Ernst Riegel (1871–1939) had worked from 1890 onwards in the workshop of Fritz von Miller, a goldsmith and chaser in Munich, who was famous for his large centrepieces and occasional silver in traditional styles. Before he went to Darmstadt in 1907, Riegel was a teacher at the municipal craft school for goldsmiths in Munich. He made various mounts for the Grand Duke of Hesse's collection of nephrite and agate bowls, as a modern interpretation of objects that were formerly kept in princely curiosity cabinets. His interest in old silversmithing techniques and ornament is clearly to be seen in his numerous prize cups, which are decorated all over with chased and embossed flowers and foliate scrolls.

Other objects by Riegel are more modern in appearance, in some cases because of the spiral motifs soldered on to them, in others

123

125

129

Design for a covered bowl by Professor Paul Haustein, Stuttgart. The bowl was made for the Brussels Exhibition of 1910 by P. Bruckmann & Söhne, Heilbronn. From *Deutsche Goldschmiede-Zeitung*, 1911

Fruit bowl with flat-chased ornament, by Ernst Riegel. From *Dekorative Kunst*, 1908.

because of the use of semi-precious stones as colourful accents on node, bowl or foot. Riegel belonged among the small group of artists before the First World War who were capable of executing their own designs. He was made a professor at Cologne in 1912 and from 1920 was in charge of the goldsmiths' shop of the Institute of Religious Art there.

Emanuel Josef Margold (1888–1962) and Theodor Wende (1883–1968) were the last artists to settle in Darmstadt. Margold was a pupil of Josef Hoffmann in Vienna and had worked at the Wiener Werkstätte. In Darmstadt he made countless designs for furniture, glass and porcelain and in 1913 some silverwork designed by him was made by Bruckmann's.

Theodor Wende was Ernst Riegel's successor. He began his training at jewelry firms in Berlin and Dresden. From 1908 onwards he studied first at the Königliche Preussische Zeichenakademie (Royal Prussian Drawing Academy) at Hanau and then under Bruno Paul, who had been appointed director of the applied art school in Berlin in 1907. He revealed a strong predilection for large hammered surfaces, which, under the influence of Cubism, were decorated with abstract, sometimes spidery ornament. From 1921 onwards he was a professor at the Badische Kunstgewerbeschule (Baden Art and Craft School) at Pforzheim.

The First World War put an end to the activities of the artists' colony at Darmstadt. Many architects and designers had taken their first steps there along the road to national and even international fame, but Darmstadt did not reap the rewards of their activities.

WEIMAR UP TO 1914 The name of Weimar is closely linked at this period with that of Henry van de Velde (1863–1957), the versatile Belgian artist, who was active as a designer in every imaginable field of architecture and the applied arts. He was the most international of all the European artists, working in Belgium, Berlin, Weimar, Hagen and the Netherlands. In 1926 he settled in Belgium again, but after the Second World War moved to Switzerland, where he died at an advanced age. Around 1890 he had abandoned his career as a painter in order to concentrate on the applied arts and sculpture. In 1895 he designed, decorated and furnished a house for himself at Uccle, a suburb of Brussels, and at the end of the same year his first interiors were exhibited at Siegfried Bing's Maison de l'Art Nouveau in Paris. The French critics slated his furniture, but a year later the same designs scored a great success in progressive German circles at the Kunstgewerbe Austellung (Arts and Crafts Exhibition) in Dresden.

At the end of 1901 Van de Velde settled in Weimar, where he had been appointed by the Grand Duke of Saxe-Weimar a consultant for the promotion of industry and the applied arts in Thuringia. To this end the Grand Duke established a Kunstgewerbliches Seminar, where modellers and draughtsmen could produce new, properly conceived designs under Van de Velde's guidance, which were meant to serve as models for industry. Van de Velde did not reject industrial production, but he did hold that the choice of materials and the creation of models for it should be left to artists.

One of the first silver projects was the designing of a 335-piece dinner service (cutlery, plates and large objects such as fruit-stands, candelabra and jardinières) on the occasion of the Grand Duke's marriage. Weimar was a small provincial town of only 28,500 inhabitants (Darmstadt had 72,000, Munich 498,500) and with only four jewelry shops.[9] Since Theodor Müller, the court jeweller there, did not employ enough silversmiths at that time to be able to carry out such a commission, the service could not be made in Thuringia, although this had actually been the reason for inviting Van de Velde there. Thus the prestigious commission was given to the firm of Koch & Bergfeld at Bremen. In hindsight Van de Velde did not consider the results very satisfactory. This was due partly to his own inexperience and unfamiliarity with the silver techniques of chasing and embossing, so that he failed to make the right demands, and partly to the shortness of the time allowed for the project.[10]

Under the direction of Theodor Müller's two sons, who succeeded their father in 1902, the modest workplace soon grew into a large workshop where thenceforth all the important silver designs were executed in close collaboration with Van de Velde. All the objects made there from 1903 onwards are characterized by undulating rounded forms accentuated by abstract, flowing lines. In order not to mar these soft forms, the spout and handle flanges of hollow-ware were not soldered on, as was customary, but were made in one piece. Although it is easy enough to draw something like that, it is a real art to execute it.

These unusual objects attracted attention everywhere at national and international exhibitions. They were mostly made in silver higher than the 0.800 standard that was customary in Germany, because their supple forms also demanded a more pliable alloy. Naturally, Van 133,134 de Velde also designed flatware. One of his models, a modern adaptation of a classic, undecorated eighteenth-century example, was made at the Vereinigte Silberwarenfabrik (United Silverware Factory) Franz Bahner at Düsseldorf, as well as at Weimar.[11]

In 1906 Van de Velde founded the Institut für Kunstgewerbe und Kunstindustrie (Institute of Arts and Crafts and Art Industry), where students could be introduced to his ideas about adequate functional forms based on logical principles (*vernunftgemässe Gestaltung*). This institute, the precursor of the Bauhaus, which was to play a pioneering role in industrial design in the twenties, had, among other facilities, a silversmiths' workshop, where Albert Feinauer was the teacher. He made various services after designs by Van de Velde, which 'are incomparable in their craftsmanship and belong among the best things I have designed in my life'.[12] In 1901, on the occasion of the exhibition 'A Document of German Art', at Darmstadt, Van de Velde had written that for two years he would use no more ornament, but would simply search for form.[13] The strong forms he found, like the sober decorations, herald the twenties.

For Van de Velde, as for the Darmstadt artists, the First World War signalled a break. In 1920 he and his family settled in the Netherlands, where the Kröller-Müllers had commissioned him to build a house and a museum for their extensive collection of paintings. His design of 66 1922 for a tea-set for his own use in his new house at Wassenaar shows how his ideas about form and construction had been simplified. Only in the handles and finials is anything still to be found of the undulating lines which had formed a fundamental part of his designs before the war. The Danish silversmith Christian Fjerdingstad, whom he had met in the Netherlands, was faced with an easier task than the Weimar silversmiths. He made the set for Van de Velde after he had started working in Paris. When the Kröller-Müllers had to abandon their grand plans because of the economic crisis of 1924, Van de Velde returned, after many years, to his native Belgium.

HAGEN   Hagen, in the Ruhr, had no royal patron like Darmstadt or Weimar, but artistic developments in this small, dreary industrial town were also due to the efforts of an individual, Karl Ernst Osthaus, the son of a banker. He wanted to give his fellow-townsfolk a chance to see the new developments in both the fine and applied arts and thus to teach them good taste. He had a museum built in which, in an interior designed by Henry van de Velde, he exhibited a permanent collection of modern art and a comprehensive array of functional objects of all periods and countries. Temporary exhibitions were also held there, with great regularity.

In 1909 the Königliches Preussisches Handfertigkeitsseminar (Royal Prussian Manual Skills Training College) was founded in Hagen for the purpose of instructing teachers in artistic crafts. The Dutch architect J.L.M. Lauweriks was appointed director. At that time he was working in Düsseldorf as a teacher of architecture at the Kunstgewerbeschule, of which Peter Behrens was then the director. On Lauweriks's recommendation the Dutch silversmith Frans Zwollo was appointed to teach silversmithing and to direct the Hagener Silberschmiede (Hagen Silver Workshop). The aim was 'to execute chasing and embossing perfectly after designs by our best artists and in this way to create an institute capable of equalling the Wiener Werkstätte'.[14]

Lauweriks was responsible for most of the designs executed by the Hagener Silberschmiede under Zwollo. He believed that an object's expressivity depended on the correctness of the mathematical proportions of its basic form or module. For silver designs he often used spiral forms, because these resulted in supple organic shapes and contours. But just as with Henry van de Velde's tea-sets from Weimar, the drawing of them is not so difficult, yet the execution demands great expertise.

162

Osthaus's attempts to sell silver and obtain commissions for the workshop met with little success, despite all the publicity and the exhibitions in which it participated. When the First World War broke out, Zwollo returned to the Netherlands and the workshop was closed. Lauweriks's designs were expressionistic experiments in three-dimensional form which attracted scarcely any interest.

BERLIN UP TO 1914

In contrast to other countries in Europe, where the capital cities were also centres of much activity aimed at the renewal of the applied arts, Berlin played only a minor role in this respect, even though it was the new capital of the recently created empire. In 1906 it was even stated that Berlin no longer belonged among the leading artistic centres.[15] There were one or two qualifications to this judgement, however. One was the bibliophile periodical *Pan*, although, apart from Peter Behrens, its contributors never ventured on designs for the applied arts. Behrens had gone to Berlin from Düsseldorf in 1907 on the invitation of Emil Rathenau, the founder of AEG (Allgemeine Elektricitäts-Gesellschaft). There he was occupied in designing everything connected with the firm, from a turbine factory to an electric kettle, from worker's housing to advertising stickers. This was the first time a firm had taken on an artist to take charge of all aspects of industrial design and mass production; to create what we would now call a house style. However, AEG was not a silver factory, so no silver objects were involved.

Naturally, there were some activities in Berlin in the field of modern silver. For example, some striking objects were made by the court jeweller Friedländer after designs by the painter Wilhelm Lucas von Cranach (1861–1918), who lived in Berlin from 1893 onwards. A common motif on them was a sinuous serpent, sometimes winged, like that on the arms borne by one of the designer's remote forbears, the painter Lucas von Cranach, in the early sixteenth century. The motif naturally accorded equally well with the Symbolist movement in painting around the turn of the century. 132

In 1905 Emil Lettré (1876–1954) set up on his own as a silversmith in Berlin, after having completed his training at the Königliche Preussische Zeichenakademie in Hanau and worked under Fritz von Miller in Munich. His work had revealed individual character from the start, as is apparent from the two bottles illustrated. It is scarcely conceivable that such decorations could already have been shown at an exhibition in Dresden in 1906. The severe, compact forms and the stylized animals suggest a much later period. 130,13

Lettré soon confined himself to designing objects, all of which were made in his workshop. They are always hand-made in a highly personal, extremely simple style. The smooth forms are decorated with finely chased linear ornament. Lettré was an original artist who stood outside all the national and international movements of his day. The London silversmith H.G. Murphy worked as an apprentice in his workshop.

The Hohenzollern Kunstgewerbehaus in Berlin sold objects by modern foreign silversmiths like Henry van de Velde and Jan Eisenloeffel, and after 1904 by the Wiener Werkstätte. At the same time jewellers could order any number of modern-looking objects for their customers from countless large and small silver factories. The imperial court, however, had no stimulating influence on artistic developments in the capital.

Cocktail shaker designed by Emil Lettré, Berlin, and shown at the Exposition Universelle in Paris in 1937.

FACTORIES UP TO 1914

Around 1900 there were more than 160 factories scattered all over Germany, which were devoted exclusively to making functional objects in silver.[16] They were not limited to a given town or region for the sale of their products, but worked for jewellers throughout Germany, who naturally sold what their customers wanted. For this reason the catalogues of these factories always exhibit a strange mixture of old and new styles.

The oldest factory of all was that of P. Bruckmann & Söhne at Heilbronn, already mentioned, which was established in 1805. It had been the first to introduce a steam engine and had grown during the nineteenth century into the biggest silver factory in the country. The fame it also acquired internationally was due to Peter Bruckmann (1865–1937), who became director in 1887 at a period he once described as 'the great style-copying course of art industry'.[17] At the Paris Exhibition of 1900 Bruckmann's objects with floral ornament were judged much more favourably than the traditional prize cups and 'monstrous goblets',[18] but he sought more than that, namely, a synthesis of artistic forms and commercial requirements. He wanted not only to give artists special commissions for important exhibitions, as had been customary up to then, but also to improve the design and quality of simple utensils.

127,128,135

In the sculptors Huchler, Rudolf Rochga and Josef Lock, Bruckmann had found artists who understood the requirements that an object had to meet for normal factory production, 'without obtrusive, stuck-on ornament, but conceived on the basis of form'.[19] But however important he considered this collaboration to be commercially, his efforts were not very productive. Most artists were too little aware of the possibilities of the materials and techniques, or the designs were too eccentric and thus too expensive. Therefore most of the objects designed by modern artists were only fit for display in exhibitions.

In his striking display at the International Exhibition of 1910 in Brussels, which won a Grand Prix, Bruckmann exhibited designs by a large number of artists.[20] The showpiece was a festive tureen by Paul Haustein. The bowls designed by Peter Behrens were much more classic in form and stately in appearance. The whole display evinced the return of ornament; linear and geometric motifs on simple, severe forms were things of the past. These special exhibition objects with their remarkable ornament, which constituted a reaction to the undecorated, functional forms of Van de Velde, are the first examples of the decorative Art Deco style of the twenties.

137

In view of Bruckmann's renewed interest in pleasing ornament, it is not surprising that in 1913 he had some designs made by Josef Margold, who was working in Darmstadt at that time. As a pupil and assistant of Josef Hoffmann, Margold was thoroughly familiar with the playful ornament that had been coming into vogue in Vienna for a number of years. Fine beading, fluting and heart-shaped leaves were some of the decorations he inspired Bruckmann's draughtsmen to use.

The other big factories, Koch & Bergfeld (established in 1829) and Wilkens & Söhne (established in 1810), both in Bremen, attached less importance to collaboration with renowned independent artists. The anonymous designers they employed were sufficiently acquainted with fashionable trends and production possibilities, so commissions to freelance artists were rare there.

The sculptor Hugo Leven (1874–1956), who is mainly known for his designs for the Kayserzinn pewter factory, succeeded Heinrich von der Cammer as head of the design studio of Koch & Bergfeld in 1904. In 1909, after he was appointed director of the Königliche Preussische Zeichenakademie at Hanau, he was succeeded by Gustav Elsass, but he was kept on by the firm as an artistic adviser. A world-famous designer who had his first drawing lessons in this Bremen factory was Wilhelm Wagenfeld, whom we shall meet later in discussing the Bauhaus. Around 1910 Albin Müller of Darmstadt designed silver for Koch & Bergfeld's display at the International Exhibition in Brussels.

The painter and graphic artist Heinrich Vogeler was the best-known freelance designer for M.H. Wilkens & Söhne. Around 1900 he designed candelabra and other table ornaments and cutlery. His Tulip model was also sold at La Maison Moderne, Julius Meier-Graefe's shop in Paris. Illustrations also survive of massive table ornaments of curious form and indeterminate style by the designers H. Bulling, A. Donant and C. Krauss.

The firm Orivit AG of Cologne-Braunsfeld made silver hollow-ware for only a short time. It registered its mark in 1901, but silver production had already ceased four years later, when the firm was taken over by the Württembergische Metallwaren Fabrik (WMF). The silver was made by a machine called a 'Huberpresse', a new invention, in which hollow objects with simple ornament could be stamped out by hydraulically produced water pressure.[21] The service illustrated was made in this way and a similar one was to be seen at the exhibition at St Louis in 1904.

With the exception of Orivit, a great deal of flatware, in addition to hollow-ware, was made in the above-mentioned factories. No other country in the world had so many specialized flatware factories. More than thirty-five are mentioned in the *Adress und Handbuch für das Deutsche Goldschmiedegewerbe* of 1903. Thanks to the low price of silver and good export markets in neighbouring countries, production soared. Flatware with classic stems and forms with eclectic Rococo and Louis XVI motifs predominated, but after 1900 many factories gradually went over to using modern motifs as well: mainly floral ornament at first, but soon followed by linear and geometrical designs. Since the bowls of the various ladles and spoons were generally produced to a standard pattern, they seldom harmonized with the modern stems. A number of factories soon followed Bruckmann's example and attracted extra publicity with designs by 'Professor So-and-so' (as Van de Velde put it). But, by comparison with traditional patterns, the number of modern models was small, about ten per cent. Half of these were designed by freelance artists.[22]

The need for collaboration between artists, workmen and manufacturers became increasingly clear to many throughout Germany. In a lecture given in Berlin in 1906, Hermann Muthesius, who had returned from London in 1903, stressed that it was important for the economic development of the German Empire to get away from the provincialism of the regional cultural centres. This idea caught on and on 5 October 1907 the Deutscher Werkbund (German Work Association) was founded in Munich. Among its first members were Peter Behrens, Peter Bruckmann, Muthesius himself, Josef Olbrich and Richard Riemerschmid, – a combination of artists and manufacturers.

Bruckmann, who had already been working with a wide variety of artists for years, became the first president. Two years later membership had risen to over seven hundred, including Van de Velde and a young architect by the name of Walter Gropius. The members had widely differing ideas, on the one hand about individual forms and on the other about industrial norms, so that heated discussions often took place. But there was one thing on which all were agreed: the quality of German products must be improved, both technically and artistically, if they were to compete successfully with goods from abroad.

In 1914 the Werkbund organized its first exhibition in Cologne, in which it aimed to show 'what art, hand-work and industry can achieve'. Karl Johann Bauer, Emil Lettré, Ernst Riegel, Adolf von Mayrhofer, Gertraud von Schnellenbühel, Carl Weishaupt and M.T. Wetzlar sent in pieces, which ranged from simple, plain models to richly decorated objects with applied ornament. The Hagener Silberschmiede and Peter Bruckmann & Söhne were represented by a great many objects, Bruckmann's contribution being awarded a gold medal. Only a small proportion of the objects he exhibited were intended for serial production. It is little appreciated that Walter Gropius, later to become famous as an architect and the founder of the

THE DEUTSCHER WERKBUND

Standing dishes, centrepiece and bowls, designed by Walter Gropius for the Berndorfer Metallwarenfabrik for the Deutscher Werkbund exhibition held in Cologne in 1914. From *Dekorative Kunst*, 1916.

Bauhaus at Weimar, designed table silver for this exhibition. Indeed, is is difficult to associate the design of these objects, which were inspired by Viennese silver of the period, with his functional architecture.

148

This exhibition had been eagerly awaited and much was expected of it. It opened in July 1914, but in August the First World War broke out, so that although the event brought the best results of German craftsmanship and industry together under one roof, it provided no more than a fleeting picture of the current situation and afforded no stimulus for further developments.

1918–14   'Through war, revolution and other factors a deep caesura has been knocked in our lives', wrote Walter Gropius to Richard Riemerschmid in 1921.[23]Slowly but surely the country overcame the worst effects of the war. Thanks to the new art schools that had been founded all over Germany before 1914, there were now more well-trained silversmiths. Exhibitions were organized and interest in modern silverwork grew. Since there was no central regulation of the registration of silver marks and many archives were lost in the Second World War, it has unfortunately often proved impossible to attribute marks to particular silversmiths.

In the early twenties designs frequently showed Viennese influence, with playful, imaginative motifs and wavy rims. Later, heavy, hand-raised forms, decorated at most with chased or engraved lines, gained the upper hand, the German silversmiths, like their English counterparts, emphasizing their craft skills here. Only occasionally are found zigzag motifs and angular forms inspired by Cubism. At this period spherical and cylindrical forms played a leading role and ornament was of minor importance. Munich still remained an important cultural centre, but Berlin also played a prominent part in the interwar years.

MUNICH   The first important postwar exhibition, the Deutsche Gewerbeschau, was held in Munich in 1922. Various of the workshops there, which have already been mentioned, T. Heiden, Carl Weishaupt, M.T. Wetzlar and E. Wollenweber, also had modern silver designed at this time. Adolf von Mayrhofer, by now an old man, also made various objects in the twenties after both designs of his own and those of Else Wenz-Viëtor and Hermann Haas, who had been engaged in designing silver since 1915. The collaboration between Von Mayrhofer and

Box with enamelled cover, by Franz Rickert, Munich, 1933.

Haas resulted in a number of striking functional objects with a character all their own: strong, simple, hand-raised forms with floral ornament on feet and finials as a playful contrast.

Franz Rickert (b. 1904) worked as an apprentice in Adolf von Mayrhofer's workshop from 1921 to 1924 and then studied for three years at the Staatsschule für angewandte Kunst (National School of Applied Art) in Munich, before setting up on his own as a silversmith. In the twenties he developed into the most important silversmith in the city. Various of his designs were to be seen at the Paris Exhibition of 1937. He had a command of all aspects of silversmithing and was an outstanding enameller. From 1938 onwards he taught at the Akademie für angewandte Kunst (Academy of Applied Art) in Munich.

Not until the twenties did Berlin develop into one of the most important cultural centres in Europe, an ascendancy that can also be seen in silverwork. Before the war Emil Lettré had smoothed the path for a number of young silversmiths, who were active there in the twenties and thirties and thus contributed to the flowering of cultural life in the capital. Good professional training was offered by the Reimann Schule and the Kunstgewerbeschule. At the former, craft training, and metalwork in particular, played an important role. The students not only learned embossing, mounting and chasing, but were also given a good grounding in business. Moreover, each was required to take a subsidiary course in a second workshop at the school, in, for example, cutting precious stones.

Bruno Paul, one of the founders of the Deutscher Werkbund, had been director of the Kunstgewerbeschule in Berlin since 1907, while, silversmithing was taught there by Josef Wilm, a skilled craftsman. At the Deutsche Gewerbeschau in Munich in 1922 two of Wilm's pupils, Waldemar Rämisch and Alfred Kopka, attracted attention with strikingly chased services. Walter von Nessen, who emigrated to the United States in 1923, and Karl Emanuel Martin ('Kem') Weber of California also learned the craft at the school.

At the well-known firm of H.J. Wilm worked Ferdinand Richard Wilm (1880–1971) who was active in many ways after the war in the development and improvement of silversmithing. To this end, in 1932, in collaboration with, among others, Ludwig Roselius of Bremen, Peter Behrens and Wilhelm Wätzoldt, director of the Staatliche Museen in Berlin, Ferdinand Wilm founded the Gesellschaft für Goldschmiedekunst (Society for Goldsmiths' Work), of which practically all the independent German silversmiths became

BERLIN

Fruit dish designed by Emmy Roth, Berlin. From *The Studio*, September 1929.

181

members. From 1924 onwards Ludwig Riffelmacher (b. 1896) directed H.J. Wilm's workshop. Under his supervision various hand-raised pieces were made, massive in form and with carefully detailed engraved ornament.[24]

During the First World War Emmy Roth had set up on her own as a silversmith in Berlin. She had trained in Anton Beumer's workshop in Düsseldorf. At first she was still influenced by the Baroque decoration current at that time, but she soon became convinced that ornament was 'a distribution of planes'.[25] She was a member of the Deutscher Werkbund and participated in various exhibitions at home and abroad. Like many of her colleagues, she hammered her rational designs into functional utensils, searching more than other silversmiths for a variety of practical applications for objects: lids which could be inverted to form fine fruit bowls or two-light candelabra which could be combined to form a larger whole, for example. Her work attracted notice everywhere for its good proportions and original forms. Before she emigrated to the United States, she worked for a few years in the Netherlands where, at the invitation of Carel Begeer, she designed silver for industrial production.

NORTHERN GERMANY

153

151

In the twenties and thirties there were a number of independent silversmiths working in the prosperous North German ports of Bremen and Hamburg. The best known are Franz Bolze, August Haarstick and Arnold Meyer. A mocha service made by the first of these in 1927–8 after a design by the sculptor Bernhard Hötger was not conceived on the basis of the material; rather it looks like an abstract sculpture. This effect is primarily achieved by the ebony handles, which clasp the mocha pot and milk jug. A cup and cover by Haarstick is a good example of the general trend in German silver around 1930: large, hammered, rounded surfaces devoid of ornament. In the Bremer Werkstätte für kunstgewerbliche Silberarbeiten (Bremen Workshop for Craft Silverwork) candelabra were made in a similar manner after a design by Wilhelm Schultze, in addition to countless bowls. Silversmiths working in Hamburg at this time were Josef Arnold, Christoph Kay and Otto Stüber.

In neighbouring Lüneberg the first fully qualified woman silversmith in Germany, Marga Jess, had been active since 1912. She was a pupil of Karl Johann Bauer at the Debschitz-Schule in Munich. In contrast to the work of Emmy Roth in Berlin, her silver designs showed scarcely any modern tendencies. She remained faithful to the bosses and spirals of her Munich training. Only in her designs for flatware did she achieve very modern and individual motifs.

Nuremberg, in southern Germany, was one of the oldest centres of silversmithing. There in 1919 Josef Pöhlmann (1882–1963) was appointed to teach gold- and silversmithing at the Kunstgewerbe- schule. One of his pupils was Ludwig Riffelmacher, mentioned above. Pöhlmann's designs of the early twenties are often simple forms decorated with enamelled three-dimensional columbines and lark- spur in a distant echo of the style of Nuremberg's greatest silversmith of the sixteenth century, Wenzel Jamnitzer.

Friedrich Schmid-Riegel also made some imaginative de luxe silver objects at this time, somewhat in the manner of Dagobert Peche of Vienna. His designs of the thirties, on the other hand, were created under the influence of the Bauhaus. It would be difficult to imagine a greater contrast.

Schwäbisch Gmünd was the most important centre of the silver industry, with countless large and small factories, but two indepen- dent silversmiths, Robert Fischer and Fritz Möhler, also worked there. Robert Fischer's work was to be seen at all the exhibitions of the thirties and his designs regularly won awards. At Paris in 1937 he exhibited various objects in robust, hand-raised forms, sometimes with an unobtrusive, but surprisingly structured surface. Fritz 154 Möhler (b. 1896) initially worked as a steel engraver in his father's firm, Gebrüder Kutler, which made gold and gold-plated jewelry. After his studies in precious metal at the technical school for workers in his birthplace and at the Kunstgewerbeschule at Munich, he set up on his own as a silversmith in 1923. He was given many commissions for ecclesiastical silver and also produced a large amount of secular work. As a skilled enameller, he often used *cloisonné* or *champlevé* enamel as a decoration. In the years before the Second World War he was regarded as one of the most important silversmiths in Germany, who had contributed much to the 'renaissance of the goldsmith's craft with the spirit of our own day'.[26]

In Stuttgart Erna Zarges-Dürr (b. 1907) was active as an indepen- dent silversmith in the thirties. From 1924 to 1927 she had been the first woman in the silversmiths' department of Peter Bruckmann's factory at Heilbronn and subsequently studied at the Kunst- gewerbeschule at Pforzheim, under, among others, Theodor Wende. After having worked for two more years in the workshops of Ernst Treusch in Leipzig and H.J. Wilm in Berlin, she set up her own workshop at Heilbronn in 1933, moving to Stuttgart three years later. She won various prizes at international exhibitions for her designs, which are outstanding in their carefully considered proportions and original modernistic ornament. Erna Zarges-Dürr's masterpiece of 1932, a wine jug, was awarded a gold medal at the Paris Exhibition of 1937.

THE MODERNISTIC
MOVEMENT

After the First World War two leading modern art schools were founded in Germany, the State and Municipal Art School at Burg Giebichenstein in Halle and the Bauhaus, which was first at Weimar and then at Dessau. In both institutions art, education, manufacture and commerce were closely linked. Halle was more geared to practice and the approach there was more commercial than that of the Bauhaus. Exhibitions were staged at which the exhibits were sold and commissions from outside were executed. The first director of the school at Halle was Paul Thiersch, who was succeeded after his death by Gerhard Marcks. The achievement of the various workshops in Halle in the twenties and thirties have passed into oblivion, but fine objects in contemporary architectural forms were made in the metal workshop under the direction of Karl Müller and the enamelling course was also of a high standard. Many bowls and boxes were made, decorated with brightly coloured geometric borders and planes, which form an abstract composition.

Karl Müller numbered two women silversmiths among his pupils, Eva Mascher-Elsässer and Hildegard Risch, both born in Halle. They learned there how to realize design ideas during the actual process of hand-raising and chasing, so that starting on a new object was a stimulus to further experimentation. After they had set up a joint workshop in Halle in 1929, they both undertook further training. Following a study trip to Italy, Eva Mascher-Elsässer took a course under Richard Riemerschmid at the Kunstschule in Cologne and worked in the workshop of Hermann Schmidhuber, while Hildegard Risch worked under the architect and designer F.A. Breuhaus at Düsseldorf. The two women worked together from 1929 to 1935. At the first exhibition in which they took part they scored a success with a tea-set, which was bought by the museum in Leipzig. After Eva Mascher-Elsässer married in 1935, Hildegard Risch continued the workshop on her own and turned to making jewelry.

THE BAUHAUS IN WEIMAR
AND DESSAU

During the First World War Henry van de Velde had suggested that Walter Gropius (1883–1969), whom he had met at the Deutscher Werkbund, should be his successor in Weimar. After his architectural training Gropius had become Peter Behrens's chief assistant in Berlin, where Le Corbusier and Ludwig Mies van der Rohe were already working at that time. From 1910 onwards he had an architect's office of his own in Berlin in collaboration with Adolf Meyer, a pupil of J.L.M. Lauweriks at Hagen.

In 1918 Gropius became director of the Grossherzogliche Kunstgewerbeschule and the Hochschule für bildende Kunst, which were merged in 1919 under the name Staatliches Bauhaus Weimar. This was intended to be an advisory art centre for industry and commerce, in which the abolition of the distinction between 'fine' and 'applied' art was a guiding principle. Gropius succeeded in attracting as teachers a number of leading modern artists capable of developing the personal creativity of the students in the age of the machine. 'The Bauhaus believes the machine to be our medium of design and seeks to come to terms with it.'[27]

The aim was to achieve purely functional forms in which ornament was superfluous. The form and material must speak for themselves; they were the basis for beauty. The training at the Bauhaus was divided into two parts, each student being obliged to take the preliminary course, in which he or she learned to handle a wide variety of materials and gained an insight into colour experimentation and form. Since the Bauhaus courses were geared to practice, the workshops occupied a prime place there. Each of them was directed by two teachers, a 'form master' and a 'craftmaster'.

The setting-up and direction of the metal workshop posed great problems at first. In 1922 Christian Dell (1893-1974) was made its craft master. He was an accomplished silversmith, who had worked under Henry van de Velde. At that time the metal workshop was still a true gold- and silversmiths' shop, where, for preference, precious metals were used. The experiments in the preliminary course led to a unique, playful style, in which the objects were built up out of various stereometric forms, such as cones, spheres, cubes and cylinders. This type of designing had nothing to do with the practical industrial design for which the metal workshop was later to become famous.

The design of the numerous wine jugs, tea- and coffee-sets, tea glasses and tea balls, which were made at the workshop, was more 155 important than the value of the material. Under the direction of László Moholy-Nagy, who was appointed by Gropius in 1923 to take charge of the design side, the workshop developed into a model of serial production. Chromium, nickel and steel were used in place of silver and the students were trained in both craft skills and industrial production techniques.

After endless difficulties with the authorities and conservative artists in Weimar, the Bauhaus moved to Dessau on 1 April 1925. The designs for electric lamps in particular proved a great hit and were taken into production by factories. Since Germany did not take part in the Paris Exhibition of 1925, it became apparent only in 1927 at the International Art Trade Exhibition at Monza how surprisingly modern German design was. The exhibition Europäisches Kunstgewerbe held that year in Leipzig offered Germans themselves an opportunity to compare modern designs from various countries. It also became apparent then how advanced was the idea of keeping to simple, impersonal forms for objects which were easy to produce in series. The Werkbund Exhibition in Paris in 1930 was a great success, particularly because of the Bauhaus contribution.

Bauhaus influence is found in all aspects of industrial design with the sole exception of silver production. Silver was made exclusively to order, the designs of the Dessau period often being lighter in weight and more conventional in form than those of the Weimar. It is not known who was responsible for these designs. They were intended for serial production, but the German silver industry failed to adopt them. There was little severe, modernistic design in Germany as there was in the Netherlands, notably in the work of Carel Begeer and Christa Ehrlich.

The impersonal, mechanical appearance of the silver made in the metal workshop at Dessau was felt by many to be incompatible with the nature of the material, a soft metal that was easy to work. Thus silversmiths and customers preferred a hammered surface, even if the model had been made by machinery. Only in the dominant role played by simple form in the contribution to the Paris Exhibition of 1937, and also in the disc-shaped finials and handles, was there something to be found of the Bauhaus influence. However, the Bauhaus itself had already been forced to close in 1933.

The Bauhaus trained a whole series of silversmiths. The best-known are Marianne Brandt and Wilhelm Wagenfeld, but Josef Albers, Josef Knau, Gyula Pap, Hans Przyrembel, Naum Slutzky and Wolfgang Tümpel also made their mark in this field.

Marianne Brandt (1893–1983) entered the metal workshop in 1924 as its first woman student on the advice of Moholy-Nagy. When he left the Bauhaus in 1928, she succeeded him as director of the workshop. Her designs for services were based on simple geometric forms and she took account of the fact that pots must pour well and not drip, so that all hers have straight spouts which are higher than the rims. The lids are placed off-centre in the flat tops to prevent the tea from running out under them during pouring.

Two other Bauhaus students, Wolfgang Tümpel (1903–78) and Hans Przyrembel, worked as independent silversmiths in Cologne and Leipzig in the thirties. They were members of the Gesellschaft für Goldschmiedekunst and contributed good hand-raised objects to the Paris Exhibition of 1937. When the Bauhaus moved to Dessau and the accent came to lie heavily on industrial design, Wolfgang Tümpel continued his training at the workshop at Burg Giebichenstein at Halle as a pupil of Karl Müller. He set up on his own in Halle in 1927 and three years later settled in Cologne. He always kept in touch with various of the Bauhaus artists.

Coffee and tea service designed by Marianne Brandt at the Bauhaus, Dessau. Shown at the Europäisches Kunstgewerbe exhibition in Leipzig in 1927. From *Dekorative Kunst*, 1928.

Tea trolley designed by F.A. Breuhaus for the Vereinigte Werkstätten A.G., with tea service designed by Marianne Brandt. Shown in *Dekorative Kunst*, 1928.

Wilhelm Wagenfeld (b. 1900), one of the most important industrial designers of this century, began his training as a silversmith in the design office of Koch & Bergfeld in Bremen.[28] After two years of courses at the Staatliche Zeichenakademie at Hanau, he became a student at the Bauhaus in 1923. He gained his silversmith's diploma there, but afterwards concentrated on designing for industrial production rather than on silverwork. At the metal workshop of the Bauhochschule in Weimar he mainly designed prototypes for desk and hanging lamps and ceiling lights.

157

FACTORIES

The large factories followed the modern movement in silver hesitantly and late in the day. Only rarely did manufacturers give independent artists special commissions. In the drawing offices of the factories anonymous draughtsmen worked on designs for industrial production, adapted to the tastes of the day. Their designs were influenced on the one hand by hand-made forms with hammered surfaces and on the other by the smooth, mechanical forms of the Bauhaus and modernism.

The firm of Bruckmann & Söhne at Heilbronn played a leading role after the war, as it had done before. Josef Lock was still designing for this factory, his objects now being decorated with zigzag motifs. Much more original in conception is a chased and hammered mocha service after a design by Gerta Schröder. In 1923 Peter Bruckmann was succeeded by his son Dietrich, who had had a sound technical training as a student at a technical college and an artistic one as a pupil of Adolf von Mayrhofer in Munich. After 1925 Paula Strauss designed hand-raised silver in stereometric forms, which was made at Bruckmann's, 161 but the firm's customers had little interest in such modernism and preferred classic models.

Koch & Bergfeld and Wilkens & Söhne in Bremen did not make much modern silver either. At Koch & Bergfeld production of hollow-ware was so minimal that Ludwig Koch, whose arrival strengthened the board of directors in 1928, decided to abandon serial production and concentrate on hand-work. Gustav Elsass was put in charge of the workshop.[29] At the exhibition in Munich in 1922, mentioned earlier, the firm of Wilkens & Söhne showed a number of objects after designs by H. Bulling and Karl Müller, both of whom were on the factory's staff as designers. The design of these prestige pieces still reveals Viennese influence, while a candelabrum of *c.* 1925 has the characteristics of the international geometrical style in Art Deco. 159

Around 1930, when the craft tendencies became clearly apparent, various smaller factories followed suit by hammering spun or stamped objects to achieve the essential 'hand-made look'. The flatware industry was increasingly rationalized by improvements in technical production. The new models designed at this time have rectangular contours accentuated by longitudinal mouldings. Many of these designs are anonymous.

A survey of the development of German silverwork of this period leads to the conclusion that within two generations it succeeded in winning a pre-eminent position in both the craft and the industrial fields. The creation of a large, unified German market and the application of machinery led to great prosperity, which in turn led to a great demand for silver. Stylistic innovation, including that of silver, originated in regional centres, where the development of the new art was often determined by the initiative of a leading figure. The rise of the factories, which saw the whole of Germany as their market, and the country's growing national consciousness gradually resulted in the blurring of regional boundaries. For the first time since the seventeenth century Germany became a land of great silversmithing again, while the modernism of the Bauhaus even lent it an international influence.

NOTES
1 *Dekorative Kunst*, XX (1912), p. 510.
2 ibid., XII (1904), p. 232.
3 Among pupils of the Debschitz-Schule were Anny Hystak, M. von Ortloff, Olga Reynier and E. Nori.
4 *Dekorative Kunst*, XXII (1914), pp. 279–80.
5 *Liste des récompenses décernées aux exposants*, Brussels 1910.
6 Exhibition catalogue *Peter Behrens in Nürnberg*, Bayerisches National-museum, Munich, 1980, pp. 114, 158 and 159.
7 Dr Heinrich Podor, 'Künstlerische Besteckformen', *Deutsche Goldschmiede-Zeitung*, 1902, p. 281.
8 Among pupils of the Königliche Lehr- und Versuchswerkstätte at Stuttgart were J. Arnold and J. Vrabec.
9 *Adress und Handbuch für das Deutsche Goldschmiedegewerbe*, Verlag Wilhelm Diebener, Leipzig 1903.
10 Henry van de Velde, *Geschichte meines Lebens*, Munich 1962, pp. 240, 248 and 489.
11 Reinhard W. Sänger, 'Massenfabrikation in Silber' in exhibition catalogue *Der westdeutsche Impuls 1900–1914*, Museum Folkwang, Essen, 1984, p. 214.
12 Henry van de Velde, op. cit., p. 295.
13 ibid., p. 488.
14 Exhibition catalogue *Franz Zwollo en zijn tijd*, Museum Boymans-van Beuningen, Rotterdam, 1982, p. 53.
15 Erich Hänel, 'Die Dritte Deutsche Kunstgewerbeausstellung', *Dekorative Kunst*, XIV 1906, p. 30.
16 Sänger, op. cit., p. 200.
17 Peter Bruckmann, 'Einiges über die Ausstellung meiner Firma in Brussel 1910', *Die Goldschmiedekunst*, 1911, p. 18.

18   Paul Vitry, 'L'orfèvrerie à l'exposition', *Art et Décoration*, 1900, p. 176.
19   Otto Grauthoff, 'Streifzuge durch Architektur und Kunstgewerbe in München', *Dekorative Kunst*, XII (1904), p. 120.
20   Other freelance designers for Bruckmann for this exhibition were Friedrich Adler, Franz Böres, Friedrich Felger, Otto Rieth, Karl Wahl and Bernhard Wenig. The designers Adolf Amberg, Hélène Brandt, Josef Lock, Karl Stock and Karl Zeller worked in Bruckmann's design office at Heilbronn. See *Die Goldschmiedekunst*, 1911, pp. 18–26.
21   Sänger, op. cit., p. 207.
22   ibid., p. 215.
23   Exhibition catalogue *Richard Riemerschmid von Jugendstil zum Werkbund*, Munich, Nuremberg, Cologne, 1983, p. 498.
24   Frau Wilm, *Ferdinand Richard Wilm, 11 Oktober 1930*.
25   *Die Goldschmiedekunst*, 1927, p. 452.
26   *The Studio*, March 1936, p. 153.
27   Walter Gropius, 'The Theory and Organization of the Bauhaus' [Weimar 1923], reprinted in *1919–1928 Bauhaus*, Museum of Modern Art, New York, 1975, p. 25.
28   Alfred Lohr, *Bremer Silber*, Bremen 1981–2, p. 31.
29   *125 Jahre Koch & Bergfeld*, Bremen [1954], p. 14.

XIII Cigarette box with enamelled lid. Maker's mark: Alphons Ungerer, Pforzheim, *c.* 1930. The abstract motif shows the influence of the painter Wassily Kandinsky. Width: 18.1 cm (8½ in.). Museum für Kunst und Kulturgeschichte der Stadt Dortmund.

XIV Three ivory boxes with silver *cloisonné* enamelled lids, designed and made by Adolf von Mayrhofer, Munich, *c.* 1920. One is set with an amethyst, one with an amazonite, and one with an opal. Height: 4 cm (1½ in.), 5 cm and 5 cm (2 in.). Private collection.

XIII

XIV

116

115 Flower vase. Signed 'A. Ofterdinger fec.' and marked 'M. Föhr, Stuttgart 1900'. Bought at the Paris Exhibition of 1900. Height: 16.3 cm ($6\frac{1}{2}$ in.). Museum für Kunst und Gewerbe, Hamburg.

116 Jug by A. Daum, Nancy, with a silver mount by N. Trübner, Heidelberg, c. 1896. Height: 25 cm ($9\frac{3}{4}$ in.). Museum für Kunsthandwerk, Frankfurt am Main.

117 Caviar dish. Design attributed to Bernhard Pankok and made by the Vereinigte Werkstätten für Kunst im Handwerk, Munich, c. 1900. The dish shows the influence of Charles Robert Ashbee's designs for silver. Height: 11.5 cm ($4\frac{1}{2}$ in.). Württembergisches Landesmuseum, Stuttgart.

XV Tea caddy set with amethysts, designed by Josef Maria Olbrich, Darmstadt, c. 1901. Maker's mark: P. Bruckmann & Söhne, Heilbronn. Height: 28 cm (11 in.). Hessisches Landesmuseum, Darmstadt.

117

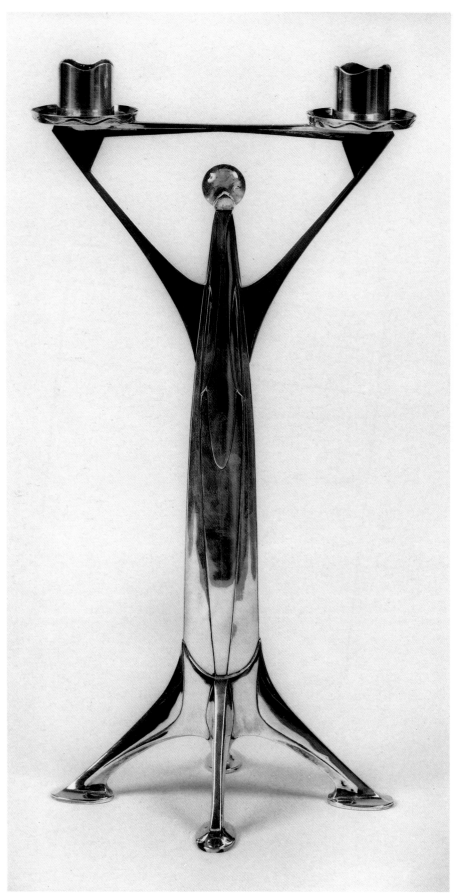

118 Candelabrum designed by Josef Maria Olbrich for the exhibition 'Ein Dokument Deutscher Kunst' in Darmstadt. Maker's mark: P. Bruckmann & Söhne, Heilbronn, 1901. Height: 34.7 cm (13¾ in.). Hessisches Landesmuseum, Darmstadt.

119 Niello beaker designed by Peter Behrens. Maker's mark: Vereinigte Werkstätten für Kunst im Handwerk, Munich, 1906. Height: 9 cm (3½ in.). Württembergisches Landesmuseum, Stuttgart.

120 Service designed by Fritz Schmoll von Eisenwerth. Maker's mark: P. Bruckmann & Söhne, Heilbronn. 1913. Württembergisches Landesmuseum, Stuttgart.

121 Three parts of a desk set designed by Peter Behrens, Darmstadt, and made by Martin Mayer, Mainz, c. 1901. Height of seal: 8.7 cm (3½ in.). Length of letter opener: 29.5 cm (11½ in.). Height of blotter: 7 cm (2¾ in.).

122 Electric bell-push designed in 1904 at the Königliche Preussische Zeichenakademie, Hanau. Made by Neresheimer, Hanau. Length: 10 cm (4 in.). Electric bell-push designed by Patriz Huber. Both with maker's mark: Martin Mayer, Mainz, c. 1901. Length: 8 cm (3¼ in.). Enamelled beaker, c. 1895, and small box, c. 1900. Private collection.

118

△

123

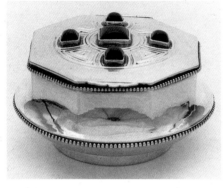

124

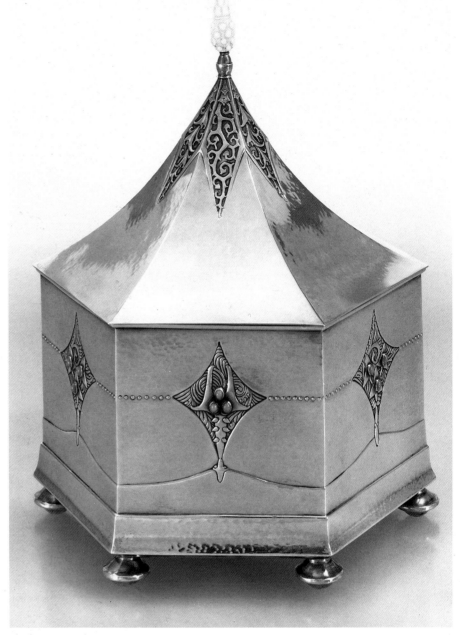

12

123 Blue and violet enamelled-copper inkpot with a silver mount, designed by Paul Haustein, 1901. Maker's mark on mount: Badische Silberwarenfabrik Baer & Deibele, Pforzheim. Height: 8.8 cm (3½ in.). Hessisches Landesmuseum, Darmstadt.

124 Covered box. Maker's mark: Carl Weishaupt, Munich, c. 1910. Height: 5 cm (2 in.). Private collection.

125 Box designed by Paul Haustein. Maker's mark: P. Bruckmann & Söhne, Heilbronn, 1906. Height: 25 cm (9¾ in.). Württembergisches Landesmuseum, Stuttgart.

127, 128 Flatware designed by Hans Christiansen. Maker's mark: P. Bruckmann & Söhne, Heilbronn, c. 1901. Length of fish server: 29.5 cm (11½ in.). Private collection.

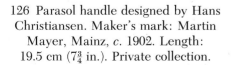

126 Parasol handle designed by Hans Christiansen. Maker's mark: Martin Mayer, Mainz, c. 1902. Length: 19.5 cm (7¾ in.). Private collection.

126

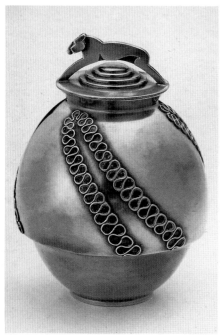

129 Coffee and tea service designed by Albin Müller. The lids have aventurine finials. Maker's mark: Koch & Bergfeld, Bremen, 1909–10. Height of coffee pot: 17.5 cm (7 in.). Bremer Landesmuseum, Bremen.

130, 131 Bottles. Maker's mark: Emil Lettré, Berlin, 1906. Height: 6.5 cm and 7 cm ($2\frac{1}{2}$ in. and $2\frac{3}{4}$ in.). Württembergisches Landesmuseum, Stuttgart.

130

131

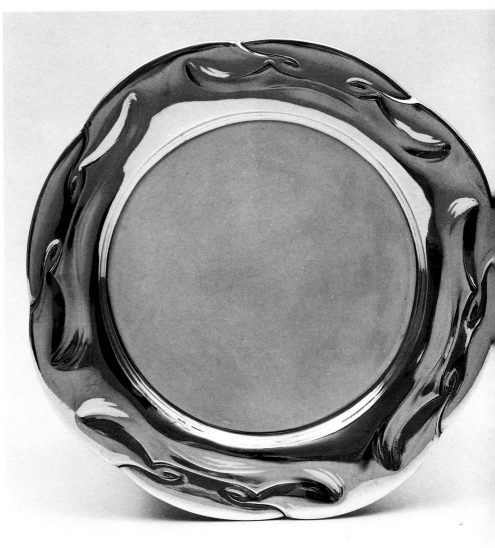

132 Wine jug designed by Lucas Wilhelm von Cranach for Friedländer, Berlin, before 1903. Height: 37.9 cm (15 in.). Badisches Landesmuseum, Karlsruhe.

133 Plate designed by Henry van de Velde, *c.* 1906. Maker's mark: Th. Müller, Weimar. 21 cm × 21.5 cm ($8\frac{1}{4}$ in. × $8\frac{1}{2}$ in.). Private collection.

134 Round bowl designed by Henry van de Velde. Maker's mark: Th. Müller, Weimar, 1906. Diameter: 22 cm ($8\frac{3}{4}$ in.). Württembergisches Landesmuseum, Stuttgart.

135

135 Tea service. Design attributed to
Huchler. Maker's mark: P.
Bruckmann & Söhne, Heilbronn,
c. 1900. Height of teapot: 20 cm
(4 in.). Private collection, Zurich.
Photograph: Marlen Perez.

136 Jam or butter dish. Maker's
mark: P. Bruckmann & Söhne,
Heilbronn, *c.* 1902. Height: 9 cm
($3\frac{1}{2}$ in.). Diameter of stand: 17.5 cm
(7 in.). Private collection.

137 Centrepiece designed by Carl
Wahl for the Brussels Exhibition of
1910. Maker's mark: P. Bruckmann &
Söhne, Heilbronn. Height: 47 cm
($18\frac{1}{2}$ in.). Limburg Collection,
Amsterdam.

137

138 Coffee service. Maker's mark: Koch & Bergfeld, Bremen, *c.* 1900. Bremer Landesmuseum, Bremen.

139 Tea-kettle. Maker's mark: Koch & Bergfeld, Bremen, *c.* 1906. The shape was influenced by that of kettles designed by Jan Eisenloeffel for Hoeker & Zn. for the Paris Exhibition of 1900. Height: 12 cm (4¾ in.). Bremer Landesmuseum, Bremen.

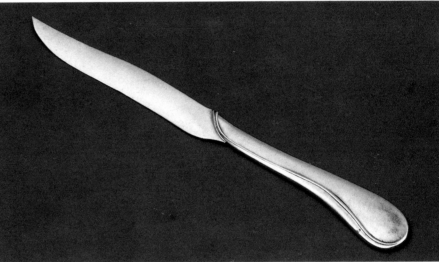

140 Letter opener designed by Heinrich Vogeler for Julius Meier-Graefe's Paris shop 'La Maison Moderne'. Maker's mark: M. H. Wilkens & Söhne, Bremen-Hemelingen, *c.* 1900. Length: 17.5 cm (7 in.). Private collection.

141 Soup ladle designed by Heinrich Vogeler. Maker's mark: M.H. Wilkens & Söhne, Bremen-Hemelingen, *c.* 1900. Length: 34.8 cm (13¾ in.). Private collection.

142, 143 Pair of candelabra, 'Night' and 'Day'. Maker's mark: M.H. Wilkens & Söhne, Bremen-Hemelingen, *c.* 1900. Height: 27 cm (10¾ in.). Württembergisches Landesmuseum, Stuttgart.

144 Coffee and tea service with tray. Maker's mark: Orivit A.G. Cologne-Braunsfeld. An identical service was shown at the Louisiana Purchase Exposition in St Louis in 1904. Height of coffee pot: 15.2 cm (6 in.). Width of tray: 41.3 cm (16¼ in.). Rijksmuseum, Amsterdam.

142

143

144

145 Silver-mounted moss-agate dish with green enamelled lobsters on the handles and 'Nordic' ornament on the feet. Design attributed to Hugo Leven. Maker's mark: C.A. Beumers, Düsseldorf, c. 1900. Diameter: 22.8 cm (9 in.). Stadtmuseum Düsseldorf. Photograph: Landesbildstelle Rheinland.

146 Silver-mounted purse. Maker's mark: Carl Forster & Graf, Schwäbisch Gmünd. Import mark: Birmingham 1904. Width: 12 cm (4¾ in.). Private collection.

147 Luncheon set comprising two meat forks, butter knife, and cheese knife. The pieces show the strong influence of Darmstadt. Maker's mark: Gebr. Köberlin, Döbeln, c. 1905. Length of forks: 20 cm (8 in.). Length of butter knife: 17 cm (6¾ in.). Length of cheese knife: 14.7 cm (5¾ in.). Private collection.

148

19

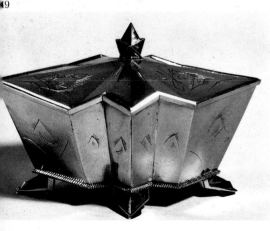

50

151

148 Candlesticks. The design was influenced by Walter Gropius's designs of 1914 for the Berndorfer Metalwarenfabrik. Retailer's mark: Hoeting, Amsterdam. Height: 19 cm (7½ in.). Private collection.

149 Bonbonnière with ivory finial. Made for the Deutsche Werkbundausstellung in Cologne in 1914. Maker's mark: P. Bruckmann & Söhne, Heilbronn. Height: 8 cm (3¼ in.). Private collection.

150 Bonbonnière designed by Philippe Oberle, Pforzheim, 1925. Height: 8 cm (3¼ in.). Badisches Landesmuseum, Karlsruhe.

151 Covered cup with agate finial. Maker's mark: August Haarstick, Bremen, c. 1930. Height: 22 cm (8¾ in.). Private collection.

152

152 Mocha service with carved ivory handles. Maker's mark: Theodor Wende, Pforzheim, 1930. Height of coffee pot: 23 cm (9 in.). Width of tray: 37.5 cm (14¾ in.). Badisches Landesmuseum, Karlsruhe.

153 Mocha service designed by Bernhard Hötger. Maker's mark: Franz Bolze, Bremen, 1927/8. Height of pot: 16.5 cm (6½ in.). Width of tray: 31.9 cm (12½ in.). Kunstgewerbemuseum, Cologne. Photograph: Rheinisches Bildarchiv, Cologne.

15

154

154 Tea service. Maker's mark:
Robert Fischer, Schwäbisch Gmünd,
c. 1935. Height of teapot: 17 cm
(6¾ in.). Width of tray: 39 cm (15¼ in.).
Museum für Kunsthandwerk,
Frankfurt am Main.

155 Coffee and tea service. Maker's
mark: Christian Dell, Weimar, 1925.
Height of coffee pot: 26.5 cm
(10½ in.). Width of tray: 50 cm
(19¾ in.). Victoria & Albert Museum,
London.

156 Stand with four tea balls, made
by the Bauhaus pupils Otto Rittweger
and Wolfgang Tümpel, Weimar, 1924.
Germanisches National Museum,
Nuremberg.

156

157

157 Plate. Maker's mark of Wilhelm
Wagenfeld's metal workshop at the
Staatliche Hochschule für Baukunst
und Handwerk, Weimar, c. 1928.
Diameter: 24.5 cm (9¾ in.). Private
collection.

158 Cigarette box designed by F.A.
Breuhaus. Maker's mark:
Württembergische Metallwaren
Fabrik, Geislingen, c. 1930. This box
is one of the few objects executed in
silver by this firm. Height: 9.3 cm
(3¾ in.). Kunstgewerbemuseum,
Cologne. Photograph: Rheinisches
Bildarchiv, Cologne.

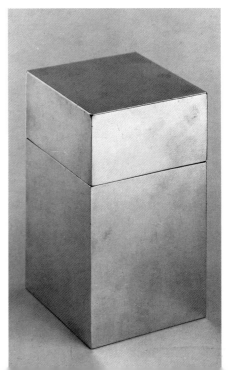

158

159

159 Candelabrum. Maker's mark:
M.H. Wilkens & Söhne, Bremen-
Hemelingen, *c.* 1925. Height: 40 cm
(15¾ in.). Germanisches National
Museum, Nuremberg.

160 Black enamelled cigarette box.
Maker's mark: Louis Kuppenheim,
Pforzheim, *c.* 1925. Height: 5.8 cm
(2¼ in.). Private collection.

161 Pitcher designed by Paula
Strauss. Maker's mark: P. Bruckmann
& Söhne, Heilbronn, *c.* 1930. Height:
17.5 cm (7 in.).
Kunstgewerbemuseum, Cologne.
Photograph: Rheinisches Bildarchiv,
Cologne.

160

XVI Enamelled asparagus server and butter knives. Maker's mark: J.M. van Kempen, Voorschoten, 1906. The design for these objects is shown on p. 179. Length: 22 cm, 16.5 cm and 6 cm (8½ in., 6½ in. and 6¼ in.). Private collection.

XVII Tea service with bright-green enamelled chequered border. Maker's mark: J.M. van Kempen, Voorschoten, 1904. Height of teapot: 11.5 cm (4½ in.). Private collection.

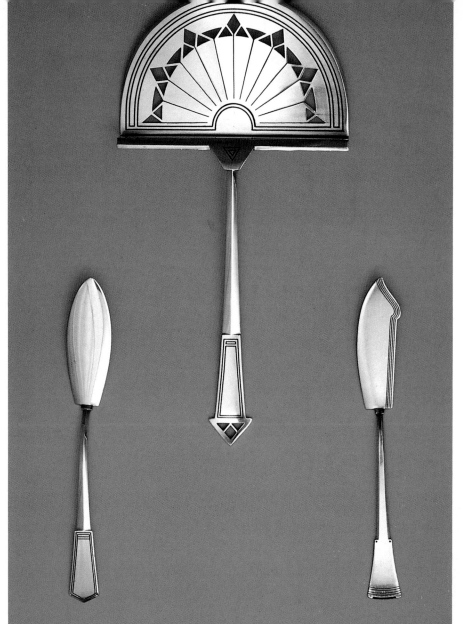

XVI

XVII

VIII

XVIII Enamelled spoons, ladle, and napkin-ring, designed by Jan Eisenloeffel. Maker's mark: C.J. Begeer, Utrecht, 1905. The shape of the spoon with the round bowl was influenced by that of Russian enamelled spoons. Length of ladle: 24.5 cm (9½ in.). Private collections.

XIX Jewelry box with gilt-silver cut-card ornament, set with amethysts. Designed by J.J. Warnaar. Maker's mark: J.M. van Kempen, Voorschoten, 1916. Private collection.

XIX

6

THE NETHERLANDS

T HE new ideas in the field of decoration and design took a long while to catch on in the Netherlands. Moreover, the development there followed a somewhat different course from that in neighbouring countries. This also applied to modern silver, which lacks not only the elegant, flowing lines of French Art Nouveau, but also the busy repoussé ornament sometimes found on German, Austrian and American silver around 1900. In the Netherlands at that time there was already a preference for geometric ornament derived from Ancient Egypt and Assyria, and a strong resistance to floral and curvilinear Art Nouveau. At the Paris Exhibition of 1900 pieces with severe formal ornament, which laid the foundation for the geometrical style, had already been shown, although objects in the current international decorative style were to be seen there as well.

The decorative style offered Dutch silversmiths an opportunity for unbridled experimentation, in which the forms became increasingly fluid, until the contours seem to melt into their surroundings. This style reached its apotheosis in the tea service by J. Steltman which was shown at the Paris Exhibition of 1925. The abstract, individual style, in which form and ornament had become indistinguishable from one another, blossomed during the First World War and continued into the thirties. It was the style of the craftsman silversmith and it was diametrically opposed to the severe, smooth forms that were creating an international furore at that time. The silversmiths in the Netherlands did not get stuck in the forms and ornament that characterized hand-made silver of the beginning of the century, as did some of their English counterparts.

The geometrical style began virtually simultaneously, but developed in a completely different direction, because of the desire on the

166

part of a group of young designers to improve machine production. They wanted to make designs for new, contemporary forms, in which the construction and the manufacture by machinery were clearly expressed. This movement paved the way for the severe, modernistic design of the end of the twenties under the influence of De Stijl in the Netherlands and the Bauhaus in Germany. Nieuwe Zakelijkheid, the Dutch version of Functionalism, demanded forms whereby the objects were geared to the requirements of mass production.

THE DECORATIVE STYLE

The most influential among the group of artists who wanted to reduce the dominance of the machine was Frans Zwollo Sr (1872–1945). As a teacher of silversmithing for nearly forty years at various applied art schools, he had a great influence on the form and decoration of Dutch hand-made silver up to the Second World War. As the son of the silversmith in charge of the workshop of As. Bonebakker in Amsterdam, which was known for the high quality of its hand-made silver, he too began his training there. After further developing his skills in Brussels (under Delheid) and Paris, he set up on his own as a silversmith in Amsterdam in 1897. In nearby Haarlem, where an applied art school had been founded in 1880, he became the first teacher of 'art metalwork' in the Netherlands. In 1910, at the invitation of Karl Ernst Osthaus, he went to Hagen in Germany, where he was appointed teacher of silversmithing at the Königliches Preussisches Handfertigkeitsseminar and put in charge of the Hagener Silberschmiede. When the First World War broke out, he returned to the Netherlands, becoming the first teacher in the new metalwork department to be set up at the Academy of Fine Art in the Hague.

At first Zwollo's designs had traditional forms and were decorated with asymmetrical naturalistic motifs, but after 1900 the ornament became more abstract. Between 1910 and 1914 he executed designs by J.L.M. Lauweriks (1864–1932), a Dutch architect who had been appointed director of the Königliches Preussisches Handfertigkeitsseminar in 1909. Zwollo and Lauweriks had known each other for a long time, both had taught in Haarlem and both were also members of the Theosophical Movement, which was influential at that time. Under Lauweriks's influence the contours of Zwollo's objects became more and more fluid and his forms and ornament indistinguishable from each other. A sweetmeat dish creates a highly plastic impression, owing to the fascinating effects of light and shade produced by its whirling spiral form. After his return to the Netherlands Zwollo carried out various commissions for the Philips, the Kröller-Müllers

164

162

and other leading Dutch families. Between 1916 and 1918 he designed for Mr R.J. de Visser a large dinner service, including candelabra, fruit dishes, a wine cooler and trays. An extensive 163 canteen of cutlery also formed part of this big commission. From 1900 onwards Zwollo took part in international exhibitions, winning awards for his work at several, such as the Turin Exhibition of 1902 and the Paris Exhibition of 1925.

Many of Zwollo's pupils were strongly influenced by him. The work of silversmiths such as G.H. Lantman, A.C. Fontani and J. van Schouwen, who were active in and around Amsterdam, L. Bosch and F.A. Hoogendijk of Schoonhoven, A. Peddemors, who succeeded Zwollo at the School of Applied Art in Haarlem, and W.P. Regenspurg, who was active in the east of the country, displays sound craftsmanship, although it is often not particularly original. Spirals and undulating ornament on a hammered surface are characteristic of such work. Zwollo's son, Frans Zwollo Jr, originally collaborated with his father in his workshop in The Hague, but later settled in Arnhem.

169 A flower vase made in 1919 at Bonebakker's, a famous Amsterdam 165 jeweller, and a bonbonnière made in 1922 by J.A. Jacobs (1885–1968) have all the characteristics of the plastic ornamentation which is also found in the Expressionist Dutch architecture of the Amsterdam School. Jacobs became a teacher in the silver department of the Institute of Applied Art, later the Quellinus School, in Amsterdam in 1917. J.L.M. Lauweriks, who had returned to the Netherlands from Hagen in 1916, had been made the new director there. He carried out a radical reorganization of the education offered by the school. The students were now required to take a compulsory first year of theory, in which the foundation was laid for methodical designing, before being given a thorough practical training in one of the newly introduced technical classes.

Johannes Steltman (1891–1961), who had trained at the Königliche Preussische Zeichenakademie in Hanau in Germany and who established his workshop, Joaillerie Artistique, in The Hague in 1917, was the designer of the most extreme example of this plastic manner 166 in silver. The tea-set which he exhibited in Paris in 1925 was inspired by the racing car in which Malcolm Campbell had broken the world speed record in 1923. Thus it was appropriate that it won a Grand Prix at the exhibition. Spouts, bodies and handles flow smoothly into each other like a modern, streamlined version of the work of the famous Dutch silversmiths of the seventeenth century, Paulus, Adam and Christiaan van Vianen and Johannes Lutma. After creating an impression of speed with his racing-car set, Steltman moved into calmer waters, designing mostly smooth, severe modern forms, sometimes varied by services in the Danish style, for the influence of Georg Jensen was all-pervasive at that point.

Just as in England, the decorative style in the Netherlands finally ran aground; not, however, because people kept on repeating themselves, but because there were too few wealthy customers for so many good silversmiths.

The most important exponent of the geometrical style in the Netherlands was Jan Eisenloeffel (1876–1957). From the end of 1896 onwards he worked as a draughtsman for the firm of Hoeker, a well-known Amsterdam jeweller, acquiring practical experience in the workshop. After a stay of several months in St Petersburg and Moscow, where he not only learned enamelling, but was also introduced to forms and ornament unusual in Western Europe, he became artistic director in October 1899 of Amstelhoek, the new workshop that Willem Hoeker had set up for modern silver.

Eisenloeffel tried to arrive at new, pure forms by means of highly surprising designs. The sparse geometric ornament served to emphasize form and construction. Hand-made objects were decorated with enamelled or pierced squares and rectangles, spun pieces with machine-engraved concentric circles round the edges. These severe forms are also found in the early work produced at the Wiener Werkstätte from 1903 onwards, after designs by Josef Hoffmann and Koloman Moser. They knew Eisenloeffel's work, which had been shown for the first time at the Paris Exhibition of 1900 and illustrated in various foreign periodicals.[1] It attracted so much attention that Tiffany's of New York bought a number of the objects during the exhibition. The largest and most prestigious commission acquired by Amstelhoek during the four years of its existence was a 97-piece dinner service commissioned by the City Council of Amsterdam for presentation to Queen Wilhelmina on her marriage in 1901.

Hoeker's exhibits won awards both in Paris in 1900 and Turin in 1902, but since his name was not mentioned as the designer, Eisenloeffel soon left the firm. Hermann Hirschwald in Berlin was interested in his work and some small silver objects had already been sent there in October 1901[2] A great deal of Eisenloeffel's brass and copperwork in particular was sold at Hirschwald's Hohenzollern Kunstgewerbehaus in Berlin.[3] Not only did Hoeker show his designs in Turin, but Eisenloeffel also sent in under his own name objects borrowed from earlier patrons and these too were awarded a gold medal.[4]

168

167

After leaving Hoeker, Eisenloeffel formed a company with J.C. Stoffels, who had a workshop in Amsterdam. However, because it lacked proper marketing facilities, the firm was disbanded nine months later. During that time Eisenloeffel experimented with his logo, which he registered as his new maker's mark in January 1903[5] and which is thereafter repeatedly found on his objects as a decorative motif. His work in both brass and silver was to be seen at, among other exhibitions, that at St Louis in 1904, where it again won an award.

XVIII
171

In the autumn of 1904 Eisenloeffel signed a contract with the firm of C.J. Begeer at Utrecht, which wanted to put his silver designs into large-scale production. Commercially the collaboration was not a success, since the designs proved extremely difficult to sell, but the objects attracted much attention at all the exhibitions and brought the factory renown both at home and abroad. Eisenloeffel's work was much imitated in Germany in particular. In 1908, at the invitation of Richard Riemerschmid, he went to Munich, where at the Vereinigte Werkstätten für Kunst im Handwerk he was given the opportunity to execute larger designs in other materials.

In 1909 Eisenloeffel was back in the Netherlands, where thenceforth he concentrated on making expensive one-off pieces. His endeavour to achieve a better mass product in the only possible way, by the use of machinery, no longer seemed to him to be the most important task of the modern applied art movement. Nevertheless, his earlier pioneering work continued to have a great influence on the design of machine-made objects in Dutch and German silver factories.

SILVER FACTORIES
XVI, XVII

The oldest and largest factory in the Netherlands was that of J.M. van Kempen & Zn at Voorschoten. It was run on traditional lines: quality came first and the names of the individual designers on its staff were not revealed. Since the factory did not take part in any big exhibitions after that held at Paris in 1900, it is little known that here too modern objects of very high quality were made with astonishing forms and decoration. As was universally the case, the objects designed around 1900 display all the characteristics of international Art Nouveau. From 1904 onwards geometric forms and ornament were used for hollow- and flatware. These are hand-made pieces with extremely refined enamelling or precisely executed pierced squares, lozenges and circles. Unfortunately, although the factory had good designers and skilled silversmiths capable of making these exceptional objects, it could not find enough customers to ensure their sale. It therefore fell back on the production of uninspired classic models. Who designed

172–175

Design for the tea service illustrated on p. 184. The service was made by J.M. van Kempen, Voorschoten, in 1902.

this modern silver is, sadly, unknown, as the surviving drawings are unsigned.

176   Equally problematical is the identity of the designer of a service of 1919. Although it bears all the characteristics of Bauhaus designs of the twenties, research in the firm's archives has shown that it was designed in 1918 – that is, before the Bauhaus was founded. Since Voorschoten is so near to Leiden, where the periodical *De Stijl* was first published in 1917 under the editorship of Theo van Doesburg, it would seem obvious to look in that direction for the designer, but as far as is known none of the De Stijl artists made silver designs. The various parts of the service are easy to make by machinery and have lucid, stereometric forms: an oval intersected by a rectangle.

During the First World War a number of expensive one-off pieces were made at Van Kempen's after designs by J.J. Warnaar (1868– XIX 1960). He had entered the firm in 1880, been trained as an engraver and subsequently worked in the design office. His work is character- ized by luxuriant ornament, generally of an oriental cast, and is often set with precious stones. In a jewel box after his design, the craftsmanship in its construction is emphasized by the use of cut-card work, an old decorative technique dating from around 1700. The name of this Van Kempen staff designer has been rescued from oblivion by virtue of the fact that various of his designs formed part of

Design for an asparagus server and two butter knives. The pieces, made by J.M. van Kempen, Voorschoten, in 1906, are shown on p. 171. Stichting Van Kempen en Begeer Museum, Zoetermeer.

XVIII
171

a contribution to an exhibition. Yet it was only after 1918 that independent artists made a few special objects and the names of the designers were made known.

At the Utrechtsche Fabriek van Zilverwerk (Utrecht Silverwork Factory) C.J. Begeer the importance of effective collaboration between artists and manufacturers was recognized early on. In emulation of Peter Bruckmann of Heilbronn, the names of all the designers were proudly made known, however much (like Jan Eisenloeffel) or little (like Professor A.F. Gips) they had designed for the firm. It was around 1895 that the first designs in the new style appeared at this factory. For this Cornelis L.J. Begeer (b. 1868), not to be confused with his later much better known half-brother Carel J.A. Begeer, was largely responsible. A good professional training not being available in the Netherlands, he had learned the craft at the Königliche Preussische Zeichenakademie at Hanau. In 1893 he made a journey of some months' duration around the United States, where, among other things, he visited the World's Columbian Exposition in Chicago. He returned from America full of impressions and new ideas. Under his direction new models were designed with motifs derived from nature, which were often strongly stylized, as in other countries. The orchid motif he used in some designs is scarcely distinguishable from that of Wolfers of Brussels, a firm with which he had business contacts.

The silverwork sent by Begeer to the Paris Exhibition of 1900 was well received, especially a fine tea-set specially designed for the occasion by Professor A.F. Gips. The elegant stand of the tea-kettle 177 seems to have little that is Dutch about it. In 1904 Cornelis L.J. Begeer left the firm and established a silver factory of his own, the Stichtsche Zilverfabriek. Thenceforth he confined himself mainly to the design and manufacture of smaller objects.

Carel J.A. Begeer (1883–1956), who had also trained at Hanau, took over the artistic direction of the firm from his half-brother and set up a special workshop, for which various leading artists supplied designs. The most important example of this is the above-mentioned contract with Jan Eisenloeffel. Most of the objects made at the Begeer factory after his designs bear his logo and the factory mark.

As at many other silver factories, there was at this Utrecht firm a drawing class, which was taught by Carel Begeer himself. The best-known pupil who 'took his first steps along the artist's path' here was the furniture maker and architect Gerrit Thomas Rietveld (1888–1964).[6] No designs for silver objects are known by him, but he did design some medals.

Carel Begeer was an influential man with many international contacts. Silver by Georg Jensen, Josef Hoffmann and Adolf von

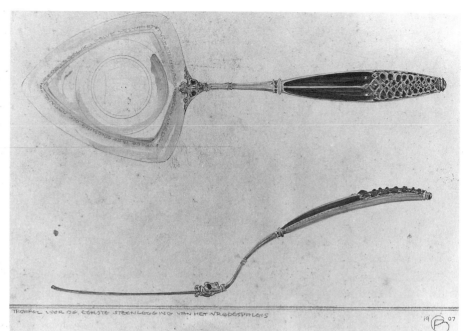

TROFFEL VOOR DE EERSTE STEENLEGGING VAN HET VREDESPALAIS

Mayrhofer, among others, was sold in his shops. He himself was also a gifted silversmith, who was not averse to experiments in the field. Initially his work was strongly influenced by German silversmiths such as Ernst Riegel. He made use of various old ornaments and techniques, but gradually the sharp contours and linear articulations of the objects became more and more fluid, until they were divested of any decorative motifs and only painterly undulating surfaces remained. Begeer was a great advocate of good collaboration between artists and manufacturers, which he tried to achieve in numerous ways.

In 1919 the former competitors Van Kempen and Begeer merged with the jewelry firm of Vos. This resulted in some years of great internal tensions, which were certainly not conducive to further developments in the artistic field. But when the concern entered calmer waters in 1925, under the name Zilverfabriek Voorschoten, there was once more an opportunity for new developments. Under the aegis of Carel J.A. Begeer, who had meanwhile become director of the merged and reorganized firms, a modern deep-drawing press was acquired. With this it was possible to make objects such as teapots which 'retained a beautiful shape, although this consisted of only four parts, body, lid, handle and spout, instead of twelve'.[7]

After Begeer himself had had some experimental designs carried out, he took on Christa Ehrlich to develop these ideas further. Born in Vienna in 1903, she had been a pupil of Josef Hoffmann at the Kunstgewerbeschule. Thereafter she had become an assistant in his

Standing cup with flat-chased ornament, designed by Carel J.A. Begeer. Maker's mark: C.J. Begeer, Utrecht, 1911. Compare this with the fruit stand shown on p. 186. Height: 19.5 cm (7¾ in.). Private collection.

179

162 Sweetmeat dish designed by
J.L.M. Lauweriks, Hagen. Maker's
mark: Frans Zwollo Sr and the
Hagener Silberschmiede, *c.* 1913.
Height: 11 cm (4¼ in.). Private
collection.

163 Fish slice. Maker's mark: Frans
Zwollo Sr, The Hague, 1916. Length:
32 cm (12½ in.). Private collection.

164 Silver-gilt tea caddy. Maker's
mark: Frans Zwollo Sr, Amsterdam,
1899. Height: 10.2 cm (4 in.).
Museum Boymans-van Beuningen,
Rotterdam.

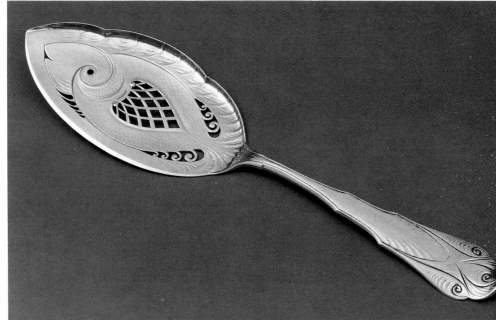

164

165

165 Bonbonnière. Maker's mark: J. Jacobs, Heemstede (near Amsterdam), 1922. Height: 13.5 cm (5¼ in.). Private collection.

166 Tea service. Maker's mark: J. Steltman, The Hague, 1925. Made for the Paris Exhibition of 1925. Height of teapot: 10.5 cm (4¼ in.). Haags Gemeentemuseum, The Hague.

167 Tea service and milk jug designed by Jan Eisenloeffel. Maker's mark: Fa. Stoffels & Co., 1903. Height of kettle (with stand): 21.5 cm (8½ in.). Diameter of tray: 28 cm (11 in.). Private collection.

167

168

168 Oval bowl designed by Jan Eisenloeffel. Maker's mark: Hoeker & Zn., and Amstelhoek monogram. Amsterdam, 1902. Shown at the Turin Exhibition in 1902. Width: 21 cm (8¼ in.). Private collection.

169 Flower vase. Maker's mark: As. Bonebakker, Amsterdam, 1919. Height: 21 cm (8¼ in.). Private collection.

170 Bag clasp. Maker's mark: Firma J. Heuvelmans, Bois-le-Duc, 1902. The ornament, derived from the Vienna Secession, is very unusual for Dutch silver. Width: 11 cm (4¼ in.). Private collection.

171 Bottle stand designed by Jan Eisenloeffel. Maker's mark: C.J. Begeer, Utrecht, 1906. Height: 11.3 cm (4½ in.). Private collection.

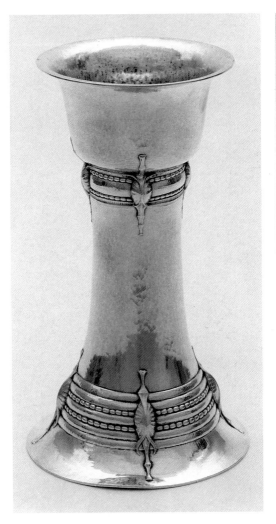

169

△ 1

1

172

173

172 Jardinière. Maker's mark: J.M. van Kempen, Voorschoten, 1899. Width: 44.5 cm (17½ in.). Museum Boymans-van Beuningen, Rotterdam.

173 Tea service. Maker's mark: J.M. van Kempen, Voorschoten, 1902. The small vase is for teaspoons. Height of teapot: 12.3 cm (4¾ in.). Width of tray: 41.5 cm (16¼ in.). Private collection.

174 Pastry server and beaker with dark-blue enamel, fish servers with bright-green enamel. Maker's mark: J.M. van Kempen, Voorschoten, 1904 and 1905. Height of beaker: 8.5 cm (3¼ in.). Length of fish slice: 28 cm (11 in.). Private collection.

175 Pastry server, sugar sifter and sugar tongs. Maker's mark: J. M. van Kempen, Voorschoten, 1905. Length of pastry server: 17.5 cm (7 in.). Private collection.

176 Tea service with spoon vase. Maker's mark: J. M. van Kempen, Voorschoten, 1919. Height of teapot: 11.6 cm (4½ in.). Width of tray: 33.3 cm (13 in.). Private collection.

177 Coffee and tea service designed by Professor A.F. Gips for the Exposition Internationale in Paris in 1900. Maker's mark: C.J. Begeer, Utrecht, 1900 and 1908. Height of kettle (with stand): 42.5 cm (16¾ in.). Width of trays: 51.5 cm and 27.2 cm (20¼ in. and 10¾ in.). Museum Boymans-van Beuningen, Rotterdam.

178 Fruit stand designed by Christa Ehrlich. Maker's mark: Zilverfabriek Voorschoten, 1928. Diameter: 25 cm (9¾ in.). Private collection.

179 Communion service designed by Carel J.A. Begeer in 1926 to be made with the new deep-drawing press. Maker's mark: Zilverfabriek Voorschoten, 1927. Height of wine jug: 30.3 cm (12 in.). Private collection.

180 Tea service and boxes designed by Christa Ehrlich in 1927 for the Zilverfabriek Voorschoten. The cylindrical forms were made in a limited number of diameters, with and without covers, spouts, and ears, in several heights. Thus it was possible to produce a wide variety of vessels from only four basic shapes. Height of taller biscuit box: 16.5 cm (6$\frac{1}{2}$ in.). Height of teapot and shorter biscuit box (without knob): 8 cm (3$\frac{1}{4}$ in.). Width of tray: 51.5 cm (20$\frac{1}{4}$ in.). Taller biscuit box: Stichting Van Kempen en Begeer Museum, Zoetermeer. Other objects: private collection.

181

181 Saucière and salt cellars designed by Emmy Roth in 1938 for the Zilverfabriek Voorschoten. Height of saucière: 6 cm (2¼ in.). Height of salt cellars: 2.5 cm and 4.5 cm (1 in. and 1¾ in.) Van Kempen en Begeer Museum, Zoetermeer. Saucière in private collection.

182 Teapot designed by Gustav Beran for the Paris Exhibition of 1937. Maker's mark: Gerritsen en Van Kempen, Zeist. Van Kempen en Begeer Museum, Zoetermeer.

182

architect's office and had done the decorations for Sonja Knip's house shown on page 201. She also painted the interior of the Austrian Pavilion at the Paris Exhibition of 1925. In 1927 she had been responsible for the installation of the Austrian section designed by Josef Hoffmann for the Europäisches Kunstgewerbe exhibition at Leipzig. It was there that Carel Begeer met her and although she had never designed metalwork in Austria, he invited her to come to the Netherlands to design models for modern silver for the Zilverfabriek Voorschoten. These were functional objects, 'designed for serial production, starting from deep-drawn basic forms, which could then be finished on the lathe'.[8]

178,180   This machine technique led to highly characteristic designs, which had features in common with the Functionalist Movement in architecture and interior decoration. The beauty of the objects was governed by the elementary factors of form, material and technique. The first objects made at the Zilverfabriek Voorschoten in particular are extremely severe in form, with sharp corners and edges, but

Catalogue cover for an exhibition of Austrian paintings and applied art designed by Christa Ehrlich shortly after arriving in Holland in 1927.

Christa Ehrlich would not have been Viennese had she not managed to introduce a little playful decorative accent here and there.

One of the other silversmiths whom Carel Begeer had met at Leipzig was Emmy Roth, who since 1916 had had a workshop in Berlin-Charlottenburg. She produced superb hand-made silver in very carefully considered forms. She had learned the craft from C.A. Beumers in Düsseldorf and had worked for some years in Palestine, but she was not very keen on the filigree technique which was used there for jewelry. In 1938–9 she lived in the Netherlands, designing for the Zilverfabriek Voorschoten table silver which seems almost to 181 herald the silverwork produced in Scandinavia after the war.

At the Paris Exhibition of 1937 Gerritsen en Van Kempen of Zeist, another big Dutch silver factory, sent in work designed by Gustav Beran. He too came from Vienna and had been a pupil of Josef Hoffmann. His award-winning design for a tea-set clearly shows his 182 teacher's influence.

Just as at the beginning of the century, artists and designers in the thirties were aiming for generalized objective forms and rejecting emotional elements. Around 1900 formal purity was the result of a systematic simplification, whereas around 1930 it resulted from a consistent application of mechanical techniques to design. Yet the ideal of bringing these objects within the reach of the widest possible circle of users by economical production remained unattainable, even though most of the designs were executed not only in silver, but also in the cheaper electroplate. The modern forms were much admired, but seldom bought.

1   See, for example, *Kunst und Kunsthandwerk* IV (1901), pp. 124 and 125 and NOTES
Revue de la Bijouterie, Joaillerie et Orfèvrerie, 1900, pp. 82–7.
2   J.J. Seekles, *Overzicht van bij de Rijksarchiefdienst berustende archief-bescheiden van de kantoren van de waarborg voor platina, gouden en zilveren werken 1815–1930*, The Hague, August 1985, 'Register van geëxporteerde gouden en zilveren werken, 1893–1908'.
3   Dr Hermann Warlich in *Dekorative Kunst*, 1909, pp. 205–8.
4   Letter of 6 April 1935 from J.W. Eisenloeffel to Carel J.A. Begeer.
5   Seekles, op. cit., 'Register van werkmeesters', no. 4642, 30 January 1903.
6   Letter of 15 July 1954 from G.T. Rietveld to Carel J.A. Begeer.
7   *Edelmetaal*, 1948, p. 167.
8   *Jaarboek VANK*, 1930, p. 150.

7

AUSTRIA

FRANZ Josef, Emperor of Austria, and King of Bohemia and Hungary, reigned over a vast area in Central Europe from 1848 to 1916. It was home to at least twelve different nationalities, from Italians to Poles, from Slovaks to Ukrainians. The capital of this huge empire was Vienna, in which, in the second half of the nineteenth century, there was a population explosion. The old ramparts were demolished, the Ringstrasse was laid out, and various public buildings in eclectic styles, such as the Opera and the city hall, overlooked the new quarters along the ring road. Historicist styles predominated in all fields of fine and applied art in Vienna until in the 1890s.

One of the leading architects up to that time in this conventional Viennese mode was Otto Wagner (1841–1918). He proved to be one of the few in his generation who was capable late in life of applying new techniques and forms in architecture. Hence he was appointed professor of architecture in 1894. With the maxim that appeared in his book on modern architecture in 1895, 'Nothing that is not practical can be beautiful', he indicated the way forward for his pupils, Josef Hoffmann and Josef Maria Olbrich among them. In 1902 he designed silver, which was executed by the firm of Klinkosch in Vienna. It formed part of the Austrian display at the Turin Exhibition of 1902 and was also to be seen at the winter exhibition in Vienna's Österreichisches Museum für Kunst und Industrie.

THE VIENNA SECESSION
AND *VER SACRUM*

In 1897 Vienna was shaken out of its artistic torpor. A number of artists led by Gustav Klimt made a radical break with the academic style of painting which had been current until then and founded the Vereinigung bildender Künstler Österreichs (Association of Austrian Artists) – Secession, generally known as the Vienna Secession, in emulation of groups of artists in Munich and Berlin. In 1898 they published the first number of their periodical *Ver Sacrum* (Sacred Spring), in which they ventilated their ideas. In that same year they also built a modern exhibition gallery of their own on Karlplatz after a design by one of the members, the architect Josef Maria Olbrich. A stained-glass window and the decorations of the interior were designed by another member, the graphic artist Koloman Moser. Over the entrance could be read an inscription by Ludwig Hevesi, *Der Zeit ihre Kunst/Der Kunst ihre Freiheit* ('To time its art, to art its freedom').

In 1899 Josef Olbrich accepted an invitation from Ernst Ludwig, Duke of Hesse, to go to Darmstadt. His *Ideen*, a portfolio with 154 pages of photographs and designs, which he dedicated to the duke on that occasion, shows what an artistic loss to Vienna his departure was.

At their exhibitions, which were held several times a year, the Secessionists showed both their own work and that of various foreign honorary members. Fine and applied arts were exhibited together in order to emphasize the ideal of the *Gesamtkunstwerk* (total work of art). The eighth exhibition of the Secession in 1900 in particular was of great importance for modern Viennese applied arts. There for the first time it was possible for people in Austria itself to encounter the modern applied arts of other European countries. Julius Meier-Graefe, owner of the Paris shop La Maison Moderne, and Henry van de Velde had been invited to take part in this exhibition, but the designs which attracted the most attention were those of Charles Robert Ashbee of London and Charles Rennie Mackintosh and his wife Margaret, of Glasgow. Various jewels and silver objects by Ashbee were again to be seen in 1906 at the twenty-seventh exhibition of the Secession. His silver designs were a great success in Austria in those years. For example, a Dr Mandello of Pressburg (now Bratislava) ordered flatware and table silver from Ashbee, while his influence can be seen in some of Josef Hoffmann's designs, not in the forms of the objects, but in the ornament used, such as wire nodes and bases and heart-shaped leaves.

187

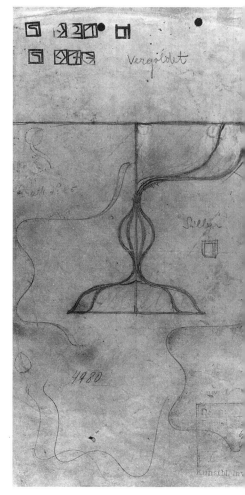

Design for the tazza illustrated on p. 206. Österreichisches Museum für angewandte Kunst, Vienna.

THE KUNSTGEWERBESCHULE

With the appointment in 1899 of Felician von Myrbach as director of Vienna's Kunstgewerbeschule a new day dawned at that institution as well. Koloman Moser and Josef Hoffmann, who like von Myrbach were members of the Secession, were appointed professor of painting and of architecture, respectively. The chasing and embossing workshop was directed by Professor H. Schwartz, the enamelling workshop by Adèle von Stark. Their progressive artistic ideas enabled the younger generation to free itself from the straitjacket of the traditional style. Of this new generation of teachers Hoffmann remained at the school the longest, until his retirement in 1936. During those years around four hundred students from Austria and elsewhere took courses under him.

The Kunstgewerbeschule wanted to broaden public interest in contemporary crafts in Vienna, so the students not only learned drawing, but were also given practical instruction in various techniques such as weaving, pottery, metalwork and fabric printing. Sometimes renowned firms in Vienna bought designs made at the school and put them into production. In order to stimulate an interest in the modern applied arts among a wide public, the Museum für Kunst und Industrie organized an annual winter exhibition up to 1914, at which it also acquired objects itself.[1]

The Kunstgewerbeschule took part in international exhibitions too. The first was the Paris Exhibition of 1900, where a room decorated and furnished by Josef Hoffmann could be admired. The furniture is dark and emphatically decorated with typical Vienna Secession ornament: pierced circles, curved lines and naturalistic motifs in squares. Flowing, undulating lines over walls, floor and furniture were used to bring them into harmony, but this ornament stifled the forms. In 1900 the Viennese artists had not yet achieved the breakthrough to simple, undecorated forms, the most striking characteristic of the applied arts in Vienna between 1903 and 1908. Opinions on this display differed widely. A. Pit, the then director of the Rijksmuseum in Amsterdam, for example, thought that Austria's role was insignificant.[2] Others were full of praise: 'Austria certainly takes first place in the field of the decorative arts. Here one finds harmonious unity, both in the way in which everything is exhibited and in the pieces themselves. Austrian art: strong, elegant simplicity and distinction.'[3]

Naturally, the Kunstgewerbeschule also took part in the Turin Exhibition of 1902. The silverwork designed by the students for this occasion was executed by the firm of Alfred Pollak in Vienna. A now rather neglected colleague of Hoffmann and Moser, Professor Rudolf Hammel, who had likewise been appointed in 1899, had also designed silver for this exhibition. It was made by the firm of Josef Bannert.

Apart from these designs for international exhibitions, other silver designs by students are also known to have been put into production. For example, around 1900 Oskar Thiede designed a tea-kettle and stand which were made by the Viennese firm of Brüder Frank.

Antoinette Krasnik, a pupil of Koloman Moser, designed glass and porcelain as well as silver and jewelry at this time. The cigarette-case illustrated, with a stylized dragonfly in blue *plique à jour* enamel, which was made by the firm of Alexander Sturm, was shown at the winter exhibition of 1902–3 at the Museum für Kunst und Industrie. Some years later Hans Ofner (b. 1880), a pupil of Josef Hoffmann and Adèle von Stark, designed various objects and jewelry: a centre piece, baskets in simple forms with pierced squares and straight lines and boxes with enamelled decoration, all showing the great influence of his teacher.

183

It proved no simple matter continually to convince firms afresh of the importance of the production of good modern designs. Therefore designers took the production of furniture and other domestic articles into their own hands and in 1903, with the financial backing of Fritz Wärndorfer, Josef Hoffmann and Koloman Moser, founded the Wiener Werkstätte. Because Moser worked there for only a few years, a separate description of his role in the silver designs for that enterprise is given below first. Josef Hoffmann's work as professor at the Kunstgewerbeschule and as architect and designer is so closely bound up with the Wiener Werkstätte, of which he was artistic director until it closed in 1932, that he will be discussed under that heading.

KOLOMAN MOSER

Koloman Moser (1868–1918) began his training as a painter at the Academy in Vienna in 1886. After that he was a student at the Kunstgewerbeschule from 1892 to 1895, concentrating on graphic art. He was one of the founders of the Vienna Secession and his numerous illustrations in the first number of *Ver Sacrum*, which appeared in 1898, show his close involvement with the genesis of this important periodical, which continued to exist until 1903. His early decorations consisted of stylized naturalistic ornament on a square grid, but from 1901 onwards these were replaced by the well-known 'chequer-board pattern'. In contrast to the black-and-white squares which had been used in the Netherlands since 1898[4] and which were derived from Assyrian and Egyptian art, Moser's square ornaments and forms were the product of a consistent abstraction of floral motifs. The souvenir booklet he designed to the commission of the City of Vienna for the ball in 1901 illustrates his development perfectly. The mount is still Secessionist, with organic and abstract motifs and lines, and seems to be influenced by Charles Rennie Mackintosh. The endpapers exhibit naturalistic motifs in squares which alternate with square fields in a light colour.

184

Of all the artists appointed as professors at the Kunst-gewerbeschule in 1899, Moser was the most versatile. He designed furniture and textiles, leather objects and book covers, ceramics, glass and metalwork, stained-glass windows, stage sets and even toys. He also designed countless exhibitions. As a graphic artist he designed postage stamps and banknotes, as well as posters and lettering. Since he not only designed, but also had practical experience in all these different fields, Moser was in an unrivalled position to train his pupils in all aspects of modern design. He also had contacts with various firms, who executed designs by him and his pupils.

In 1903 Moser founded the Wiener Werkstätte in company with Josef Hoffmann and Fritz Wärndorfer, because, as he once said, 'We are living in the times of automobiles, electric cars, bicycles and railways; what was good style in stage-coach days is not so now, what may have been practical then is not so now, and as the times are, so art must be.'[5] Modern times and ideas demanded different, practical, functional objects, while contemporary art appeared to best advantage in a light interior.

During these years Moser worked very closely with Josef Hoffmann and it is not possible on stylistic grounds to accurately attribute objects to either. Both designed silver with hammered surfaces and the familiar borders with pierced squares, the so-called *Quadratmuster*. In such cases only the monogram on the object or the drawing identifies its designer. How close the collaboration was between the two men is revealed, for example, by the fact that Hoffmann designed a 'jardinière for the Moser service'.[6] In Moser's use of cabochon-cut stones, as on the two objects illustrated, one sees the influence of Ashbee, who often used these in his designs. The form of the vase of 1905 has points in common with a milk jug of 1900 by Liberty's: both have the same flat, round foot, but the cylindrical form is stricter in Moser's vase.

185,188

23

Moser left the Wiener Werkstätte in 1907 for three distinct reasons: the financial problems, the fact that, in his opinion, too many different things were being tackled at the same time, and because the enterprise was too dependent on the taste of important patrons.[7] His designs continued in production for years, although he did not design any silver after 1907, but devoted himself to painting. He died in 1918, the same year as Gustav Klimt, Otto Wagner and Egon Schiele.

THE WIENER
WERKSTÄTTE, 1903–14

The Wiener Werkstätte, Productiv-Genossenschaft von Kunsthand-werkern in Wien was entered in the commercial register in Vienna on 19 May 1903. The maker's mark for gold and silver was registered a few weeks later. The metal and silver workshops were the first to be fully equipped. The latter was directed by Karl Kallert and other silversmiths of this early period were Josef Hossfeld, Josef Czech, Adolf Erbrich, Augustin Grötzbach, Josef Husnik, Alfred Mayer and Josef Wagner. They executed the designs of Josef Hoffmann and Koloman Moser, who had the courage to design forms without ornament for a generation born in houses stuffed with an extraordinary variety of bric-à-brac. They were encouraged in this by Charles Rennie Mackintosh who, when he heard of their plans to found the enterprise, enthusiastically urged them to 'Embark on it today.'[8] He advised them to concentrate at first entirely on high-quality objects and to make them exclusively to order. Only after that could they aim to produce well-designed objects for daily use at prices which everyone could afford. That is why the famous 'latticework' design did not make its first appearance until 1905.   186

This latticework pattern (*Quadratmuster*), which was punched elsewhere, was used in the silver and metal workshops as the semi-manufactured basis for the production of series of inexpensive functional objects in surprisingly new forms. These, like nearly all the other early designs of the Wiener Werkstätte, were derived from the square, rectangular prism, cube and cylinder. For this reason the geometrical Art Nouveau style of Vienna is often regarded as one of   XX the precursors of the modernism of the thirties. Functionality, good proportions and honest handling of the material were the most important criteria. Hence use was made only of ornament appropriate to the material and technique employed. This meant that only hand-made objects had hammered surfaces or were decorated with semi-precious stones.

In the close collaboration that always existed between Hoffmann and Moser, the latter must in many instances be seen as the source of ideas. But as soon as the spark had jumped across to Hoffmann, Moser's partner developed those ideas in a highly individual way.[9] As has already been noted above, it is often not possible to determine precisely who the designer was in the case of hollow-ware that bears no monogram. This problem does not, however, apply to flatware, which, with but one exception, was all designed by Hoffmann. The earliest design for cutlery was the 'flat model', first produced in December 1903. This resembles a model designed by Charles Rennie Mackintosh at the same time, of which he presented a variant to his godson, F.E. Muthesius, the son of the German architect Hermann Muthesius, in 1904. Hoffmann's design has a less forbidding aspect,   189,190 by virtue of the beading at the end of the stem. The set consisted of thirty-one different parts, plus a salt cellar. The initials LFW show this striking set to have been made for Fritz Wärndorfer, the financial backer of the Wiener Werkstätte, and his wife Lily. Hoffmann and Moser also each possessed two place settings of this model.[10]

In 1904 the Wiener Werkstätte took part in an exhibition for the first time. It was held in Hermann Hirschwald's Hohenzollern Kunstgewerbehaus in Berlin, where a wide variety of objects were sold, ranging from classic English furniture to furniture by Henry van de Velde and silver by the Dutchman Jan Eisenloeffel. Silver and metal objects formed an important part of the Wiener Werkstätte's contribution. It included the 'flat model' cutlery, but we do not know what visitors thought of it. We are better informed as to the reactions it evoked in England two years later. The Viennese correspondent Amelia S. Levetus remarked in connection with the Imperial Royal Austrian Exhibition in London in 1906 that she was afraid that it might not find many admirers. The large knives and forks were very heavy and the bowls of the spoons were too much like shovels in shape. She was better pleased with a tall, elegant dessert stand.

In Germany the work of the Wiener Werkstätte was held in much higher esteem. In November-December 1906, two years after the exhibition in the Hohenzollern Kunstgewerbehaus, another was held, in Hagen, at which various silver objects were bought by Karl Ernst Osthaus.

Some weeks before this successful exhibition the Wiener Werkstätte also attracted great attention on its home territory with an exhibition entitled 'The Laid Table', in which a number of tables were laid for various occasions, ranging from a wedding to a gathering of artists. Here, for the first time, the Viennese public was introduced to the great variety of objects and forms designed by the artists of the Wiener Werkstätte over the previous three years. Jardinières and flower vases, candlesticks and fruit-stands with an array of flowers and fruit adorned all the tables, but, as in London, it was the flatware that attracted the most attention. At this exhibition a second design, the 'round model' with slightly domed stems, could be admired. In a silver-plated version this was used in, among other places, the Cabaret Fledermaus designed by Hoffmann in 1907.

The most important patron Josef Hoffmann and his collaborators at the Wiener Werkstätte ever had was the Belgian industrialist Adolphe Stoclet. In 1905 he commissioned Hoffmann to build a house for him in Brussels and to decorate and furnish it throughout. Building began in 1906 and the house was completed in 1911; not, as Stoclet had hoped, in two years. A large number of objects were specially designed, such as various parts of an extensive dinner service, jardinières, flower vases, dishes, vegetable dishes, sauceboats and soup tureens, all decorated with a border of elliptical ornaments formed by beading. The same motif is also found on the set of cutlery

with three dozen place settings. Naturally, it was not just for the dining room that silver was made. In contemporary photographs of the interior, various silver objects can be recognized as part of the overall décor. The unity of form created here between architecture and interior decoration resulted in an unsurpassed *Gesamt-kunstwerk*.

Moser's departure in 1907 marked the end of the first phase of the Wiener Werkstätte, that of strong geometric forms and ornament. Subsequently the forms became less austere, and ornaments such as bell-flowers, heart-shaped leaves and spiralling tendrils determined the decorative pattern. Two new young designers, ex-students of the Kunstgewerbeschule, had already arrived on the scene before Moser's departure: Carl Otto Czeschka (1878–1960) in 1905 and Eduard Josef Wimmer-Wisgrill (1882–1961) a few years later. Czeschka left in 1907, the same year as Moser, to take up an appointment as a professor in Hamburg, but he continued to produce many designs for the Wiener Werkstätte. Josef Wimmer-Wisgrill is chiefly known as the director of the fashion department there, but he also produced various designs for silver.

Dining room in the Stoclet Mansion, Brussels, designed by Josef Hoffmann in Vienna and built 1905–11. Silverware on dining table and sideboards made at the Wiener Werkstätte. From *The Studio*, April 1914.

The connections between the Kunstgewerbeschule, the Wiener Werkstätte and Hoffmann's architectural practice are sometimes difficult to disentangle, partly because he often gave talented pupils a place in one of the workshops or in his practice, which was itself situated in the Kunstgewerbeschule from 1912 onwards. Hoffmann was an outstanding teacher, but he never gave strictly defined assignments. 'It is all one to me what is attempted or aimed for, as long as there is a result to be seen.'[11] He encouraged his students to experiment and pointed out their mistakes, but left it to them to find an effective solution.

OTHER SILVER MANUFACTURERS IN VIENNA

One of the most conspicuous characteristics of the factory-made Art Nouveau silver produced in Austria before 1900 is the busy embossed decoration. The factories also eagerly imitated the ornament applied by the artists of the Secession, a combination of floral and abstract motifs and undulating lines.

191,19

The work of Georg Adam Scheid constitutes an exception to this, because it was already characterized by simple forms before 1900. In this workshop beautiful enamel was made, such as the candlestick illustrated, with its enamelled mistletoe leaves. The *Journal der Goldschmiedekunst* wrote of the application of this ornament in 1900, 'The use of mistletoe as an artistic ornament is of very recent date and uncommonly fruitful. The mistletoe sprig with its soft curves and the characteristic structure of its leaves cries out particularly for use as a motif for gold and silverwork and has thus also found general application recently.'[12] Before the Wiener Werkstätte was founded, a number of enamelled objects were also made after designs by Koloman Moser at G.A. Scheid's. A silver object designed by Hoffmann before the foundation of the Wiener Werkstätte has also survived: a cup and cover in which the bowl and cover constitute a sphere and the stem is formed by an ellipsoid between four narrow cylinders. This was made by the firm of Würbel & Czokally.

I

195

In connection with an exhibition of Viennese applied art, which was held in London in 1902 and naturally included silver, it was stated in *The Studio*, 'The novel, the "modern" became the fashion and an activity set in, which has brought discredit on the best of things. Imitation set in; the external characteristics of Otto Wagner, of Olbrich, of Kolo Moser were seized upon; their original ideas were done to death; their individual methods of expression were openly plagiarized.'[13] Under the influence of the Wiener Werkstätte these

Candelabrum designed by Hans Bolek. Maker's mark: Alfred Pollak, Vienna, 1912. Österreichisches Museum für angewandte Kunst, Vienna.

ornaments gradually disappeared and various firms switched to producing simple geometrical forms and decorations.

The striking silver made by the Wiener Werkstätte has attracted so much attention everywhere that it is scarcely realized that there were countless other factories and workshops at that time. Bannert, Brüder Frank, Klinkosch, A. Pollak and A. Sturm have already been mentioned, but Oskar Dietrich and Eduard Friedmann also executed designs by leading artists such as Hans Bolek and Otto Prutscher. Professor Franz Delavilla, A.O. Holub and Milla Weltmann, all three ex-students of the Kunstgewerbeschule, likewise made fine designs for these two firms, which link up with the forms and ornament of the Wiener Werkstätte. However, just as in other countries, these firms made only a few objects in the new style in proportion to their total output.

196

The geometric forms of the early years of the Wiener Werkstätte, which had already become less strict after Moser's departure, partly under the influence of Czeschka and Wimmer-Wisgrill, disappeared in this later period. This radical change was brought about by the advent of Dagobert Peche (1887–1923) who, along with Hoffmann, was the most important designer at the Wiener Werkstätte at this time. In contrast to Moser, Peche thought in terms of ornament and rich decoration. He introduced completely new, playful forms and ornament and imaginative decorative objects, which, certainly in the war years, were made of simple materials like painted tin and cardboard.

After the First World War Peche designed, in addition to functional objects in silver, a number of silver ornaments in which decoration played the leading role and which clearly reflect his playful imagination. A good example is the present given to Josef Hoffmann on his fiftieth birthday by the Wiener Werkstätte. The three fruits, which can be opened, symbolize architecture, painting and sculpture. Etiolated, lanceolate leaves and zigzag motifs are the most common characteristics of his decorative style.

Influencing Hoffmann, too, an innate feeling for richness of colour and ornament now gained the upper hand and governed Viennese art in the years between 1914 and 1930. Fluting, horizontal and vertical mouldings, accolades and twisted facets enlivened the softly gleaming surfaces of the silver objects of this period. Hoffmann was an unconventional artist with his own ideas about forms and ornament. At first he was ahead of modernism, but when smooth, undecorated forms became generally accepted, he began decorating. Only at the

THE WIENER WERKSTÄTTE, 1914–32

Ornamental piece designed by Dagobert Peche and presented to Josef Hoffmann for the latter's fiftieth birthday, in 1920. The fruits open to reveal symbols for architecture, painting and sculpture. Illustrated in *Dekorative Kunst*, 1923.

99,200
01,204

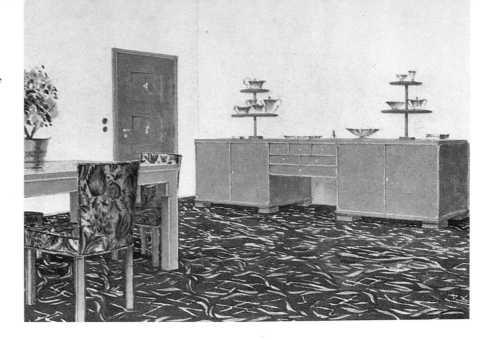

Watercolour by Oswald Härdtl of the dining room in the villa designed by Josef Hoffmann for Sonja Knips. On the sideboard, depicted in deep red, silver made by the Wiener Werkstätte. Interior decoration by Christa Ehrlich. From *The Studio*, June 1929.

end of the twenties did he design some simple hammered objects with rounded angles, which shared the characteristics of the international style.

In the twenties the Wiener Werkstätte also took part in various exhibitions in other countries. Unlike Germany, Austria participated in the Paris Exhibition of 1925, Hoffmann being commissioned to design the pavilion in collaboration with Oswald Härdtl. The showcases, which went right up to the ceiling, were painted by Christa Ehrlich, one of Hoffmann's assistants at that time. She was also in charge of the construction and installation of the Austrian section of the Europäisches Kunstgewerbe exhibition held in the Grassi Museum in Leipzig in 1927. At these two exhibitions a great deal of silver was shown. After the Leipzig event was over, Christa Ehrlich went to the Netherlands where, for the Zilverfabriek Voorschoten, she designed modern silver which could be produced efficiently by the most modern machines.

180

Hoffmann was an individualist. He aimed at exclusivity, even though this proved commercially unattainable in a country which had lost its dominion over all the lands around it as a result of the First World War. Hoffmann's ideas did not bring commercial success. Despite publicity in all the leading international periodicals and participation in countless exhibitions at home and abroad, the Wiener Werkstätte had from the start been faced by great financial problems. Like most artists, Hoffmann was no businessman. Three different backers had tried to put the enterprise on a firm financial footing. The first was Fritz Wärndorfer, followed, after his bankruptcy, by Otto Primavesi.

Through the efforts of Josef Urban, who founded the Wiener Werkstätte of America Inc. in 1921, the Wiener Werkstätte won great renown in the United States too, but even there sales remained below par. Primavesi died in 1926 and again the enterprise found itself teetering on the edge of a financial abyss. Once more at the last moment, a backer, Kuno Grohmann, was found who was prepared to try to keep it in being. However, his efforts at reorganization were unavailing. The financial difficulties of the Wiener Werkstätte can be deduced from the continual reduction in the number of silversmiths. At the beginning of the twenties there were still twenty-six, but the great exodus began in 1925 with the departure of thirteen of them. In the years that followed this trend continued and by 1931 the last silversmith had left.

The political and economic situation in Austria was not such as to allow an institution geared to luxury like the Wiener Werkstätte to come to fruition in the twenties. The workshop was famous all over the world and its objects attracted great attention at exhibitions time and time again, and yet both the enormous variety of its products and the many difficulties of its financial management forced its closure in the adverse economic climate of 1932. What remain are a large number of applied art objects in the most divergent materials and techniques and, happily, the archives, which are now deposited at the Österreichisches Museum für angewandte Kunst (Austrian Museum of Applied Art).

Just as before the First World War, the silver made by other firms in the twenties was again generally influenced by the Wiener Werkstätte. Only incidentally does one find de luxe French Art Deco or the simple functional forms of the Bauhaus. Oskar Dietrich was one of the Viennese firms which showed silver at the Paris Exhibition of 1925. The disappointing results of this big exhibition led to violent denunciations of Josef Hoffmann in Vienna. In future, it was felt, architects and artists should take more account of the commercial requirements of manufacturers and craftsmen.

Art and commerce remained difficult things to combine, but around 1930 two more factories commissioned designs for modern silver. Klinkosch made a number of silver objects after designs by Oswald Härdtl (1899–1959), who had been first a pupil of Hoffmann 202 and then an assistant in his architectural practice. In 1925 he was appointed professor at the Kunstgewerbeschule and a few years later became Hoffmann's closest collaborator. When the silver workshop of the Wiener Werkstätte closed down, the firm of A. Sturm made silver after designs by Hoffmann. Brüder Frank was the only firm in 203 Vienna to make silver that could rival good French Art Deco silver in both form and quality.

In the thirties Austrian silver lost its unique character. In a country with many political and economic problems it is impossible for new

One of the showcases in the Austrian pavilion at the Paris Exhibition of 1925, containing several pieces of silver made by the Wiener Werkstätte. Decoration of showcases by Christa Ehrlich.

impulses from a young generation of artists to develop. At international exhibitions it was now French and Danish silversmiths who were attracting all the attention.

NOTES 1 Waltraud Neuwirth, *Wiener Gold- und Silberschmiede und ihre Punzen*, Vienna 1976.
2 A. Pit, 'De Nederlandsche Kunstnijverheid op de Parijsche Tentoonstelling', *Tweemaandelijksch Tijdschrift*, September 1900, pp. 296–308.
3 Henri Evers in *Das Interieur*, 1901, p. 26.
4 See, for example, Dr L. Gans, *Nieuwe Kunst*, Utrecht 1966, p. 233; K.P.C. de Bazel, *Bouw- en Sierkunst* 1898.
5 A.S. Levetus, 'Koloman Moser', *The Studio*, November 1904, p. 114.
6 Archives of the Wiener Werkstätte, Inv. no. 12038/8, Österreichisches Museum für angewandte Kunst.

7   Werner Fenz, *Koloman Moser*, Salzburg/Vienna 1984, pp. 36, 37.
8   Thomas Howarth, *Charles Rennie Mackintosh and the Modern Movement*, London 1971, p. XXXIX.
9   Werner J. Schweiger, *Wiener Werkstätte, Kunsthandwerk 1903–1932*, Vienna 1982.
10 Waltraud Neuwirth, *Josef Hoffmann, Bestecke für die Wiener Werkstätte*, Vienna 1982, p. 32.
11 Eduard Sekler, 'Josef Hoffmann als Mensch, Künstler und Lehrer', *Josef Hoffmann Wien*, Museum Bellerive, Zurich, 1983, p. 29.
12 *Journal der Goldschmiedekunst*, 21, no. 2, 15 January 1900, p. 10.
13 T.G. in *The Studio*, 25 (1902).

183 Cigarette-case with *plique à jour* enamelled dragon-fly, designed by Antoinette Krasnik. Maker's mark: A. Sturm, Vienna, 1902. 8 cm × 7.8 cm (3¼ in. × 3 in.). Badisches Landesmuseum, Karlsruhe.

184 Souvenir ball book with velvet, silk and metal, designed by Koloman Moser, Vienna, 1901. Private collection.

183

184

185 Flower vase set with oval amber cabochons, designed by Koloman Moser. Maker's mark: Josef Hossfeld and Wiener Werkstätte, Vienna, 1905. Height: 22 cm (8½ in.). Österreichisches Museum für angewandte Kunst, Vienna.

186 Flower basket with glass liner, designed by Josef Hoffmann, c. 1906. Maker's mark: Wiener Werkstätte. Height: 25.5 cm (10 in.). Private collection.

187 Tazza designed by Josef Hoffmann, c. 1908. Maker's mark: Wiener Werkstätte. The open thread-work stem shows the strong influence of some of Charles Robert Ashbee's designs for the Guild of Handicraft. The design for this object is shown on p. 192. Height: 12.5 cm (5 in.). Diameter: 18.5 cm (7¼ in.). Christie's, Amsterdam, 27 October 1983, no. 448.

188 Inkpot set with chrysoprase cabochons, designed by Koloman Moser. Maker's mark: Konrad Koch and Wiener Werkstätte, Vienna, c. 1904. An identical inkpot was made for Adolphe Stoclet of Brussels. Height: 11 cm (4¼ in.). Badisches Landesmuseum, Karlsruhe.

185

△186

187

189, 190 Flatware designed by Josef Hoffmann and made in the Wiener Werkstätte in 1905 for Lily and Fritz Wärndorfer. Initialled 'LFW'. Length of soup ladle: 37.3 cm (14¾ in.). Length of egg spoon: 10.5 cm (4¼ in.). Österreichisches Museum für angewandte Kunst, Vienna.

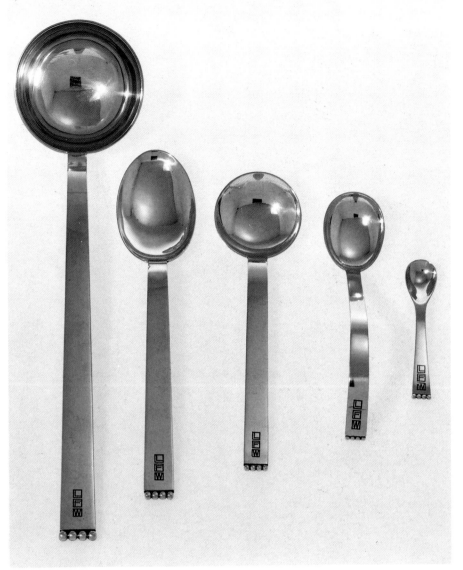

189

190

191

191 Pair of pitchers, signed 'Bachruch', Budapest, *c.* 1900. Height: 41.5 cm (16¼ in.). Limburg Collection, Amsterdam.

192 Tea caddy made in Vienna. Design attributed to Rudolf Hammel. Bears import mark of George Bedingham, London, 1902. A similar caddy can be seen in the advertisement on p. 23. Height: 10.5 cm (4¼ in.). Private collection.

193 Parasol handle. Maker's mark: Johann Gross, Vienna, *c.* 1900. Length: 21 cm (8¼ in.). Private collection.

194 Bowl. Maker's mark: Eduard Friedmann, Vienna, *c.* 1900. 46 cm × 32.5 cm (18 in. × 12¾ in.). Rijksmuseum, Amsterdam.

195 Candlestick with green enamelled mistletoe leaves, shown at the Paris Exhibition of 1900. Maker's mark: Georg Adam Scheid, Vienna, 1899. Height: 22.5 cm (8¾ in.). Württembergisches Landesmuseum, Stuttgart.

196 Oval centrepiece designed by Hans Bolek. Maker's mark: Eduard Friedmann, Vienna, *c.* 1910. Height: 24.5 cm (9¾ in.). Badisches Landesmuseum, Karlsruhe.

192

194

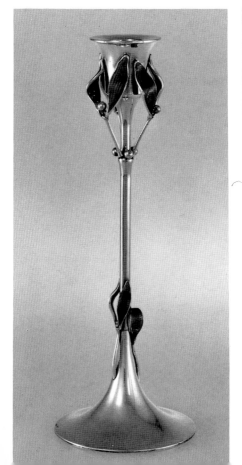

196

197

198

197 Candelabra. Maker's mark: J.C. Klinkosch, Vienna, *c.* 1910/1922. Height: 21.5 cm (8½ in.). Rijksmuseum, Amsterdam.

198 Oval basket with glass liner. Maker's mark unknown. Vienna, *c.* 1920. Height: 13.5 cm (5¼ in.). Rijksmuseum, Amsterdam.

199 Fruit basket and standing dish designed by Josef Hoffmann. Maker's mark: Wiener Werkstätte, Vienna, 1916. Basket: 16.8 cm × 16.8 cm (6½ in. × 6½ in.). Height of dish: 24 cm (9½ in.). Badisches Landesmuseum, Karlsruhe.

200 Flower vase designed by Dagobert Peche, *c.* 1922. Maker's mark: Wiener Werkstätte. Height: 32.2 cm (12¾ in.). Badisches Landesmuseum, Karlsruhe.

201 Tea service designed by Josef Hoffmann on a tray designed by Dagobert Peche. Maker's mark: Wiener Werkstätte, Vienna, 1918. The service was shown at the Paris Exhibition of 1925. Width of tray: 43 cm (17 in.). Sotheby's, Monaco, 9 October 1983, no. 290.

199

201

200

204

202

203

202 Bottle-stop designed by Josef Hoffmann. Maker's mark: Wiener Werkstätte, Vienna, *c.* 1918. Height: 8 cm ($3\frac{1}{4}$ in.). Coffee pot designed by Oswald Härdtl. Maker's mark: J.C. Klinkosch, Vienna, *c.* 1930. Height: 19 cm ($7\frac{1}{2}$ in.). Private collection.

203 Candlesticks designed by Josef Hoffmann. Maker's mark: A. Sturm, Vienna, *c.* 1930. Height: 29.5 cm ($11\frac{1}{2}$ in.). Badisches Landesmuseum, Karlsruhe.

204 Cigarette-case with niello ornament, designed by Josef Hoffman. Maker's mark: Wiener Werkstätte, *c.* 1918. 8.2 cm ($3\frac{1}{4}$ in.) × 4.9 cm (2 in.). Badisches Landesmuseum, Karlsruhe.

XX Plate designed by Josef Hoffman, *c.* 1905. Maker's mark: Wiener Werkstätte. 15.5 cm × 15.5 cm (6 in. × 6 in.). Galerie Torsten Bröhan, Düsseldorf.

8

SCANDINAVIA, FINLAND AND RUSSIA

J UST as Celtic art was a source of inspiration in England, so in the Scandinavian countries, under the influence of the nationalist movements, was grateful use made of the rich store of motifs of the Viking period. As far as silverwork was concerned, this renewal of interest in the Vikings, sometimes referred to as the 'Viking revival', played a part in Denmark and above all in Norway, but the silver in these two countries also had distinct characteristics of its own: in Denmark heavy forms with abstract ornament and in Norway enamelled objects. In Finland and Sweden modern silver played only a minor role around the turn of the century.

After 1925 there gradually developed in all these countries a common Scandinavian style, which had a great influence on modern design in Europe after the Second World War. The simple, undecorated, smooth and streamlined forms proved better suited to execution in silver than the modernistic forms produced under the influence of the Bauhaus.

DENMARK

XXI *Plique à jour* enamelled vase, designed by Gustav Gaudernack. Maker's mark: David-Andersen, Christiania (Oslo), *c.* 1907. Height: 27 cm (10¾ in.). Kunstindustrimuseet, Oslo. Photograph: Teigens Fotoatelier A.S.

Georg Jensen is generally credited with being the first to design or make modern silver in Denmark, but in fact that honour belongs to the architect and designer Thorvald Bindesbøll (1846–1908) and the famous silver factory of A. Michelsen. Bindesbøll's first designs for silver date from 1899 and were shown by Michelsen at the Paris Exhibition of 1900. They are objects with simple forms and powerful abstract decoration. Bindesbøll was the most important designer in Denmark from the 1890s onwards, and not only in the field of silver.

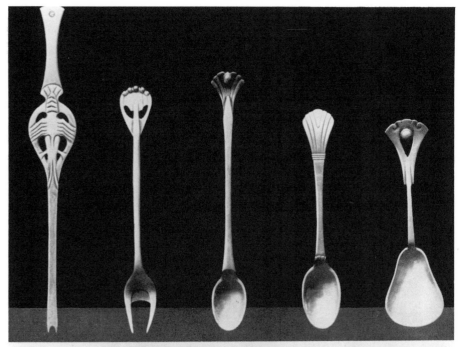

OGENS BALLIN UND GUDMUND HENTZE ● HANDGESCHMIEDETE SILBERNE VORLEGEGABELN UND LÖFFE
AUSGEFÜHRT IN MOGENS BALLINS WERKSTATT, KOPENHAGEN

He also produced many designs for ceramics, textiles and furniture, always with heavy, undulating abstract ornament. These motifs derived from clouds or seaweed, with their erratic, amorphous contours, are the most striking characteristic of modern Danish silver around the turn of the century. Thorvald Bindesbøll had a great influence on the work of a whole generation of young Danish artists. The highly personal way in which he brought a silver surface to life found many imitators in Denmark. For example, the designs of Fr. Hegel, who worked for Michelsen from 1906 onwards, were influenced by Bindesbøll, as was the work of Holger Kyster of Kolding.

A. Michelsen, the only Danish firm to exhibit silver at Paris in 1900, also showed designs by Niels Georg Henriksen and Harald Slott-Møller there. The sculptor Niels Georg Henriksen (1855–1922) was the firm's artistic director. He designed objects decorated with chased and embossed naturalistic flowers, thistles, irises and poppies, which were popular in many other countries at that time. He also designed the silver mounts for a number of objects made by the Royal Porcelain

205,206

Silver by A. Dragsted, shown at the Brussels Exhibition of 1910. The beaker on the left is decorated with lotus motifs, that on the right is in Viking-revival style. From *Deutsche Goldschmiede-Zeitung*, 1911.

Kettle and stand made by Peter Hertz and shown at the Brussels Exhibition of 1910. The heavy abstract ornament was influenced by Thorvald Bindesbøll and Mogens Ballin. From *Deutsche Goldschmiede-Zeitung*, 1911.

Manufactory Ltd in Copenhagen. His work was awarded a gold medal in Paris. The designs of the painter Harald Slott-Møller (1864–1937) are marked by a combination of abstract, capricious ornament borrowed from Bindesbøll and narrative motifs.

Mogens Ballin (1871–1914) had a workshop of his own, where copper and pewter objects were made, as well as silver. One of his assistants was Gudmund Hentze. Georg Jensen too, worked for Ballin, before setting up on his own as a silversmith, and the influence of Ballin and Bindesbøll is unmistakable in some of his early work.

Flatware designed in Denmark at this time frequently bears the same heavy motifs. These decorations were so popular that they continued to be used until late in the twenties and were even copied abroad.

The firm of Peter Hertz, the oldest silver factory in Denmark, also executed designs by Bindesbøll. Thus it is not surprising that his influence is to be seen in the form and ornament of the tea-kettle and stand illustrated. A coffee pot after a design by Just Andersen, which

207

was made at Peter Hertz's four years later, is quite different in those respects. The severe horizontal and vertical articulations, which divide it into large planes, foreshadow the Cubist forms of the twenties. Johan Rohde, who worked mainly with Georg Jensen, also made some designs for Hertz at this time.

212

Modern Danish silver owes its great international renown to a newcomer in the field of silverwork, Georg Jensen (1866–1935). He created a style all his own, which found many followers the world over. He had originally wanted to be a sculptor and it was only after 1901 that he made his first jewelry in the workshop of Mogens Ballin, who allowed him to exhibit it under his own name. In 1904 he opened a small workshop of his own, where he made only silver jewelry. A year later he sold his first pieces to a foreign museum, the Folkwang Museum at Hagen, in Germany[1], and made his first hollow- and flatware. It is notable that these models are still completely devoid of ornament. The curving outlines and hammered surface were enough. In the designs that followed, simplicity was already abandoned and decoration appeared in the form of the familiar finials, feet and handles with bunches of flowers and fruit. These offer a fine contrast to the matt finish of the hammered surface, which characterizes his simple, well-balanced forms. In Jensen's early designs for beakers, vases and boxes he often made use of semi-precious stones. As with many of his contemporaries in Denmark, the influence of the great Bindesbøll is sometimes found in his early work.

214

216

Like Arthur Lasenby Liberty in London, Jensen realized that machines, employed in the right way, could be a useful aid in the making of beautiful objects.[2] He combined old-fashioned quality with contemporary, partly mechanical, production methods and in order to be able to meet the ever-growing demand for his articles, he built a factory on Copenhagen's Ragnagade in 1918.

During the First World War the Georg Jensen Sølvsmedie became a highly profitable concern, with a great deal of interest in its products in Sweden in particular. Around 1918, just as was the case at Van Kempen's in the Netherlands, a number of expensive pieces were designed, such as the well-known five-light candelabrum with bunches of grapes and garlands and the fruit stands on high, twisted stems, also with bunches of grapes. But the optimistic expectation of a greatly improved economic situation after the war, an idea cherished by many neutral countries, soon proved an illusion.

From 1906 onwards Georg Jensen worked in close collaboration with Johan Rohde (1856–1935), the painter, sculptor, architect and designer. Dissatisfied with the silver on offer in the shops, Rohde had designed silver for his own house and had had it made at Jensen's in 1905.[3] After that he supplied the firm with a great many designs, from

1913 onwards as its permanent designer. Compared with those of his friend Georg Jensen, Rohde's forms are lighter in general and his ornament more restrained. His best-known designs are the Konge flatware model, known in English as Acorn, and a jug. Acorn, which dates from 1916, was the firm's most famous cutlery design and is still

211 in production today. In 1920 Rohde designed a pitcher so far ahead of its time that only five years later did the firm dare to put it into production. It was the first 'streamlined' design in silver and it

166 symbolized speed, but in quite a different way from the service by J. Steltman of The Hague.

Jensen's brother-in-law Harald Nielsen (1892–1977) came to work for the firm in 1909 as an apprentice, but soon proved to be a gifted designer. In the twenties he developed a style of his own, which became characteristic of Jensen's modern silver, his designs being marked by smooth, undecorated forms with sharp angles and straight edges. After Jensen's death Nielsen succeeded him as artistic director. He was the designer of the famous Pyramid flatware model,

214 the most successful Art Deco cutlery design, along with Relief, known in English as Parallel.

Parallel was designed in 1931 by the sculptor Gundorph Albertus (1887–1970), who went to work for Jensen's in 1911 and soon acquired a command of all aspects of the trade. As director of the silver factory on Ragnagade, he was responsible for the high quality that characterizes all the Jensen products. The designs made by the Swedish Prince

217 Sigvard Bernadotte (b. 1907) for Georg Jensen from 1931 onwards are imbued with the spirit of thirties' modernism: severe, smooth forms, often with horizontal, vertical or diagonal linear decoration. Other designers who worked for Jensen were the architect O. Gundlach Pedersen, the sculptor Arno Malinowski (1899–1976) and Jensen's son Jorgen.[4]

Just as Jensen himself had been allowed to exhibit under his own name by Mogens Ballin, so he too always gave the names of his designers. Hollow-ware often bears the initials or signature of the designers. These must not be confused with the assayer's marks sometimes found on Danish silver. In the period covered by this book the assayers were Simon Groth (to 1903), C.F. Heise (1904–32) and J. Sigsgaard (1933–60).

Jensen's path to international recognition was a long one. In 1910, at the age of forty-four, he won a gold medal at Brussels, the first of a long series of awards showered upon him from that time onwards at all the international exhibitions, the last coming in 1935, the year of his death. By that time his modest workshop had grown into a firm with its own outlets in Brussels, Barcelona, Berlin, Geneva, London, New York and Paris. In other countries well-known jewellers were made

his sole representatives. In the Netherlands, for example, a contract was signed in 1929 by P.A. Pedersen (business director of the Sølvsmedie since 1924) and Carel J.A. Begeer.[5] Jensen's workshop developed into the only firm in the world which made modern silver to the exclusion of all else.

In the twenties and thirties numerous new models were also made in the other silver factories in Denmark after designs by a young generation of artists, who had distanced themselves from the heavy forms and ornament of around 1900. Alongside Jensen, the firm of A. Michelsen maintained its prominent position. Here in the twenties and thirties designs by various leading artists were executed. Kay Fisker was the first of a new generation of architects who designed modern forms for silver around 1925. The bonbonnières and fruit basket illustrated above still have connections with the international decorative Art Deco style, but Fisker's later designs have the smooth, round, undecorated forms characteristic of modern Danish silver. Two other architects who made modern designs in the thirties were Kay Gottlob and Palle Svenson.

From 1928 onwards the silversmith Svend Weihrauch (b. 1899) designed silver for Franz Hingelberg of Aarhus. These objects were shown abroad for the first time at the big exhibition in Brussels in 1935. For hot drinks or dishes Weihrauch often combined silver with strips of wood over handles and under bases.

In 1907 Carl M. Cohr of Fredericia had commissioned the architect Knud von Engelhardt to design a new flatware model. This was the precursor of the completely plain modern cutlery of the thirties and fifties with the rounded contours which are so characteristic of Scandinavian design. The designs of the thirties for machine-made objects have links with the international modern movement.

Evald Nielsen (1879–1958) showed his jewelry and silver at exhibitions from 1911 onwards. At first his work was influenced by

Candelabra designed by Palle Svenson
for A. Michelsen, Copenhagen. From
The Studio, May 1936.

208,209

210   Jensen, but in the twenties his designs became severe and decorated only with subdued stylized ornament.

    Just Andersen (1884–1943), who was originally a painter and sculptor, set up as a silversmith in 1915. He regularly sent objects in pewter and bronze as well as silver to exhibitions. In contrast to the invariable characteristic style of Jensen's designs, Andersen's work

212   shows an obvious development, reflecting the period in which it was made. His wife was a pupil of Jensen at the same time as Kaj Bojesen and Inger Møller.

    Kaj Bojesen (1886–1958) was apprenticed to Georg Jensen around 1907 and set up on his own as a silversmith in 1913.[5] His early work naturally shows his teacher's influence. At that time he executed designs not only of his own, but also by the painter Harald Slott–Møller. Around 1930 he broke away from the 'Jensen style' and concentrated increasingly on making simple, undecorated objects, in which he clearly wanted to indicate the mechanical nature of their production. For these modern designs he also brought in freelance designers, such as architect Magnus Stephensen, the designer of the

221   tea-kettle illustrated.

    Inger Møller (1886–1966) worked at Jensen's from 1909 onwards and set up on her own in 1922. Her work was shown abroad for the first time in the Danish Pavilion at the Paris Exhibition of 1925. It is characterized by simple motifs soldered on to smooth forms, as in the

219   tureen illustrated.

    The modern 'Danish style', which did not go to extremes, reigned supreme in the twenties and thirties and the expertise of Danish silversmiths was everywhere highly appreciated abroad. Some firms commissioned designs from Danish artists, others took on Danish silversmiths at their factories. For example, the American silver

105,108   factory Gorham Manufacturing Co. invited Erik Magnussen (1884–1961) to the United States in 1925. He had trained as a modeller and silversmith and afterwards studied for two years at the Kunstgewerbeschule in Berlin, before setting up a workshop of his own in Copenhagen. Like that of all the other young Danish artists, his early work is influenced by Bindesbøll.

    Although Carl Christian Fjerdingstad (1891–1968) was born at Kristiansand in Norway, he regarded himself as a Danish silversmith, as is evident from the title of his autobiography, *Escapade dans le passé ou la vie d'un Danois en France*. From 1918 to 1921 he worked in the Netherlands at Blaricum near Amsterdam. Towards the end of that time he met Henry van de Velde, probably through H.P. Bremmer, artistic adviser to the Kröller-Müllers. Van de Velde had entered their service in 1920, to build, among other things, a museum for their already world-famous art collection with its nucleus of works by Vincent van Gogh. Van de Velde must have admired Fjerdingstad's work very much, since he commissioned him to make a service designed for his own use. Fjerdingstad produced it in 1922, 66 when he was already working in Paris.

The international movements in Art Nouveau and Art Deco never took root in Denmark. The Danish silversmiths had their own ideas about the possibilities of the material, which, in their view, lent itself neither to sharp, naturalistic ornament nor to angular, mechanical designs, but to simple, rounded forms. Hence geometric forms and stepped ornament only appeared at a late stage, and to a limited extent, in Denmark. The Danish silversmiths succeeded as no others in combining artistic and technical perfection in harmonious, logical utensils.

Since 1809 Finland had formed part of the Russian Empire as an autonomous Grand Duchy and in the nineteenth century many able Finnish silversmiths, attracted by its wealth, settled in nearby St Petersburg (Leningrad). To keep the old craft traditions alive at a time when industrialization was gaining ground in Finland too, the School of Arts and Crafts (later known as the Institute of Industrial Art) was opened in 1872. Three years later, in 1875, came the founding of the Finnish Society of Crafts and Design, which organized exhibitions. At that time silversmithing was not a high priority, as is evident from, among other things, the fact that there was no silver to be seen in the Finnish Pavilion at the Paris Exhibition of 1900, which was designed by the architects Gesellius Lindgren and Eliel Saarinen.

From 1900 onwards exhibitions were held twice a year in Helsinki, mainly of paintings and sculpture, but with some applied art as well. A box with chased and embossed stylized flowers inside a border of rather wild interlacing, which was exhibited in 1910, shows that, just as in Sweden, silverwork had not yet reached the standard found in other branches of applied art at this time.

All the more surprising, then, is the communion set made by Erik Ehrström (1881–1934) for Tampere Cathedral in 1904. This design, plain, with slightly curved outlines and stepped bases, such as were to be seen everywhere in the thirties, was way ahead of its time. Ehrström, a pupil of first the well-known Finnish painter and designer Akseli Gallén-Kallela and then a Paris silversmith, was the most important silversmith of that period. When a metal department was established in the Institute of Industrial Arts in 1904, he was appointed to teach there.

FINLAND

XXII, XXIII Two *plique à jour*
enamelled standing dishes, designed
by Thorolf Prytz. Maker's mark: Fa.
J. Tostrup, Christiania (Oslo). Bought
at the Paris Exhibition of 1900.
Height: 14.5 cm and 15.5 cm ($5\frac{3}{4}$ in.
and 6 in.). Württembergisches
Landesmuseum, Stuttgart.

XXII

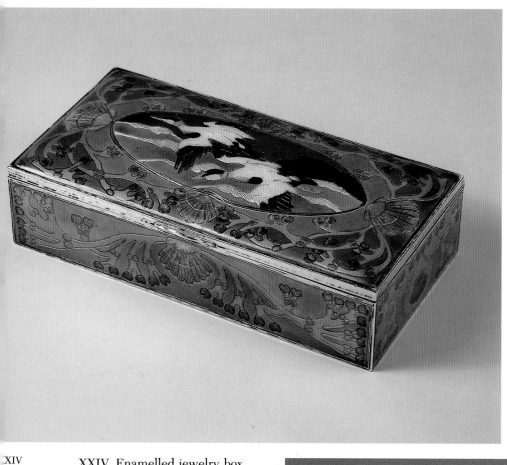

XXIV Enamelled jewelry box designed by Jacob Prytz, *c.* 1914. Maker's mark: J. Tostrup, Christiania (Oslo). Width 20 cm (8 in.). Private collection.

XXV Silver-gilt and enamelled spoon. Maker's mark: Gustav Gustavovich Klingert, Moscow, 1889. Jan Eisenloeffel from Holland was influenced by this champlevé enamel technique. Length 19 cm ($7\frac{1}{2}$ in.). Private collection.

XXIV

XXV

206

205

205 Bowl designed by Thorvald
Bindesbøll. Maker's mark: A.
Michelsen, Copenhagen, 1898.
Height: 9 cm (3½ in.). Museum of
Decorative Art, Copenhagen.

206 Tea caddy designed by Thorvald
Bindesbøll. Maker's mark: A.
Michelsen, Copenhagen, 1900.
Height: 8 cm (3¼ in.). Museum of
Decorative Art, Copenhagen.

207 Bowl designed by Harald Slott-
Møller and made by A. Michelsen,
Copenhagen, 1899. Height: 13.5 cm
(5¼ in.). Museum Bellerive, Zurich.
Photograph: Marlen Perez.

207

208

208 Saucière designed by Svend Weihrauch. Maker's mark: Franz Hingelberg, Aarhus, 1931. The handle, partly in wood, is decorative as well as functional. Height: 31 cm (12¼ in.). Museum of Decorative Art, Copenhagen.

209

209 Pitcher designed by Svend Weihrauch. Maker's mark: Franz Hingelberg, Aarhus, 1931. Height: 16 cm (6¼ in.). Museum of Decorative Art, Copenhagen.

210 Tea strainer and meat fork, signed 'Evald Nielsen', Copenhagen, c. 1920 and c. 1915. Length of fork: 15 cm (6 in.). Private collection.

210

211 Pitcher designed by Johan Rohde in 1920. Made five years later as it was at first thought too modern. Maker's mark: Georg Jensen, Copenhagen, 1925–1932. Height: 23 cm (9 in.). Private collection.

212 Coffee pot designed by Just Andersen. Maker's mark: P. Hertz, Copenhagen, 1914. Height: 19.5 cm (7¾ in.). Museum of Decorative Art, Copenhagen.

213 Pastry server. 'Acorn' or 'Konge' pattern, designed by Johan Rohde in 1915. Maker's mark: Georg Jensen, Copenhagen, 1927. Length: 21.5 cm (8½ in.). Spoon. Maker's mark: Svend Toxvaerds Sølvsmedie, Copenhagen, 1913. Cream spoon. Copenhagen, 1924. Private collection.

213

SCANDINAVIA, FINLAND AND RUSSIA · 227

214

215

216

214 Coffee and tea service designed by Georg Jensen, Copenhagen, in 1905 (Model no. 1). All pieces were made between 1915 and 1927. Height of coffee pot: 15 cm (6 in.). Cake server in 'Parallel' or 'Relief' pattern, designed by Oscar Gundlach Pedersen in 1931. Maker's mark: Georg Jensen, Copenhagen. Length: 17 cm (6¾ in.). Private collection.

215 Different flatware patterns, all with maker's mark of Georg Jensen, Copenhagen. Caddy spoon in 'Agave' or 'Elsinore' pattern, and marrow scoop designed by Harald Nielsen in 1927. Crumb scoop designed by Georg Jensen in 1906 and letter opener by Georg Jensen in 1913. Imported by George Stockwell, London, in 1924. Length of crumb scoop: 28.5 cm (11¼ in.). Length of letter opener: 27 cm (10¾ in.). Private collections.

216 Covered beaker designed by Georg Jensen in 1910. Each of the four flowers is set with an amethyst. Maker's mark: Georg Jensen, Copenhagen, 1915–1919. Height: 20.4 cm (8 in.). Rijksmuseum, Amsterdam.

217 Cocktail shaker designed by Sigvard Bernadotte in 1937. Maker's mark: Georg Jensen, Copenhagen. Height: 17 cm (6¾ in.). Rijksmuseum, Amsterdam.

217

219

218 Bowl. Maker's mark: Hans Hansen, Kolding, 1935. Height: 10 cm (4 in.). Kunstgewerbemuseum, Cologne. Photograph: Rheinisches Bildarchiv, Cologne.

219 Vegetable dish with handles wound with silver wire. Maker's mark: Inger Møller, Copenhagen, 1937. Height: 13 cm (5 in.). Museum of Decorative Art, Copenhagen.

220

220 Table bell and saucière. Maker's
mark: Carl M. Cohr, Fredericia, 1937.
Height of bell: 19.5 cm (7¾ in.).
Private collection.

221 Tea-kettle with wicker-covered
handle and ivory finial, designed by
Magnus L. Stephensen. Maker's
mark: Kaj Bojesen, Copenhagen,
1938. Height: 16 cm (6¼ in.). Private
collection.

222 Soup ladle in 'Suomi' pattern.
Maker's mark: Suomen Kultaseppät
Oy, Turku, 1908. Length: 35 cm
(13¾ in.). Private collection.

222

223 Beaker designed by Henri
Ericsson for the Barcelona Exhibition
of 1929. Maker's mark: Taito Oy,
Helsinki. The embossed decoration,
showing a bear and elk hunt, was
executed by Frans Nykänen. Ericsson,
Nykänen and Taito Oy won an award
at the exhibition. The Finnish
president presented the beaker to the
Spanish king, Alfonso XIII.

223

224 Jelly bowl with ladle, designed by
Walle Rosenberg. Maker's mark: Alm.
Porvoo, 1911. Height: 25 cm (9¾ in.).
Taideteollisuusmuseo, Helsinki.

225

225 Baptismal font designed by
Gunilla Jung c. 1935. Maker's mark:
Viri Oy. Kulosaari Church, Helsinki.

226 Cigarette box designed by
Gunilla Jung. Maker's mark: Suomen
Kultaseppäosakeyhtiö, 1938.
Taideteollisuusmuseo, Helsinki.

226

227

227 Jardinière in old Nordic or
Viking-revival style, designed by
Thorolf Prytz. Maker's mark: Fa. J.
Tostrup, Christiania (Oslo), 1900. It
was intended to be shown at the Paris
Exhibition of 1900, but was not ready
in time. Width: 53 cm (20¾ in.).
Kunstindustrimuseet, Oslo.
Photograph: Teigens Fotoatelier A.S.

228 Vase in silver-gilt and *plique à
jour* enamel, designed by Thorolf
Prytz. Fa. J. Tostrup, Oslo, 1900.
Height: 32.5 cm (12¾ in.).
Kunstindustrimuseet, Oslo.
Photograph: Teigens Fotoatelier A.S.

228

229

229 Spoon with *plique à jour* enamel.
Maker's mark: Marius Hammer,
Bergen, *c.* 1890. Length: 15.6 cm
(6¼ in.). Kunstindustrimuseet, Oslo.
Photograph: Teigens Fotoatelier A.S.

230

231

230 *Plique à jour* enamelled standing
dish. Maker's mark: Fa. J. Tostrup,
Christiania (Oslo), 1900–05. Height:
20 cm (7¾ in.). Kunstindustrimuseet,
Oslo. Photograph: Teigens
Fotoatelier A.S.

231 Three *plique à jour* enamelled
photograph frames designed by
Thorolf Prytz. Maker's mark: Fa. J.
Tostrup, Christiania (Oslo), 1895–
1900. Height: 28.8 cm (11¼ in.).
Kunstindustrimuseet, Oslo.
Photograph: Teigens Fotoatelier A.S.

232

233

232 Pitcher designed by Arthur David-Andersen. Maker's mark: David-Andersen, Oslo, 1901–04. Height: 29.5 cm (11½ in.). Kunstindustrimuseet, Oslo. Photograph: Teigens Fotoatelier A.S.

233 Cream jug and sugar bowl. The bodies are in red guilloché enamel, the rims in white opaque enamel with blue cornflowers. Maker's mark: David-Andersen, Oslo, 1903. Height: 7.2 cm (2¾ in.). Sotheby's, London, 4 December 1985, no. 106.

234 Enamelled bonbonnière and cigarette box designed by Oskar Sørensen in 1928. Maker's mark: Fa. J. Tostrup, Oslo, 1928. Height of bonbonnière: 17.5 cm (7 in.). Kunstindustrimuseet, Oslo. Photograph: Teigens Fotoatelier A.S.

235 Liqueur decanter designed by Oskar Sørensen. Maker's mark: Fa. J. Tostrup, Oslo, 1937. Kunstindustrimuseet, Oslo. Photograph: Teigens Fotoatelier A.S.

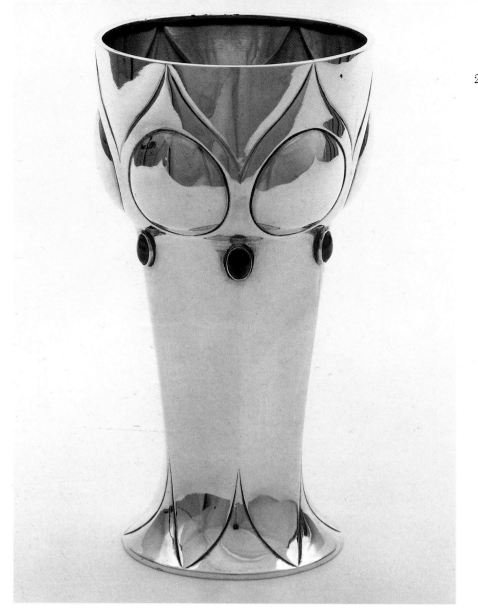

236 Flower vase. Maker's mark: C.G. Hallberg, Stockholm, 1906. Height: 16.9 cm (6¾ in.). Private collection.

236

237 Tea caddy with ebony finial. Maker's mark: Wiwen Nilsson, Lund, 1930. Height (excluding finial): 12 cm (4¾ in.). National Museum, Stockholm. Photograph: Statens Konstmuseer.

238 Cigarette box designed by Erik Fleming. Maker's mark: Atelier Borgila, Stockholm, 1935. Height: 13 cm (5 in.). National Museum, Stockholm. Photograph: Statens Konstmuseer.

237

239

239 Tea service with tray. Maker's mark: K. Anderson, Stockholm, 1910. Diameter of tray: 39.5 cm (15½ in.). Height of teapot: 18 cm (7 in.). K. Barlow Ltd, London. Photograph: Louanne Richards, London.

240 Jewel casket, 'The Three Holy Kings', designed by Jacob Ångman. Maker's mark: GAB, Stockholm, 1916. Height: 22 cm (8½ in.). National Museum, Stockholm. Photograph: Statens Konstmuseer.

240

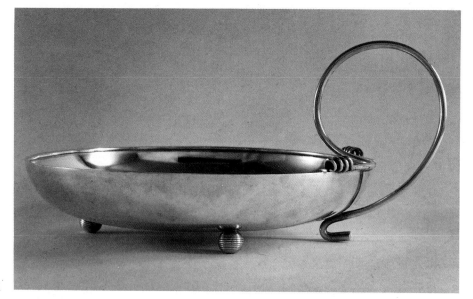

241 Plate. Maker's mark: C. Fabergé, Moscow, 1895. Diameter (without ear): 20.2 cm (8 in.). Height: 11.2 cm (4½ in.). Museum für Kunst und Gewerbe, Hamburg. Photograph: Kiemer & Kiemer.

241

242

242 Two *kovshi*. Maker's mark: P. Ovchinnikov, Moscow, *c.* 1900. Width: 11.2 cm and 12.4 cm (4½ in. and 5 in.). Sotheby's Inc., New York, 5 March 1981, no. 182.

243 Cake basket. Maker s mark: M. and S. Grachev, St Petersburg (Leningrad), *c.* 1900. Height: 15 cm (6 in.). Private collection.

243

244 Wine jug with silver mount and decorated with clematis. Made by Jan Lieberg-Nyberg. Maker's mark: Fabergé, St Petersburg (Leningrad), 1899. Height: 33.5 cm (13¼ in.). Museum für Kunst und Gewerbe, Hamburg. Photograph: Kiemer & Kiemer.

244

245

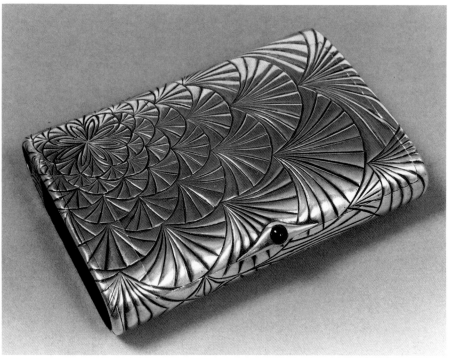

246

245 Tray. Maker's mark: V A, Moscow, 1899–1908. Width: 57.2 cm (22½ in.). Sotheby's, Belgravia, London, 24 November 1977, no. 115.

246 Cigarette-case with compartment for matches. The thumbpiece is set with a cabochon sapphire. Maker's mark: A. Tillander, St Petersburg (Leningrad), before 1899. 9.8 cm × 6.5 cm (3¾ in. × 2½ in.). Oy A. Tillander, Helsinki.

After 1906 there was an increasing influence from German artists, especially in designs for serial production, such as that of flatware. The ladle illustrated was made at Suomen Kultaseppät Oy, the oldest silver factory in Finland. 222

English and Austrian artists also influenced Finnish silversmiths and designers, as is evident from, among other things, a jelly bowl designed by Walle Rosenberg (1891–1919) in 1911 for the firm of A.A. Alm at Porvoo. The forms are simple and ornament plays only a minor role. 224

In 1917 many experienced Finnish silversmiths returned to their native land from Russia, For example, Johan Victor Aarne, one of Fabergé's workmasters, settled in Viipuri, while Alexander Tillander Jr, a well-known jeweller in St Petersburg, made a new start in Helsinki. Workshops and small factories were set up, which commissioned new designs from freelance artists. The first of these new workshops was Taito Oy, established in 1918. The most important designer there was Paavo Tynell (1890–1973), a pupil of Erik Ehrström. In Viri Oy, founded by Frans Nykänen (1893–1951), the best chaser in the country, production in small series was the aim. Nykänen also worked for others. For instance, he chased the ornament on objects designed by Henry Ericsson for Taito Oy. 223

Henry Ericsson (1898–1933) studied at the Central School of Applied Arts in Helsinki. He was a painter, graphic artist and designer, not only of silver, but also of glass and textiles. He was a friend of the famous Finnish architect Alvar Aalto, with whom he shared a studio for a time. His first silver design, a plain oval tea-set for Taito Oy resembles designs by Jacob Ångman of Sweden.

One of the most versatile designers in Finland was Gunilla Jung (1905–1939). After completing her studies at Helsinki's Central School of Applied Arts, she designed lamps, enamel and textiles as well as silver. In 1936 she studied for a year at the Institut Supérieur des Arts Décoratifs in Brussels, which had been set up by Henry van de Velde in the twenties at the request of the Belgian government. Her first designs were executed by Taito Oy, but she also worked for Viri Oy and Kultaseppät Oy in the thirties. Her biggest commission was the designing of a dinner service for the Finnish manufacturer Lennart Baumgartner. This consisted of a number of plates and tureens with simple, smooth, undecorated forms. The cutlery has shortened stems with a groove around them which accentuates their angular form.

225,226

Silver box by O. Weckmann, Helsinki. From *Deutsche Goldschmiede-Zeitung*, 1911.

In Norway, which broke away from the political union with Sweden in 1905, the Viking revival played an important part as an expression of nationalism. The borders of interlacing derived from the ornament on medieval stave churches and dragons' heads based on archaeological finds were used in adapted forms on coffee pots, candelabra and jardinières. In the last decades of the nineteenth century these types of ornament were regarded as characteristic of Norway, so a number of them were shown in the Norwegian Pavilion at the Paris Exhibition of 1900. What attracted much more attention there, however, was the *plique à jour* enamel.

The first experiments with enamel began to be made around 1880 by J. Tostrup, who was soon followed by David-Andersen and Marius Hammer. The first two firms were established at Christiania, as Oslo was then known, the last at Bergen. Initially objects were decorated with *champlevé* or *cloisonné* enamel, but in the 1890s these firms turned more and more to making objects in *plique à jour* enamel. The first results were shown at the World's Columbian Exhibition at Chicago in 1893. The showpiece of the Norwegian display was an oil lamp with a large shade in *plique à jour* enamel. This was made by David-Andersen's after a design by Johan Lund (1861–1939) and it established Norway's credentials in the field of enamel. Stylized flower motifs and symmetrical volutes were used as ornaments at first, but in the last years of the nineteenth century motifs were taken directly from nature.

Among the objects shown by Tostrup's at the Paris Exhibition of 1900 were a number of standing dishes in the form of transparent flowers on tall, elegant stems. These gave rise to so much admiration that they were bought by various museums. The local flora and fauna provided a rich source of inspiration for the designer, the architect Thorolf Prytz (1858–1938), who directed the firm from 1890 to 1912. These pieces were made by Emil Saeter, who had originally been a worker in filigree. The few objects still made by Tostrup's in *plique à jour* enamel after 1900 are far less elegant. An example is a standing dish of which the foot, with fanciful seaweed motifs, is reminiscent of Danish ornament.

At the firm of David-Andersen, where Gustav Gaudernack (1865–1914) was artistic director, experimentation went on longer than at Tostrup's. Gaudernack was born in Bohemia and had trained in Vienna, a city famous in the nineteenth century for its high-quality enamel. He had come to Norway in 1891 and worked for David-Andersen from 1892 onwards. He developed new techniques which made it possible to produce large objects in *plique à jour* enamel. The naturalistic motifs on these objects were always rendered in minute detail. In 1910 Gaudernack set up on his own as a silversmith in Oslo

NORWAY

227

XXII,XXIII
228

230

XXI

and was appointed to teach the craft at the city's School of Art and Design.

232 Apart from these special ornamental pieces, objects for daily use were made which had the naturalistic Art Nouveau decoration of the time. Sometimes these were also enamelled in a simpler way, as in the
233 sugar bowl and cream jug illustrated, which exhibit a pleasing combination of *guilloché* and opaque enamel.

Simpler objects were made in *plique à jour* enamel too. Spoons above all were extremely popular souvenirs among tourists in those years. Many of them were made at Marius Hammer's, a large firm in Bergen, which exported them in quantity. The spoons were so popular in England that in their catalogue of 'Yule-Tide Gifts' of 1896 and 1898 Liberty & Co. of London offered a whole series of spoons with
229 'Norwegian brilliant enamel work'.[6]

Emil Hoye (1875–1958), born in Denmark, settled in Bergen in 1905. From 1910 to 1916 he was director of Marius Hammer's and even after he had set up on his own continued to make designs for the firm from time to time. His early work was influenced by the Danish silversmith Mogens Ballin, while in some of his later designs the influence of Georg Jensen is detectable.

During the First World War costly one-off pieces were made in Norway, just as in Denmark and the Netherlands. Squat forms with heavy, abstract ornament combined with precious stones came into fashion. Various objects in this manner were made by David-Andersen's after designs by Ludvig Wittmann (1877–1961) and Johan Sirnes (1883–1966).

XXIV Jakob Prytz succeeded his father as director of Tostrup's in 1912. Two years later, after the death of Gustav Gaudernack, he became a teacher at the School of Art and Design. His ideas about functional forms had a great influence on the designers of the twenties and thirties. Artists such as Ivar David-Andersen, Guttorm Gagnes, Thorbjørn Lie-Jørgensen and Harry Sørby, who designed for David-Andersen's, and Oskar Sørensen, a designer for Tostrup's, knew the possibilities of the material and production. They designed simple, plain objects which could be mass-produced by machinery. In contrast to the oval forms which we shall encounter below in the streamlined designs by Jacob Ångman of Sweden, round forms were preferred in Norway.

From 1928 onwards enamel, which had gradually receded into the background after 1910, again took an important place in Norwegian silverwork. *Plique à jour* enamel was clearly no longer suited to the modern forms, so use was now made of transparent enamel in strong colours over a *guilloché* ground (*guilloché* enamel). It is remarkable that enamel should have developed in such a short time into one of the 234

Sterling silver coffee pot designed by Harry Sørby for David-Andersen, Oslo, in 1938.

most characteristic aspects of silverwork in Norway, which could boast no tradition in the field, as could, for example, France. Moreover, its development has continued right up to the present day.

In contrast to Denmark and Norway, in Sweden scarcely any modern silver was made around 1900. Nowhere else in Europe were the tried and tested Rococo and Empire models adhered to for so long. Sweden's contribution to the Paris Exhibition of 1900 consisted of ornamental pieces in eclectic styles. The architect Ferdinand Boberg, who had made his name with, among other things, elegant furniture designs for the Swedish royal family, which were shown in the Swedish Pavilion in 1900, was one of the few to design any modern silver. In contrast to the flower motifs customary in other countries, he used pine branches as decorations in his designs, which were executed by C.G. Hallberg in Stockholm, one of the leading firms in Sweden. The German influence was great, as is evident, for example, from the vase illustrated, which was made at the Hallberg factory a few years later.

The firm of K. Anderson, also of Stockholm, ventured into the production of modern models only around 1908. Here the forms were mainly traditional and the ornament of a type already regarded as outmoded elsewhere.

To promote the designing of modern silver the Föreningen Svensk Hemslöjd, the Swedish Handicraft Society, had organized a competition, but one of the aims, the designing of a new flatware model, still took years to realize.[7] This was perhaps partly because of the great success of Georg Jensen's silver, which Nils Wendel imported from 1914 onwards. The designs for hollow-ware were more successful. They were displayed at a decorative art exhibition in Stockholm in 1909. One of the services to win a prize was designed and made by the silversmith John Fährngren, but it proved unsuited to serial production. A design by David Nilsson, which was made by Anders Nilsson in Lund, was better in that respect. The third design to win a prize was executed by the firm of C.F. Carlman and drawn by Eric Lundsqvist. What attracted the most attention at this exhibition was a coffee service after a design by Jacob Ångman for the Guldsmeds-aktiebolaget (GAB). The squat, angular forms have stylized, unobtrusive Art Nouveau ornament.

After entering the service of the GAB in 1907, Jacob Ångman (1876–1942) set the pattern for modern Swedish silver. Having studied at the Stockholm Technical School (RIT) and in Germany, he worked for some time under, among others, Henry van de Velde at

SWEDEN

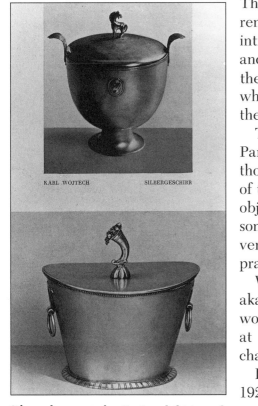

Silver shown at the Paris exhibition of 1925. Top: covered bowl designed and made by Karl Wojtech; bottom: covered bowl designed by Jacob Ångman for GAB (Guldsmedsaktiebolaget), Stockholm. From *Dekorative Kunst*, 1925/6.

Th. Müller's in Weimar. Most of his designs after 1920 evoke vague reminiscences of silver made around 1800, but he succeeded in an intriguing way in giving traditional forms a contemporary appearance, so that they appealed to modern tastes. Apart from the finials on the lids, these smooth, oval forms were undecorated. The extent to which they governed the character of Swedish silver is evident from the designs of Elis Bergh and Karl Wojtech.

The first time that Sweden showed modern silver abroad was at the Paris Exhibition of 1925. Jacob Ångman's designs for the GAB and those of Nils Fougstedt for Hallberg's were the successful forerunners of the silver that gave Sweden a fine reputation in the thirties. The objects shown in Paris by the silversmith Karl Wojtech, who sometimes collaborated with Wolter Gahn and Anna Petrus, were very severe, almost Romanesque in form and ornament. His work was praised for the beautiful matt colour of the silver.

Wiwen Nilsson (1897–1974) trained at the Staatliche Zeichenakademie at Hanau and afterwards worked in Georg Jensen's Paris workshop. In 1927 he took over the firm of his father, Anders Nilsson, at Lund. Cylinders and hemispheres, planes and sharp angles characterize the geometrical style of his jugs, vases and other objects.

237

Erik Fleming (1894–1954) was a gifted designer and silversmith. In 1920 he set up his well-known Atelier Borgila, which concentrated exclusively on hand-made silver. His designs of the twenties are still quite classic in form, but his pieces from the thirties exhibit the characteristic angular forms and stepped edges and lids of that period. In 1932 the Swedish government awarded him the prestigious commission for a complete service (of over eight hundred pieces) to be given as a wedding present to Prince Gustaf Adolf and Princess Sybilla.

238

Fleming was not the only silversmith to receive a commission for a royal gift. This honour also fell to the firm of Bolin, one of the purveyors to the Tsar of Russia up to the Revolution, when Princess Ingrid of Sweden married the then crown prince of Denmark. The painter Oskar Brandtberg designed this gift, which consisted, among other things, of a two-metre (6½ ft.) long centrepiece, candelabra, jardinières and fruit stands. Wilhelm Bolin had opened a shop and workplace in Stockholm in 1916. Ernst Hellgren worked there from 1916 to 1941 as a chaser and designer. He was responsible for the production of most of the objects made there in the twenties and thirties, which, like much other Swedish silver, were influenced by Jacob Ångman.

Elis Bergh (1881–1954) is mainly known for his designs for the Kosta glass factory, of which he was director from 1929 onwards, but during that time he also produced silver designs for the firm of C.G.

Hallberg, as did Hakon Ahlberg and Edvin Ollers. These were, without exception, sober, plain objects intended for industrial production. Sylvia Stave, who worked for Hallberg's from 1930 onwards, designed bowls and vases in which plain, spherical forms offer a surprising contrast to the straight, faceted bases.

After Helge Lindgren had taken over as artistic director of K. Anderson's in 1933, a number of useful objects were made there too in the modernistic style of the day, with smooth planes and angular forms.

Maja-Lisa Ohlsson and Folke Arström made designs for the GAB in the thirties. One of them was shown at the Paris Exhibition of 1937: a cocktail-shaker with smooth, curved facets, horizontal ribs and vertical grooves, which was highly original in its asymmetrical design.

Swedish silver won its first international recognition at the Paris Exhibition of 1925. Under the leadership of Jacob Ångman, and in the thirties also of Erik Fleming and Wiwen Nilsson, it acquired a character of its own.

RUSSIA

In Russia, as in other countries, there was in the late nineteenth century a nationalist movement which tried to keep alive traditional crafts. In 1898 the Mir Iskusstva (World of Art) movement was founded by a number of artists, among them Sergei Diaghilev. In the periodical of the same name, published until 1905, attempts were made to arouse interest in Russian folklore and at the same time to combine international movements in the applied arts with the style peculiar to Russia. A good example of this are the *kovshi*, traditional Russian drinking vessels, decorated with floral Art Nouveau ornament.

242

The two most important cities were St Petersburg (Leningrad), the capital of Russia until 1917, and Moscow. Avant-garde circles in Russia were well-informed about artistic developments in Europe and the United States. For example, in 1902 Count Stieglitz bought some jewels and a beaker by René Lalique for his museum.[8] In 1902 the Comité Français des Expositions à l'Étranger organized an exhibition in St Petersburg, in which leading French silversmiths such as Aucoc, Boin, Falize, Feuillâtre and Keller took part. Some of the glass objects on display by Émile Gallé of Nancy had mounts by Fabergé, the best-known of all Russian silversmiths of that time.

The universal fame enjoyed by the firm of Fabergé was owed to Peter Carl Fabergé (1846–1920), who from 1870 until the Russian Revolution was director of the concern, which had been founded by his father in 1842. Carl Fabergé was not a silversmith himself, but exercised technical artistic supervision. His idea of making *objets de fantaisie* caught on to an extraordinary extent. The most famous are the fifty-six Imperial Easter Eggs made by the firm, presumably from 1884 onwards. Each of these costly little gifts, which the Tsar gave to his wife and mother, contained a surprise, a miniature model of a coach, palace or ship, for example, Small gold and silver objects, such as cigarette-cases and boxes, electric bells, photograph frames and other knick-knacks, mostly in eighteenth-century French styles, made Fabergé's name renowned throughout Western Europe and the United States. He was no artistic innovator, unlike the French artist René Lalique, for example, but the objects made in his workshops are fascinating for the perfection with which even the tiniest details are executed. When these objects were enamelled, it was nearly always done in the traditional eighteenth-century way, *guilloché* enamel.

Fabergé's knick-knacks are so well-known that it is scarcely realized that the firm also made functional objects in silver in more modern designs. For instance, the Finnish silversmith Johan Viktor Aarne made the mounts for some Tiffany glasses for Fabergé. In general, however, the silver at St Petersburg was made by Josef

244

Rappoport, Jan Lieberg-Nyberg and Stephen Wäkewä. Much more silver was produced in Moscow, where Fabergé had opened a branch in 1887. At this workshop, under the direction of Michel Tchepournoff, objects were made for the wealthy bourgeoisie. Some

Plate. Maker's mark: M. Takkinen, Russia, *c.* 1900. Diameter: 44 cm (17¼ in.). Private collection.

To Mr. A. Laws
With best wishes from the Foreign and
Chinese Staff of the Chi Jung, Tobacco Co.
Ltd. Harbin, Manchuria.

of these are astoundingly functional in their simplicity, but silver was 241
also made there in the so-called Old Russian style, which came into
vogue in the second half of the nineteenth century.

However, it was not Fabergé who was the champion of traditional
Russian silversmithing, but the firm of Ovchinnikov, established in
Moscow in 1853. This concern, the most important silver factory in
Russia after that of Fabergé, was granted an Imperial Warrant in
1883. Here the old Russian enamel techniques, *cloisonné* and
champlevé were revived, the firm winning awards for its enamels at
the World's Columbian Exhibition in Chicago in 1893 and at the Paris
Exhibition of 1900. The objects made at the Ovchinnikov factory are
usually entirely covered with *cloisonné* enamel in busy patterns of
polychrome arabesques on silver-gilt grounds. Naturalistic Art Nouveau motifs were seldom used in this technique. In the *champlevé*
enamel there is often found simple geometric ornament in bright
colours derived from folk art motifs.

Ovchinnikov's example was followed by numerous other firms. In
the workshops of Fedor Rückert, from which Fabergé ordered his

cloisonné enamel, and I. Klebnikov, enamelled objects were made in which the combination of traditional ornament and contemporary Art Nouveau motifs sometimes led to original results. The fame of Russian enamel spread everywhere after 1893. For instance, the Dutch silversmith Jan Eisenloeffel, among others, worked in Fabergé's 'sweet factory'.[9] He was more interested in the *champlevé* enamel technique, however, and once back in the Netherlands he made much use of it in his silverwork, as he did of new forms based on Russian objects.

168,243
XVIII

Moscow was the centre of traditional Russian silversmithing. This applied not only to decorative techniques like enamelling, but was also evident in the choice of objects such as *kovshi*, icons and the archaic form of spoons. The example illustrated was made in the workshop of Gustav G. Klingert, which was described at the Chicago Exhibition in 1893 as one of the most important firms in Russia.

XXV

Although, as has already been seen, the internationally-orientated aristocratic clientele in St Petersburg preferred *guilloché* enamel, the firm of Grachev there made objects with *cloisonné* and *champlevé* enamel. This firm was founded in 1866 and granted an Imperial Warrant in 1896. Just as at Fabergé, silver was made there around 1900, which looks very modern by reason of its simple, undecorated forms.

243

In order to be able to cope with competition from the big firms, small workshops joined co-operatives known as Artels, which sold objects made by independent silversmiths to large concerns like Fabergé. More than twenty of these Artels are known, but only a few of them made objects with Art Nouveau ornament.

A remarkably large number of Finnish and Swedish silversmiths worked in Russia, either independently or as employees in larger workshops. For example, seventy-five per cent of the five hundred silversmiths at Fabergé came from one of those two countries,[10] while fourteen of the twenty-four foremen were Finnish.

Carl-Edvard Bolin of Sweden set up as a jeweller in St Petersburg and his brother Henrik Conrad as a silversmith in Moscow. In 1888 the latter was succeeded by his son Wilhelm, who brought some foreign designers to Moscow. These also designed silver objects in Art Nouveau style.

Alexander Tillander from Finland opened a workshop in St Petersburg in 1860. In addition to jewelry and eggs in all manner of techniques, many small objects, such as paper-knives, photograph frames and cigarette-cases, were made there.

246

International Art Nouveau had little success in Russia. In contrast to the custom in most other countries, the characteristic floral ornaments with elongated, undulating leaves, which were arranged asymmetrically over the surface, were in Russia engraved rather than chased. The Revolution of 1917 put an end to the prosperity of silversmithing in Russia at a stroke.

245

NOTES

1 Hugh Honour, *Goldsmiths and Silversmiths*, New York 1971, p. 295, and Vivienne Becker, *Art Nouveau Jewelry*, London 1985, p. 200. Note that in both these books the authors erroneously refer to The Hague instead of Hagen in this connection.
2 Jørgen Møller, *Georg Jensen, The Danish Silversmith*, Copenhagen 1985, p. 41.
3 ibid., p. 24.
4 Sales leaflet of the Georg Jensen Company, Copenhagen, *c.* 1936.
5 Archives, Van Kempen & Begeer Museum, Zoetermeer, CB 1.
6 R.W. Lightbown, *Catalogue of Scandinavian and Baltic Silver*, Victoria and Albert Museum, London 1975, p. 147.
7 'Modernes schwedisches Tischsilber', *Die Goldschmiedekunst* 32 (1911), no. 43, p. IV.
8 *Ori e Argenti dall'Ermitage*, exhibition catalogue, Villa Favorita, Lugano, 1986, nos. 155–8.
9 'De tijd wisselt van spoor, Nederland rond 1900', exhibition catalogue, Singermuseum, Laren 1981, p. 67.
10 Henry Charles Bainbridge, *Peter Carl Fabergé*, London 1966, p. 123; Alexander von Solodkov, *Russian Gold and Silverwork*, New York 1981, p. 192.

BIOGRAPHIES

A

Adic Bros, Birmingham, Great Britain Founded in 1879. Executed from 1925 modern silver designs by Harold Stabler and the Frenchman Fernand Piret.

Friedrich Adler (1878–1942) Munich, Hamburg, Germany Sculptor and designer. Pupil, then teacher at the Debschitz-Schule in Munich. From 1907 teacher at the Kunstgewerbeschule in Hamburg. Designed silver for P. Bruckmann & Söhne in Heilbronn.

E. Altenloh, Brussels, Belgium Prominent firm in Brussels. Modern silver in the twenties designed by Robert Altenloh.

Alvin Corporation, Providence, Rhode Island, USA Founded in 1886. The firm was purchased by Gorham in 1928, when the name became Alvin Corporation.

Adolf Amberg (1874–1913) Hanau, Berlin, Germany Sculptor and designer. Studied at the Königliche Preussische Zeichenakademie in Hanau and the Académie Julian in Paris. Designed silver for P. Bruckmann & Söhne in Heilbronn.

Amstelhoek, Amsterdam, the Netherlands Workshops for modern ceramics founded in 1897, for metalwork and furniture c. 1900 by Willem Hoeker. Jan Eisenloeffel was artistic director of the metal workshop and was in 1902 succeeded by J. Blinxma. In December 1903 the metal workshop closed.

Just Andersen (1884–1943) Copenhagen, Denmark Trained with Mogens Ballin and Peter Hertz and started his own firm in 1915. Andersen's wife, Alba Lykke, was a pupil of Georg Jensen.

K. Anderson, Stockholm, Sweden Designers of modern silver for the firm in the thirties were the architects Erik Ekeberg, Viking Göransson and Hans Quinding.

Jacob Ångman (1876–1942) Stockholm, Sweden Architect and designer. Studied at the Stockholm Technical School, and in Germany 1903–04. Worked for a few months with Theodor Müller in Weimar under Henry van de Velde. From 1907 artistic director of Guldsmedsaktiebolaget (GAB).

Josef Arnold (1884–1960) Hamburg, Germany Trained with his father and P. Bruckmann & Söhne in Heilbronn. Pupil of Paul Haustein in Stuttgart 1907–09. Teacher in Erbach and Hanau and from 1921 in Hamburg. Had his own workshop from 1931.

Ferdinand Arpin, Paris, France Active 1886–1916. Executed cast-silver mounts for Daum.

The Art Silver Shop, Chicago, Illinois, USA Founded in 1912 by Edmund Boker (b. 1886) and Ernest Gould (1884–1954). In 1934 the name was changed to Art Metal Studios.

Artificers' Guild, London, Great Britain Founded in 1901 by Nelson Dawson, who left in 1903 when the Guild was taken over by Montague Fordham. Chief designer was Edward Spencer. Closed in 1942.

Charles Robert (C.R.) Ashbee (1863–1942) London, Great Britain Architect, designer. Founded the Guild of Handicraft in 1888. Honorary member of the Vereinigung bildender Künstler Österreichs-Secession in Vienna and the Münchener Akademie. Professor in Cairo 1915–19 and worked in Palestine 1919–23, before returning to Britain.

Maison Aucoc, Paris, France Founded in 1836. In the 1880s René Lalique designed diamond jewelry for Aucoc. The firm executed designs by Edouard Becker c. 1900.

B

Kurt Baer, Berlin, Germany Taught silversmithing 1934–44 at the Meisterschule für das gestaltende Handwerk in Berlin.

Franz Bahner, Düsseldorf, Germany Founded in 1895. Specialist in silver flatware. Executed designs by Peter Behrens c. 1905. Closed in the 1960s.

Oliver Baker (1859–1938) Birmingham, Great Britain Painter. Designed silver for Liberty & Co., London.

Mogens Ballin (1871–1914) Copenhagen, Denmark Painter and metalworker. Georg Jensen worked for Ballin before setting up on his own. After Ballin's death, Peter Hertz took over the workshop.

Jane Barnard (b. 1902) London, Great Britain Studied at the Central School of Arts and Crafts in London. Designed silver 1923–39 for the family firm Edward Barnard & Sons.

Hermann Bauer, Schwäbisch Gmünd, Germany Founded in 1863. Specialized in small silver objects and desk and toilet sets.

Karl Johann Bauer (1877–1914) Munich, Germany Trained with Adolf von Mayrhofer and studied at the Debschitz-Schule. From 1904 teacher there.

Bauhaus (1919–33) Weimar, Dessau, Berlin, Germany Founded by Walter Gropius. In 1921 Alfred Kopka was 'handwerklicher Meister' of the metal workshop and was succeeded by Christian Dell. Famous pupils of the metal workshop were Marianne Brandt, Josef Knau, Gyula Pap, Hans Przyrembel, Otto Rittweger, Wolfgang Tümpel and Wilhelm Wagenfeld.

C.J. Begeer, Utrecht, the Netherlands Founded in 1868. Cornelis L.J. Begeer (b. 1868) studied at the Königliche Preussische Zeichenakademie in Hanau. Worked in the family firm from 1888. Founded his own firm, the Stichtsche Zilverfabriek in 1904. His half-brother Carel J.A. Begeer (1883–1956), also studied in Hanau. In 1904 he set up a workshop for modern silver in the family firm's premises and executed Jan Eisenloeffel's silver designs. In 1919 merged with the firm of J.M. van Kempen en Zoon and J. Vos. The firm's name was changed from Van Kempen, Begeer & Vos to Zilverfabriek Voorschoten in 1925.

Peter Behrens (1868–1940) Munich, Darmstadt, Düsseldorf, Berlin, Germany and Vienna, Austria Painter, designer, architect. Founding member of the Vereinigte Werkstätten für Kunst im Handwerk in Munich. Member of the artists' colony in Darmstadt. Director of the Kunstgewerbeschule in Düsseldorf 1904–07. From 1907 architect and designer for AEG in Berlin. From 1922 Professor of Architecture at the Akademie der Bildenden Künste in Vienna and from 1936 at the Preussische Akademie der Künste in Berlin. His silver designs were executed by Martin Mayer and M.J. Rückert in Mainz, Franz Bahner in Düsseldorf and P. Bruckmann & Söhne in Heilbronn.

W.A.S. Benson (1854–1924) London, Great Britain Architect and designer. Started production of metalwork in the 1880s.

Gustav Beran (b. 1912) Vienna, Austria and Zeist, the Netherlands Designer. Pupil of Josef Hoffmann at the Kunstgewerbeschule in Vienna. Went to the Netherlands in 1934 as chief designer for Gerritsen & Van Kempen of Zeist.

Arthur Berger (1892–1981) Vienna, Austria and Moscow, Russia Designer. Pupil of Josef Hoffmann at the Kunstgewerbeschule in Vienna. Designed silver for the Wiener Werkstätte.

Elis Bergh (1881–1954) Stockholm, Sweden Designed silver for C.G. Hallberg in the twenties. Artistic director of Kosta Boda Glassworks 1929–50.

H.P. Berlage (1856–1934) Amsterdam, The Hague, the Netherlands Architect and designer. The silver he designed for Mr and Mrs Kröller-Müller was executed by C.J. Begeer in Utrecht and W. Voet in Haarlem.

Sigvard Bernadotte (b. 1907) Stockholm, Sweden and Copenhagen, Denmark Son of King Gustav of Sweden. Designed for Georg Jensen from 1930.

Conrad Anton Beumers, Düsseldorf, Germany Founded in 1858. Executed modern silver designs by Hugo Leven and Paul Beumers. Workshop closed in 1928.

Bigelow, Kennard Co., Inc., Boston, Massachusetts, USA Founded in 1830. Silver manufacturers and retailers.

Wilhelm Binder, Schwäbisch Gmünd, Germany Founded in 1869. Produced modern silver hollow-ware and flatware.

Thorvald Bindesbøll (1846–1908) Copenhagen, Denmark Architect, and graphic artist. Designed silver for A. Michelsen, Copenhagen.

Siegfried Bing (1838–1905) Paris, France Erroneously known as Samuel. Born in Hamburg, Germany. Went to Paris in 1854. Dealer in Japanese art. Opened in 1895 his Maison de l'Art Nouveau. His son Marcel Bing, Edouard (Edward) Colonna and Georges de Feure designed silver for his Pavillon de l'Art Nouveau at the Paris Exhibition in 1900.

Birmingham Guild of Handicraft, Birmingham, Great Britain Founded in 1895 by the architect and designer Arthur S. Dixon. Worked with precious and base metals.

Black, Starr & Frost, New York, USA Successors to Ball, Black & Co. in 1876. Merged with Gorham Corporation in 1929.

William Thomas Blackband (1885–1949) Birmingham, Great Britain Pupil, then teacher, and from 1924 headmaster of the Vittoria Street School for Jewellers and Silversmiths in Birmingham.

Johannes Blinxma (1872–1941) Amsterdam, the Netherlands After working for Amstelhoek he opened his own workshop in 1904. His work shows the strong influence of Jan Eisenloeffel.

Bloch-Eschevêque, Paris, France Manufacturer of modern silver in the twenties and thirties.

Ferdinand Boberg (1860–1946) Stockholm, Sweden Architect and designer of glass, ceramics and textiles. Designed silver for C.G. Hallberg *c.* 1900.

Hugo Böhm & Co., Schwäbisch Gmünd, Germany Founded in 1887. Produced modern silver in the twenties and thirties.

Boin-Taburet, Paris, France Founded *c.* 1875. Participated in all important exhibitions between 1889 and 1937.

Kaj Bojesen (1886–1958) Copenhagen, Denmark Trained with Georg Jensen 1907–10. Worked as a craftsman in Paris and Copenhagen before opening his own workshop in 1913. In the thirties he worked with the architects G.B. Petersen and Magnus Stephensen and the painters Lauritz Larsen and Svend Johansen.

Hans Bolek (b. 1890) Vienna, Austria Architect. Studied at the Kunstgewerbeschule in Vienna. Designed silver for Eduard Friedmann, Oskar Dietrich and Alfred Pollak.

Franz Bolze, Bremen, Germany Worked as a silversmith in Bremen 1926–76. Also executed some designs by Bernhard Hötger.

As. Bonebakker & Zn, Amsterdam, the Netherlands Founded in 1792. Frans Zwollo Sr was trained in this workshop.

L. Bosch (1878–1960) Schoonhoven, the Netherlands Pupil of Frans Zwollo Sr. In 1918 teacher at, then director of the Vakschool voor Goud- en Zilversmeden in Schoonhoven until 1946.

Frédéric Boucheron, Paris, France Jewellers and silversmiths. Founded in 1858. Collaborated with Edouard Becker and Lucien Hirtz.

Maison Boulenger, Paris, France M. Bodereau ('le meilleur ouvrier de France') worked for this firm as a silversmith. Manufacturer of modern silver in the twenties and thirties.

Charles Boyton (1885–1958) London, Great Britain Worked in the family firm. Started a workshop for modern silver in 1934.

Emil Brackenhoff, Bremen, Germany Worked as a silversmith in Bremen 1927–81.

Marianne Brandt (1893–1983) Weimar, Chemnitz, Dresden, Berlin, Germany Painter, designer and metalworker. Studied at the Bauhaus, then was director of the metal workshop there until 1929.

Bremer Silberwarenfabrik, Bremen, Germany Founded in 1905. Specialized in silver flatware. Closed in 1981.

Bremer Werkstätte für Kunstgewerbliche Silberarbeiten, Germany Founded in 1921. Among the designers was Wilhelm Schultze.

Professor F.A. Breuhaus (1883–1960) Düsseldorf, Germany Architect and designer. Studied at the Technische Hochschule in Berlin-Charlottenburg and worked for Peter Behrens. Designed metalwork and silver for Württembergische Metallwarenfabrik (WMF) after 1927.

Bruckmann & Söhne, Heilbronn, Germany Founded in 1805. The firm trained its own designers, silversmiths, chasers and engravers. Peter Bruckmann was the first chairman of the Deutscher Werkbund. He executed the silver designs of many leading German artists. Closed in 1973.

C

J.E. Caldwell Co., Philadelphia, Pennsylvania, USA Founded in 1839. Jewellers and silversmiths. Manufacturer of silver in the Art Nouveau style.

Maison Cardeilhac, Paris, France Founded in 1802. Maker's mark registered in Paris in 1817. Showed designs by Lucien Bonvallet at the Paris Exhibition in 1900. In 1927 Cardeilhac's sons Jacques and Pierre became directors of the firm. After Pierre's death in 1944 Jacques became sole manager. In 1951 the firm merged with Orfèvrerie Christofle.

C.F. Carlman, Stockholm, Sweden Producers of modern silver designed by Per Sköld since the thirties, when Sven Carlman became head of the family firm.

Alwyn C.E. Carr (1872–1940) London, Great Britain Silversmith. Studied at the Sheffield School of Art, where he met Omar Ramsden. In 1898 they set up a workshop in London. When the partnership was dissolved in 1919 they worked independently as silversmiths.

Cellini Shop, Evanston, Illinois, USA Workshop founded by Ernest Gerlach in 1914. From 1916 to 1919 David and Walter Mulholland worked for the Cellini Shop. In the twenties Hans Gregg and Wilhelm Conrad from Germany were the most important craftsmen. In 1969 the shop was purchased by the Randahl Company.

Hans Christiansen (1866–1945) Munich, Hamburg, Germany; Paris, France; Darmstadt, Wiesbaden, Germany Painter, designer. Member of the artists' colony in Darmstadt 1899–1902. His silver designs were executed by E.L. Viëtor, Darmstadt and Martin Mayer, Mainz. His flatware was executed by Peter Bruckmann & Söhne, Heilbronn and his designs for enamelled boxes by Louis Kuppenheim, Pforzheim.

Orfèvrerie Christofle, Paris, France Founded in 1830. First firm to manufacture silver plate in France. Arnoux, 'chef de l'atelier de l'Art Nouveau' and Eugène Bourgouin designed the silver for the Exhibition in Paris in 1900. Designers in the twenties and thirties were Maurice Dufrène, André Groult, Christian Fjerdingstad, Paul Follot, Luc Lanel, Louis Süe, André Mare and Gio Ponti.

J.V. Cissarz (1873–1942) Dresden, Darmstadt, Stuttgart, Frankfurt am Main, Germany Member of the artists' colony in Darmstadt 1903–07. Silver designs executed by E.L. Viëtor, Darmstadt.

Carl M. Cohr, Fredericia, Denmark Founded in 1860. Executed modern flatware designed by Knud von Engelhardt, *c.* 1910 and modern hollow-ware after 1935.

Edward (Edouard) Colonna (1862–1948) Designer. Born in Germany as Edouard Klönne. Studied architecture in Brussels. Went to the USA in 1882, worked for Louis Comfort Tiffany's Associated Artists. Settled in Dayton, Ohio, and worked as an architect, designer and painter. Returned to Europe and designed silver for Siegfried Bing in Paris 1898–1902. On returning to the USA, worked as an interior decorator. Settled in Nice, France, in 1925.

G.L. Connell, London, Great Britain Founded before 1839. Silver manufacturers. Also retailers of foreign silver and silverware made by William Hutton & Sons and A.E. Jones.

John Paul Cooper (1869–1933) London, Birmingham, Westerham, Great Britain Architect, silversmith and jeweller. One of the first in the English Arts and Crafts Movement to revive the use of shagreen.

Elizabeth Copeland (1866–1957) Boston, Massachusetts, USA Silversmith, well known for *cloisonné* enamelled objects.

Wilhelm Lucas von Cranach (1861–1918) Berlin, Germany Painter. Designed silver and jewelry c. 1900.

Margaret Craver (b. 1907) Boston, Massachusetts, USA Silversmith and teacher. Studied at the Art School, University of Kansas. Trained as a silversmith in the thirties in Boston and in Baron Erik Fleming's workshop in Stockholm, Sweden.

Bernard Cuzner (1877–1956) Birmingham, Great Britain Studied at Vittoria Street School in Birmingham. Designed for Liberty & Co. c. 1900 and in later years for trade firms such as the Goldsmiths & Silversmiths Co. Ltd in London and Elkington & Co. Ltd in Birmingham. In 1910 head of the Metalwork Department at the Birmingham School of Art.

Carl Otto Czeschka (1878–1960) Vienna, Austria and Hamburg, Germany Painter, architect and designer. Studied at the Akademie der Bildenden Künste in Vienna; teacher at the Kunstgewerbeschule 1902–07. Was the first to introduce ornaments in silver made in the Wiener Werkstätte. In 1907 became a professor at the Kunstgewerbeschule, Hamburg.

D

David-Andersen, Oslo, Norway Founded in 1876. Famous for high-quality enamels. Arthur David-Andersen (1875–1970) and his son Ivar David-Andersen (b. 1903) designed for the family firm. Other designers were Johan Lund (1861–1939), Gustav Gaudernack (1865–1914), Thorolf Holmboe, Ludvig Wittmann (1877–1961) and Johan Sirnes (1883–1966).

Nelson Dawson (1859–1942) London, Great Britain Architect and painter. Took up metalwork in 1891 and attended enamelling lessons by Alexander Fisher. Founder and Art Director of the Artificers' Guild 1901–03. Gave up metalwork for painting in 1914.

Debschitz-Schule, Munich, Germany Founded in 1902 by Wilhelm von Debschitz and Hermann Obrist under the name of Lehr- und Versuchs-Ateliers für angewandte und freie Kunst.

Delheid, Brussels, Belgium Started production of modern silver after 1925.

Christian Dell (1893–1974) Hanau, Weimar, Frankfurt, Germany Studied at the Königliche Preussische Zeichenakademie in Hanau and the Kunstgewerbeschule in Weimar as a pupil of Henry van de Velde. In 1922 he was appointed Handwerklicher Meister of the metal workshop of the Bauhaus. In charge of the metal workshop of the Frankfurter Kunstschule 1926–33.

E. Deppe, Berlin, Germany Founded in 1853. Specialized in the production of flatware.

Jean Després (1889–1980) Paris, France Trained in Avallon and Paris. Took evening classes in drawing. After the First World War he participated in all the important exhibitions in France and other countries.

Gebrüder Deyhle, Schwäbisch Gmünd, Germany Founded in 1820. Manufacturers of flat- and hollow-ware.

Oscar Dietrich (1853–1940) Vienna, Austria Trained in his father's workshop, which he took over in 1882. Participated in the exhibitions in Paris in 1900 and 1925. Executed designs by Franz Delavilla, Emanuel Josef Margold, Dagobert Peche and the architects Hans Bolek and A.O. Holub and others. The workshop closed in 1931.

Arthur S. Dixon (1865–1929) Birmingham, Great Britain Architect and silversmith. Founder of the Birmingham Guild of Handicraft in 1895.

James Dixon & Sons, Sheffield, Great Britain Founded in 1806. Executed designs by Christopher Dresser after 1879.

A. Dragsted, Copenhagen, Denmark Founded in 1854. Executed some designs by Johan Rohde in 1913.

Christopher Dresser (1834–1904) London, Great Britain Botanist and designer of metalwork, glass and ceramics. His silver designs were executed by Elkington & Co and Hukin & Heath in Birmingham and by James Dixon & Sons in Sheffield. Many of his designs were registered at the British Patent Office under the names of the firms concerned.

Vincent Carl Dubb (1852–1922) Vienna, Austria Manufacturer of flat- and hollowware.

Fernand Dubois (1861–1939) Brussels, Belgium Sculptor, medallist and modeller of silver and bronze objects and jewelry.

Maurice Dufrène (1876–1955) Paris, France Studied at the École des Arts Décoratifs. Designed small silver objects such as umbrella handles for Julius Meier-Graefe's shop La Maison Moderne.

Jean Dunand (1877–1942) Paris, France Born in Switzerland. Studied in Geneva at the École des Arts Industriels. Went to Paris in 1897 and worked in the studio of the sculptor Jean Dampt. In 1912 the Japanese artist Sougawara taught Dunand the secrets of lacquer work. In the twenties and thirties Dunand executed furniture and small wooden and metal objects decorated with lacquered modernist motifs.

E

Hermann Ehrenlechner, Dresden, Germany Trained as a silversmith in workshops in Pforzheim, Munich and Berlin. Worked in Dresden from 1904. Most of his designs are decorated with elaborate ornament, often combined with precious stones and enamels. He executed several designs by Professor Karl Gross.

Christa Ehrlich (b. 1903) Vienna, Austria and The Hague, the Netherlands Studied at the Kunstgewerbeschule in Vienna. Assistant in Josef Hoffmann's architectural practice. From 1927 she designed modern silver for the Zilverfabriek Voorschoten.

Jan W. Eisenloeffel (1876–1957) Amsterdam, Laren, the Netherlands Silversmith, metalworker and designer of ceramics and glass. Trained with Hoeker & Zoon. Studied enamelling in Russia in 1898. Designed silver for the metal workshop in Amstelhoek. Formed a company with J.C. Stoffels in 1902, worked for De Woning in Amsterdam in 1903–04, for C.J. Begeer in Utrecht until 1907 and in 1908 in the Vereinigte Werkstätten in Munich, Germany. On returning to the Netherlands, settled in Laren.

Elkington & Co Ltd, Birmingham, Great Britain Founded in 1836 by George Richard Elkington, the inventor of electroplating. Manufactured designs by Christopher Dresser 1875–85. After 1935 executed modern designs by John Walker, Reginald Hill and Frank Nevile.

Harm Ellens (1871–1939) Groningen, Amsterdam, the Netherlands Studied at the Academy in Groningen and the Rijksschool voor Kunstnijverheid in Amsterdam. In the twenties was first director of the Vakschool voor Goud- en Zilversmeden in Schoonhoven. His silver designs were executed in the school and by E. Voet in Haarlem and H. Hooykaas in Schoonhoven.

A.R. Emerson (b. 1906) London, Great Britain Apprenticed in the trade. Taught at the Central School of Arts and Crafts in London and became head of the metalwork department.

Runar Engblom (1908–1965) Helsinki, Finland Trained as a furniture designer. Designed textiles, glass and silver in the thirties.

Ercuis, Paris, France Exhibited modern silver in the twenties and thirties.

George C. Erickson, Gardner, Massachusetts, USA Born in Sweden. Trained with Arthur J. Stone. Took over David Carlson's workshop for hand-wrought silver in 1932.

Henry Ericsson (1898–1933) Helsinki, Finland Painter and designer. Finished his studies at the Central School of Applied Arts in Helsinki in 1915. Designed silver for Taito Oy.

H.A. van den Eynde (1869–1940) Amsterdam, the Netherlands Sculptor and designer, in 1918, of modern silver for Fa. J.M. van Kempen, Voorschoten.

F

Peter Carl Fabergé (1846–1920) St Petersburg (Leningrad), Moscow, Russia Took over the family firm in 1870. Employed more than five hundred assistants, designers, modellers, goldsmiths, enamellers and gem-cutters. Among his silversmiths were Jan Lieberg-Nyberg, J. Nevalainen, J.A. Rappoport and S. Wäakewä. The firm closed after the revolution.

John Fährngren, Stockholm, Sweden Silversmith. Began teaching at the Arts and Crafts Institute in Stockholm in the twenties.

Albert Feinauer, Weimar, Germany Worked as a teacher in the silversmithing workshop in the Kunstgewerbeschule in Weimar founded by Henry van de Velde and executed a number of tea services designed by him.

Eugène Feuillâtre (1870–1916) Paris, France Sculptor and silversmith. Began experimenting in 1893 with techniques for enamelling on silver and platinum. Worked for René Lalique and set up his own workshop in 1899. He participated in all national and international exhibitions until 1910.

Georges de Feure (1868–1928) Paris, France Born in the Netherlands as Van Sluyters. Worked in Paris as a painter. Designed ceramics, furniture and silver for Siegfried Bing.

Robert Fischer (1906–41) Schwäbisch Gmünd, Germany Trained with Wilhelm Binder, and studied at the Staatliche höhere Edelmetallfachschule, Schwäbisch Gmünd. Worked in Berlin and Leipzig and settled in Schwäbisch Gmünd in 1932. Taught metalwork at the Edelmetallfachschule from 1934.

Alexander Fisher (1864–1936) London, Great Britain Painter, sculptor and silversmith. Studied at the South Kensington Schools, then went to Paris to study enamelling techniques. Taught at the Central School of Arts and Crafts in London and set up his own school in 1896.

Kay Fisker (1893–1965) Copenhagen, Denmark Architect and professor at the Academy of Art, Copenhagen. Designed silver for the firm A. Michelsen in the twenties.

W. Fitzner, Berlin, Germany Silversmith active in the thirties.

Carl Christian Fjerdingstad (1891–1968) Blaricum, the Netherlands and Paris, France Born in Kristiansand, Norway, he settled in Blaricum in December 1918. Left in March 1921 for Paris, where he worked as a designer for Orfèvrerie Christofle in the twenties and thirties and as an independent silversmith.

Baron Erik Fleming (1894–1954) Stockholm, Sweden Studied in Berlin and Munich. His Atelier Borgila, founded in 1919, became one of Sweden's leading workshops for modern silver. Worked as a teacher in the USA 1938–9.

Paul Fliege, Danzig, Poland Worked as a silversmith in the thirties in Danzig, which was at that time German.

Paul Follot (1877–1941) Paris, France Sculptor and designer. Pupil of Eugène Grasset. Designed jewelry and small silver objects for Julius Meier-Graefe's Shop La Maison Moderne. Began exhibiting as an independent artist in 1904. In the early twenties he designed silver in the decorative style for Orfèvrerie Christofle and in 1925 for Lapparra.

A.C. Fontani (b. 1895) Amsterdam, the Netherlands Trained in his father's workshop and with Frans Zwollo Sr.

Carl Forster & Graf, Schwäbisch Gmünd, Germany Founded in 1884. Manufacturer of small silver objects and silver-mounted leatherware.

Fouquet-Lapar, Paris, France Manufacturer of modern silver in the twenties and thirties.

Gebrüder Friedländer, Berlin, Germany Founded in 1829. Executed silver designed by the painter Wilhelm Lucas von Cranach *c.* 1900.

Eduard Friedmann, Vienna, Austria Founded in 1877. Executed designs by Rudolf Karger, Milla Weltmann, and by the architects Hans Bolek, Philippe Häusler, Emanuel Josef Margold (Darmstadt) and Otto Prutscher. Closed in 1920.

George T. Friend, London, Great Britain Taught engraving at the Central School of Arts and Crafts, London. Engraved designs by R.M.Y. Gleadowe and the sculptor and typographer Eric Gill.

G

Lucien Gaillard (b. 1861) Paris, France Pupil of the sculptor Henri L. Levasseur. Began working in the family firm in 1878. Influenced by Japanese metalwork he experimented with enamelling and different metal alloys. In 1892 he took over the family business. In 1900 the firm moved to bigger premises and had Japanese metalworkers brought over from Tokyo.

Carl Gehle (1884–1951) Hagen, Germany Worked as a silversmith in Hagen.

Koninklijke Gerritsen & Van Kempen, Zeist, the Netherlands Manufacturing firm founded in 1924. Gustav Beran, a pupil of Josef Hoffmann in Vienna, was head designer 1934–77. In 1960 Gerritsen & Van Kempen in Zeist merged with Van Kempen en Begeer in Voorschoten.

Eric Gill (1882–1940) London, Great Britain Sculptor and typographer whose designs for silver of *c.* 1930 were executed by H.G. Murphy.

Maurice Giot, Paris, France Painter. His designs for silver of *c.* 1900 were executed by A. Debain.

A.F. Gips (1861–1943) Delft, the Netherlands Professor at the Polytechnical School in Delft. Designed silver for the Koninklijke

Utrechtsche Fabriek van Zilverwerk C.J. Begeer for the Paris Exhibition of 1900.

R.M.Y. Gleadowe (1888–1944) London, Great Britain Designed silver for Edward Bernard & Sons, H.G. Murphy and Wakely & Wheeler in the thirties.

Frances M. Glessner (1848–1922) Chicago, Illinois, USA Social leader in Chicago in the 1880s. Amateur silversmith.

Goldsmiths' & Silversmiths' Co. Ltd, London, Great Britain Retailer and manufacturer, founded in 1898. Executed in the thirties designs by Bernard Cuzner, S.J. Day, Leslie Durbin and A.E. Harvey.

J.J. van Goor (1874–1956) Utrecht, the Netherlands Studied at the Königliche Preussische Zeichenakademie in Hanau. After returning to the Netherlands became a designer and modeller in the Koninklijke Utrechtsche Fabriek van Zilverwerk C.J. Begeer.

Gorham Mfg. Corporation, Providence, Rhode Island, USA Founded by Jabez Gorham *c.* 1815–18. In 1891 the Englishman William C. Codman became the chief designer. In 1897 he introduced the Martelé range of hollow-ware. He retired in 1914. In 1925 the Danish silversmith Erik Magnussen designed for Gorham.

Jean Goulden (1878–1947) Paris, Reims, France Settled in Paris as a painter and musician after his medical studies. After the First World War Jean Dunand taught him the technique of *champlevé* enamel. In 1928 he settled in Reims.

Mikhail and Semen Grachev, St Petersburg (Leningrad), Russia Founded in 1866. Silversmiths and enamellers. Closed after the revolution.

Jakob Grimminger, Schwäbisch Gmünd, Germany Founded in 1893. Manufacturer of fine modern silver in the early thirties.

Walter Gropius (1883–1969) Berlin, Weimar, Germany and Cambridge, Massachusetts, USA Architect. Studied in Berlin and Munich. Worked with Peter Behrens in Berlin. Designed silver for Arthur Krupp, Berndorf, for the Werkbund-Ausstellung in Cologne in 1914. Director of the Bauhaus in Weimar and Dessau 1919–28. Professor at Harvard University 1937–52.

Karl Gross (1869–1934) Dresden, Munich, Germany Sculptor and silversmith. Trained with Fritz von Miller and at the Kunstgewerbeschule in Munich. Became in 1898 a professor at the Kunstgewerbeschule in Dresden. His silver designs were executed by Theodor Heinze and Hermann Ehrenlechner in Dresden. Also designed flatware for Bruckmann & Söhne in Heilbronn.

André Groult (1884–1967) Paris, France designed silver for Orfèvrerie Christofle in 1925.

Guild of Handicraft, London, Chipping Campden, Great Britain Founded in 1888 by Charles Robert Ashbee. Some early silversmiths, mentioned in 1898, were W.A. White, William Hardiman, J.K. Baily and David Cameron. Enamellers were David Cameron and Fleetwood C. Varley. The Guild's silver was not hallmarked before 1896. Closed in 1907.

Guldsmedsaktiebolaget (GAB), Stockholm, Sweden Founded in 1867. When Jacob Ångman joined the GAB in 1907 as artistic director, the firm developed into Sweden's leading producer of modern silver. Other designers in the twenties and thirties were Just Andersen, Folke Arström and Maja-Lisa Ohlsson. Merged with C.G. Hallberg in 1961.

Knut L. Gustafson (1885–1976) Chicago, Illinois, USA Trained as a silversmith in Stockholm, Sweden, before going to the USA in 1906. Settled in Chicago *c.* 1910 and was associated with the Jarvie Shop, Lebolt & Co. and the Randahl Shop before founding the Chicago Silver Company in 1923.

H

August Haarstick (1882–1964) Bremen, Germany Trained in the family workshop in Bremen, founded in 1874. Worked as a silversmith 1913–64.

Hermann Haas, Munich, Germany Painter, architect, teacher at the Technische Hochschule in Munich. His silver designs in the twenties were executed by Adolf von Mayrhofer.

Wenzel Hablik, Itzehoe, Germany Painter, interior decorator and designer. Made silver flatware in the twenties.

W.S. Hadaway (1872–1941) London, Great Britain Worked in silver and enamel, first shown in 1904. In 1908 he left for India and worked as superintendent to the Madras Government School of Arts.

Werkstätte Hagenauer (1898–1956) Vienna, Austria Founded in 1898 by Carl Hagenauer. In 1919 his son Karl Hagenauer joined the firm. Executed designs by the architects F.J. Meckel, Josef Hoffmann and Otto Prutscher.

Hagener Silberschmiede (1910–14) Hagen, Germany Founded by Karl Ernst Osthaus. The Dutch silversmith Frans Zwollo Sr executed the silver, designed by J.L.M. Lauweriks, director of the Handfertigkeitsseminar, F.H. Ehmcke and E.H. Schneidler.

Otto Hahn, Bielefeld, Germany Executed *c.* 1910 hollow-ware designed by the sculptor Hans Parathoner. His son Otto Hahn Jr designed and made modern silver in the thirties.

Hallbergs Guldsmeds Aktiebolaget, Stockholm, Sweden Executed designs in naturalistic Art Nouveau style by Ferdinand Boberg in 1900. Designers in the twenties were Elis Bergh, Hakon Ahlberg, Niels Fougstedt and Edvin Ollers and in the thirties Sylvia Stave. Merged with Guldsmedsaktiebolaget (GAB) in 1961.

Rudolf Hammel, Vienna, Austria Architect. Appointed professor at the Kunstgewerbeschule in Vienna in 1899. Designed silverware for the firm Bannert 1898–1903 and for A. Pollak in 1902.

Marius Hammer (1847–1927) Bergen, Norway One of Norway's leading firms, known for *plique à jour* enamelled spoons. From 1905 Emil Hoye designed modern silver for the firm.

S.A. Hammond, London, Great Britain Silversmith and chaser, worked with H.G. Murphy. Teacher at the Central School of Arts and Crafts in London.

Hans Hansen (1884–1940) Kolding, Denmark Founded in 1906. Executed modern silver designs in the thirties.

Oswald Härdtl (1899–1959) Vienna, Austria Studied at the Kunstgewerbeschule in Vienna. In 1922 became an assistant, and later a partner in Josef Hoffmann's architectural practice. Professor at the Kunstgewerbeschule 1925–59. Designed silver for Klinkosch *c.* 1930.

George Hart (b. 1882) Chipping Campden, Great Britain Member of the Guild of Handicraft. Continued to work as a silversmith and designer with Huyshe and Warmington in Chipping Campden after the Guild closed in 1907.

Arthur Edward Harvey, Birmingham, Great Britain Architect. Head of the School of Industrial Design in Birmingham. Designed objects in silver and electroplate for mass production for the Birmingham firms Hukin & Heath and Deakin & Francis in the thirties.

W.H. Haseler & Co. Ltd, Birmingham, Great Britain Founded in 1850 by William Hair Haseler. From 1899 to 1927 manufacturers of the 'Cymric' silver sold by Liberty & Co. in London. Jessie Jones, Thomas Hodgetts and Charles Povey executed the first designs. Even after the dissolution of the company, continued to supply Liberty's.

Paul Haustein (1880–1944) Darmstadt, Stuttgart, Germany Studied at the Kunstgewerbeschulen in Dresden and Munich. Experimented with enamels and designed metalwork for the Vereinigte Werkstätten für Kunst im Handwerk in Munich and silver for Bruckmann & Söhne in Heilbronn. The silver he designed in Darmstadt in 1903–05, when he was a member of the artists' colony, was executed by E.L. Viëtor. From 1905 he taught metalwork at the Lehr- und Versuchswerkstätten of the Kunstgewerbeschule in Stuttgart.

H. Hébrard, Paris, France Gallery owner. Sold silver designed by the sculptor Edouard Becker and by Carlo Bugatti, Henri Husson and Frank Scheidecker.

Theodor Heiden (b. 1853) Munich, Germany Silver and jewelry firm founded in 1880.

Theodor Heinze, Dresden, Germany Exe-

cuted silver designed by Professor Karl Gross in the early twenties.

N.G. Henriksen (1855–1922) Copenhagen, Denmark Sculptor. Artistic manager of the firm of A. Michelsen.

Peter Hertz, Copenhagen, Denmark Founded in 1834. Took over Mogens Ballin's workshop in 1914.

Reginald Hill, London, Great Britain Studied at the Central School of Arts and Crafts in London in the thirties. Designed silver for Wakely & Wheeler in London and Elkington in Birmingham.

Joyce Himsworth, Sheffield, Great Britain Trained by her father. She executed small silver objects with niello and enamel decorations in the thirties.

Frantz Hingelberg, Aarhus, Denmark Founded in 1897. His son Vilhelm studied in Birmingham. Svend Weihrauch worked for the firm as a silversmith and designer from 1928.

Lucien Hirtz (b. 1864) Paris, France Worked with Boucheron from 1893. Modelled several objets d'art, which were often decorated with enamel.

David Hislop, Glasgow, Great Britain Registered at the Glasgow Assay office in 1904–05 as 'Watchmaker, jeweller and dealer in stones'. In that time he sold electroplated and silver objects designed by Charles Rennie Mackintosh.

Fa. Hoeker & Zoon, Amsterdam, the Netherlands Founded in 1854. Jan Eisenloeffel trained with the firm before he went to Russia. After Eisenloeffel's return in 1899 Willem Hoeker set up the Amstelhoek workshops for modern ceramics, metalwork and furniture.

Josef Hoffmann (1870–1956) Vienna, Austria Architect and designer. Professor at the Kunstgewerbeschule in Vienna. One of the founders of the Wiener Werkstätte in 1903 and its artistic director until 1932.

A.O. Holub, Vienna, Austria Architect. Studied at the Kunstgewerbeschule in Vienna. Designed silver for Oscar Dietrich in 1911–12.

F.A. Hoogendijk (1878–1934) Schoonhoven, the Netherlands Pupil of Frans Zwollo Sr at the Haarlemsche School voor Kunstnijverheid. Worked in Schoonhoven.

François Hooseman, Brussels, Belgium Jeweller and silversmith. Showed silver at the Paris exhibition of 1900.

H. Hooykaas, Schoonhoven, the Netherlands Founded in 1875. Executed designs for modern silver by Harm Ellens in the twenties.

Emil Høye (1875–1958) Christiania (Oslo), Norway Silversmith and designer, from 1905, for the firm of Marius Hammer, Bergen.

Patriz Huber (1878–1902) Darmstadt, Germany Studied in Mainz and Munich. Founder member of the artist's colony in

Darmstadt 1899–1902. His designs for silver objects were executed by Martin Mayer in Mainz.

Hukin & Heath Ltd, Birmingham, Great Britain Founded in 1855. Executed designs by Christopher Dresser after 1878 and by A.E. Harvey in the thirties.

Henri Husson (1852–1914) Paris, France Born in the Vosges. Went to Paris when he was young. His work was sold by the gallery owner H. Hébrard.

William Hutton & Sons, Birmingham, London, Great Britain Founded in 1800. Kate Harris designed Art Nouveau silver for the Paris exhibition of 1900. Connell and the Goldsmiths & Silversmiths Co. were among the London shops that sold these designs.

I

Helen M. Ibbotson, Sheffield, Great Britain Teacher in Sheffield who specialized in enamelling.

Regitze Ingerslev, Copenhagen, Denmark and Haarlem, the Netherlands Worked as enameller in Copenhagen. Taught enamelling at the Haarlemsche School voor Kunstnijverheid 1909–10.

Bernard Instone (b. 1891) Birmingham, Great Britain Studied at Vittoria Street School, Birmingham. Trained by Emil Lettré in Berlin and by J.P. Cooper. Well known for his enamelled silver.

International Silver Co., Meriden, Connecticut, USA Incorporated in 1898 by independent New England silversmiths. World's largest manufacturer of silverware.

J

J.A. Jacobs (1885–1968) Amsterdam, the Netherlands Silversmith and teacher at the Kunstnijverheidsschool Quellinus (after 1924, Instituut voor de Kunstnijverheid).

Robert R. Jarvie (1865–1941) Chicago, Illinois, USA Leading Arts and Crafts metalworker 1893–1917.

Georg Jensen (1866–1935) Copenhagen, Denmark Sculptor. His workshop, founded in 1904, developed into a leading producer of modern silver.

Jørgen Jensen (b. 1895) Copenhagen, Denmark Trained as a silversmith. Joined the Jensen firm only in the mid-thirties.

Marga Jess, Lüneburg, Germany Studied at the Debschitz-Schule in Munich, Became in 1912 the first qualified woman silversmith in Germany.

F.J. Joindy (1832–1906) Paris, France Sculptor and silversmith. Worked for Christofle, Falize and Harleux. Modelled silver mounts for Gallé vases.

A.E. Jones (1879–1954) Birmingham, Great Britain Studied at the Central School of Arts and Crafts and worked in the Birmingham Guild of Handicraft. Founded A.E. Jones & Co. Ltd in 1902.

K. Jordan, Darmstadt, Germany Executed umbrella handles designed by Emanuel Josef Margold c. 1913.

K

Kalo Shop, Chicago, Illinois, USA Founded by Clara Barck Welles (1868–1965) in 1900. Started production of metalwork in 1905. Closed in 1970.

Christoph Kay, Hamburg, Germany Trained in the firms of Koch & Bergfeld in Bremen and Bruckmann & Söhne in Heilbronn. Before setting up a workshop in Hamburg with Otto Stüber in 1910, was a pupil, like Stüber, of Professor Alexander Schönauer.

Gustave Keller Frères, Paris, France Started in 1857 as manufacturer of leather dressing cases. Around 1880 started to produce matching silver toilet articles and hollow-ware. Participated in all major exhibitions in France and elsewhere 1900–37.

J.M. van Kempen en Zoon, Voorschoten, the Netherlands Founded in 1789 in Utrecht, moved to Voorschoten, near The Hague, in 1858. Largest manufacturer of silver in the Netherlands. Merged with C.J. Begeer and J. Vos in 1919.

William B. Kerr, Newark, New Jersey, USA Founded in 1855. Purchased by Gorham Mfg. Co. in 1906.

Keswick School of Industrial Art, Keswick, Great Britain Evening classes began in 1884, day classes in 1898. Executed small objects in a very simple Arts and Crafts style.

Arthur Nevill Kirk (1881–1958) London, Great Britain and Cranbrook, Michigan, USA Studied at the Central School of Arts and Crafts in London and became a teacher there. In 1927 emigrated to the USA and set up the Cranbrook metal workshop, which was forced to close in 1933.

Fa. J.C. Klinkosch, Vienna, Austria Founded in 1797. Executed designs by Otto Wagner in 1902 and by Otto Prutscher and Oswald Härdtl in the twenties.

Archibald Knox (1864–1933) Isle of Man, London, Great Britain Painter and designer for Liberty's 'Cymric' silver and 'Tudric' pewter 1899–1906.

Gebrüder Köberlin, Döbeln, Germany Specialized in silver flatware.

Koch & Bergfeld, Bremen, Germany Founded in 1829. Executed 1900–10 designs by Hugo Leven, Albin Müller and Henry van de Velde and in the twenties and thirties by Gustav Elsass and Bernhard Hötger.

Alfred Kopka, Breslau, Germany In 1921 in charge of the metal workshop of the Bauhaus. Taught metalwork at the Vereinigte Staatsschulen für freie und angewandte Kunst in Berlin and, from 1926, in Breslau.

Antoinette Krasnik, Vienna, Austria Painter and designer. Pupil of Koloman Moser. Designed silver for Alexander Sturm in 1902.

Kreuter, Hanau, Germany Founded in 1842. Manufacturer of modern silver hollow-ware in the thirties.

Jan Kriege (1884–1944) Woerden, the Netherlands Sculptor and silversmith. Trained in the workshop of C.J. Begeer in Utrecht. Set up his own workshop in 1919. Taught metalwork at the Instituut voor Kunstnijverheid in Amsterdam from 1932.

A. Krupp, Berndorf, Austria Exhibited objects designed by Walter Gropius at the Deutsche Werkbund Ausstellung in Cologne in 1914.

Louis Kuppenheim, Pforzheim, Germany Leading firm of enamellers in Germany. Executed enamelled objects designed by Hans Christiansen of Darmstadt c. 1900.

Holger Kyster, Kolding, Denmark Executed silver designed by the painter and ceramist Svend Hammershoi in the twenties.

L

René Jules Lalique (1860–1945) Paris, France Silversmith, jeweller and glass-maker. Studied in London for two years after training in the workshop of Louis Aucoc. After his return to France designed jewelry for many Parisian jewellers. Experimented with glass and enamelling. Exhibited jewelry and silver with enamel and glass from 1894. After 1914 devoted himself to glass-making.

Lapparra, Paris, France Originally specialized in flatware production. Since the twenties also manufacturers of hollow-ware. One of the firm's designers was Paul Follot.

George H. Lantman (1875–1932) Amsterdam, the Netherlands Pupil of Frans Zwollo Sr at the Haarlemsche School voor Kunstnijverheid. Worked for C.J. Begeer in Utrecht. Taught metalwork at the Instituut voor de Kunstnijverheid in Amsterdam.

J.L. Mathieu Lauweriks (1864–1932) Amsterdam, the Netherlands and Düsseldorf, Hagen, Germany Architect and designer. Teacher at the Haarlemsche School voor Kunstnijverheid 1894–1903, at the Kunstgewerbeschule in Düsseldorf 1904–09, director of the Handfertigkeitsseminar in Hagen and designer of silver for the Hagener Silberschmiede 1909–15. After his return to Amsterdam, director of the Kunstnijverheidsschool Quellinus. Retired in 1929.

E. Lefèbvre, Paris, France Founded in 1895 by the jeweller Eugène Lefèbvre for the manufacture of silverware and silver jewelry.

Karl F. Leinonen (b. 1866) Turku, Finland and Boston, Massachusetts, USA Silversmith, emigrated in 1893. Director of the Handicraft Shop in Boston, founded in 1901.

Alfred Lelièvre (b. 1856) Paris, France Sculptor. His silver designs of after 1900 were executed by A. Debain.

Emil Lettré (1876–1954) Hanau, Berlin, Germany Studied in Hanau, Munich and Vienna. Worked as a silversmith in Berlin from 1905. Designed flatware for Bruckmann & Söhne, Heilbronn, in the twenties. In 1933 became director of the Staatliche Zeichenakademie in Hanau.

Hugo Leven (1874–1956) Düsseldorf, Bremen, Hanau, Germany Sculptor, designer. Designed silver for C. Beumers in Düsseldorf and for Koch & Bergfeld, Bremen. From 1909 director of the Königliche Preussische Zeichenakademie in Hanau.

Liberty & Co., London, Great Britain Shop founded in 1875 by Sir Arthur Lasenby Liberty. The silver and jewelry with their own makers' mark were sold under the name 'Cymric' 1899–1927. They were made by W.H. Haseler, Birmingham. Some of the designers were Oliver Baker, C. Carter, Maud Coggin, Harry Craythorn, A.E. Jones, Jessie King, Rex Silver, Bernard Cuzner and Archibald Knox, the last-named being the most important.

Ernst Lichtblau (1883–1963) Vienna, Austria Pupil of Otto Wagner. Architect, designed silver with enamel for Alfred Pollak in 1912. Founded his own workshop, probably in the twenties.

Walter and Charlotte Lochmüller, Schwäbisch Gmünd, Germany Silversmiths and enamellers in the twenties and thirties. Walter taught enamelling at the Fachschule in Schwäbisch Gmünd.

Josef Lock, Germany Sculptor. Designed silver for Bruckmann & Söhne in Heilbronn.

Johan Lund (1861–1939) Christiania (Oslo), Drammen, Norway Silversmith and designer for David-Andersen. Director of the Norsk Filigransfabrik 1894–98. Settled in 1899 in Drammen.

M

Charles Rennie Mackintosh (1868–1928) Glasgow, Great Britain Architect and designer. His designs for silver and electroplated flatware, in some cases bearing the mark of David Hislop, were probably all executed by Elkington and Co. in Birmingham.

Erik Magnussen (1884–1961) Copenhagen, Denmark and Chicago, Illinois, and Los Angeles, California, USA Started a workshop in Copenhagen in 1909. Went to the USA in 1925, designed silver for Gorham Mfg. Co. Opened a workshop in Chicago in 1932 and, from 1933 to 1938, in Los Angeles. Returned to Copenhagen in 1939.

Mappin & Webb, Sheffield, Great Britain Founded in 1863. The firm's chief designer until 1935 was A. Hatfield. Executed in the thirties modern silver designed by A.E. Harvey, Keith Murray and James Warwick.

Marcus & Co, New York, New York, USA Manufacturer of machine-made objects with repoussé Art Nouveau ornament.

André Mare (1887–1932) Paris, France Painter, founder, with Louis Süe, of the Compagnie des Arts Français. Designed silver for Orfèvrerie Christofle and Tétard Frères in the twenties.

Emanuel Josef Margold (1888–1962) Vienna, Austria and Darmstadt, Berlin, Germany Pupil and then assistant of Josef Hoffmann. Went to Darmstadt in 1911. Designed silver for P. Bruckmann & Söhne in Heilbronn in 1913 and umbrella handles for K. Jordan in Darmstadt. Settled in Berlin in 1929.

Gilbert Leigh Marks (1861–1905) London, Great Britain Trained with Johnson, Walker & Tolhurst. Set up as a silversmith in 1885 but registered his mark only in 1896.

Eva Mascher-Elsässer (b. 1908) Halle, Göttingen, Brunswick, Germany Studied at the Kunsthandwerkerschule Burg Giebichenstein in Halle. Founded a workshop with Hildegard Risch in 1927. In 1949 started a new workshop in Göttingen and in 1957 moved to Brunswick.

Martin Mayer, Mainz, Germany Founded in 1888. Manufacturer of small silver objects. Executed designs by Peter Behrens, Hans Christiansen and Patriz Huber.

Adolf von Mayrhofer (1864–1929) Munich, Germany Silversmith and enameller. Also executed designs by Hermann Haas and Else Wenz-Viëtor in the twenties.

Arnold Meyer, Bremen, Germany Silversmith active in the twenties and thirties.

Anton Michelsen, Copenhagen, Denmark Founded in 1841. Executed designs by Mogens Ballin and Thorvald Bindesbøll at the beginning of this century, in the twenties by Kay Fisker, and in the thirties by Palle Svenson and Kay Gottlob.

Fritz Möhler (b. 1896) Schwäbisch Gmünd, Germany Trained in his father's workshop and studied in Munich. Founded his own workshop in his native town in 1923.

Inger Møller (1886–1966) Copenhagen, Denmark Trained by Georg Jensen and worked at that firm until 1921. From 1922 had her own workshop.

Koloman Moser (1868–1918) Vienna, Austria Painter and designer. Studied at the Akademie and the Kunstgewerbeschule in Vienna. One of the founders of the Vienna Secession and the Wiener Werkstätte. His designs for enamelled boxes were executed by Georg Adam Scheid. He also designed silver hollow-ware for the Wiener Werkstätte.

Franz Mosgau, Berlin, Germany Founded in 1807. Executed a flatware design by Peter Behrens.

Latino Movio, London, Great Britain Possibly trained by Gilbert Marks. Executed silver in the style of Marks with the maker's mark of Holland, Aldwinckle and Slater.

Albin Müller (1871–1941) Darmstadt, Germany Architect and member of the artists' colony in Darmstadt. Designer of silver for Koch & Bergfeld, Bremen. Some designs were executed by Johann L. Brandner and J. Götz in Regensburg.

Karl Müller, Halle, Germany Silversmith. Taught metalwork at the Kunsthandwerkerschule Burg Giebichenstein in Halle.

Theodor Müller, Weimar, Germany Executed silver designed by Henry van de Velde.

Peter Müller-Munk (b. 1904) Germany, and New York, New York, USA Studied with Bruno Paul in Berlin. Silversmith, emigrated to the USA in 1926 and opened his workshop in New York in 1927.

Henry George Murphy (1884–1939) London, Great Britain Studied at the Central School of Arts and Crafts in London with Henry Wilson and in Berlin with Emil Lettré. Opened his own workshop in 1913 and became a teacher at the Central School.

Keith Murray (1892–1981) London, Great Britain Born in New Zealand and went to England in 1906–07. Architect. Designed glass for Stevens & Williams Glassworks, ceramics for Wedgwood and silver for Mappin & Webb in the thirties.

N

Arnold Nechanski (1888–1938) Vienna, Austria and Berlin, Germany Studied at the Kunstgewerbeschule in Vienna with Josef Hoffmann. Architect. Designed silver for A. Pollak in Vienna in 1913 and for the Wiener Werkstätte. Teacher in the metal workshop of the Meisterschule für das Kunsthandwerk in Berlin 1921–33.

Frank Nevile, London, Great Britain Designed silver for mass production for Elkington & Co Ltd in the thirties.

Evald Johannes Nielsen (1879–1958) Copenhagen, Denmark Trained in the workshop of August Fleron. After his studies in Berlin he founded his own workshop in 1905.

Harald Nielsen (1892–1977) Copenhagen, Denmark Joined Georg Jensen in 1909 and was art director of the Sølvsmedie after Jensen's death. He designed the silver in the geometrical style of the twenties and thirties.

Wiwen Nilsson (Karl Edvin Wiwen-Nilsson) (1897–1974) Lund, Sweden Trained in the workshop of his father Anders Nilsson. Studied at the Königliche Preussische Zeichenakademie in Hanau. Worked in the Paris studio of Georg Jensen while studying at the Académie de la Grande Chaumière. Designed for his father's workshop from 1923 and took it over in 1928.

Falick Novick (1878–1957) Chicago, Illinois, USA Born in Russia, emigrated to the USA in 1893. Opened a workshop in Chicago in 1909. Also worked for the Kalo Shop there.

Frans Evald Nykänen (1893–1951) Helsinki, Finland Born in St Petersburg (Leningrad). He trained in his father's workshop in Sortavala. From 1918 director of the firm Taito Oy.

O

Philippe Oberle (1877–1950) Strasbourg, Pforzheim, Germany Studied in Munich, Brussels and Antwerp. From 1904 teacher at the Kunstgewerbeschule in Strasbourg and after 1920 teacher at the Goldschmiedeschule in Pforzheim.

Hans Ofner (b. 1880) Vienna, Austria

Architect and designer. Studied with Josef Hoffmann at the Kunstgewerbeschule in Vienna and took enamelling lessons with Adèle von Stark.

August Ofterdinger (b. 1855) Hanau, Germany Trained in Schwäbisch Gmünd, Hanau, Vienna and Paris. Taught chasing and embossing at the Königliche Preussische Zeichenakademie in Hanau from 1882.

Maja-Lisa Ohlsson, Oslo, Sweden Designed silver for the Guldsmedsaktiebolaget (GAB) in the late twenties and thirties.

Josef Maria Olbrich (1867–1908) Vienna, Austria and Darmstadt, Germany Architect and designer. Studied at the Akademie der Bildenden Künste in Vienna and travelled in Italy, North Africa and France. Co-founder of the Vienna Secession in 1898. Member of the artists' colony in Darmstadt from 1899.

Max Olofs (b. 1889) Munich, Germany Silversmith and sculptor. Trained with Fritz von Miller and studied at the Academy in Munich. Founded his own workshop in 1919.

Orivit AG, Cologne-Braunsfeld, Germany Founded in 1900 by Ferdinand Hubert Schmitz for the production of silver hollow-ware. Production stopped after the firm was taken over by Württembergische Metallwarenfabrik (WMF) in 1905.

Ovchinnikov, Moscow, Russia Founded in 1853 by Pavel Akimovich Ovchinnikov and carried on by his sons Mikhail, Alexander, Pavel and Nikolai. Closed after the revolution.

P

Gyula Pap (1899–1983) Weimar, Berlin, Germany and Budapest, Hungary Studied at the Bauhaus in Weimar and worked in the metal workshop. Returned to Budapest in 1934.

Bruno Paul (1874–1968) Berlin, Germany Architect. From 1907 principal of the Berlin Kunstgewerbeschule and from 1924 to 1933 director of the same institution, renamed the Vereinigte Staatsschulen für freie und angewandte Kunst, Berlin-Charlottenburg.

Dagobert Peche (1887–1923) Vienna, Austria and Zurich, Switzerland Designer. Studied at the Academy in Vienna. Joined the Wiener Werkstätte 1915 and was leader of the Zurich branch 1917–19.

A. Peddemors, Haarlem, the Netherlands Trained by Frans Zwollo Sr at the Haarlemsche School voor Kunstnijverheid. Taught metalwork there 1907–17 and enamelling from 1912.

John Pontus Petterson (1884–1949) New York, New York, Chicago, Illinois, USA Studied silversmithing at the Royal School of Arts and Crafts in Oslo. Went to New York in 1905 and worked for Tiffany & Co. Went to Chicago in 1911, where he worked for Robert Jarvie and opened his own studio in 1914.

Francis Peureux, Paris, France Silver-

smith. Sometimes worked with the sculptor F.J. Joindy.

Josef Pöhlmann (1882–1963) Munich, Nuremberg, Germany Opened his own workshop in 1908 and became a teacher at the metal workshop of the Gewerbliche Fortbildungsschule in Nuremberg. Taught silversmithing at the Kunstgewerbeschule in Nuremberg 1919–45.

Alfred Pollak, Vienna, Austria Founded in 1878. Executed designs by Rudolf Hammel, Hans Bolek, Ernst Lichtblau, Arnold Nechanski and students of the Kunstgewerbeschule in Vienna.

Antoine Pompe (1873–1980) Brussels, Belgium Architect. Designed, c. 1903, silver flat- and hollow-ware in the style of Henry van de Velde.

Charles Douglas Price (b. 1906) Bloomfield Hills, Michigan, USA Assistant of Arthur Nevill Kirk. From 1935 to 1937 taught silver and metalwork at the Cranbrook Academy of Art and executed designs by Eliel Saarinen.

Otto Prutscher (1880–1949) Vienna, Austria Architect. Worked for Wiener Werkstätte. Designed silver for J.C. Klinkosch and L.M. Gaspardi in Vienna.

Jacob Prytz (1886–1962) Christiania (Oslo), Norway Silversmith and designer. Director of the firm J. Tostrup. From 1914 teacher at the Royal School of Arts and Crafts in Oslo.

Thorolf Prytz (1858–1938) Christiania (Oslo), Norway Architect and designer. Artistic director of the firm J. Tostrup 1890–1912.

Hans Przyrembel, Leipzig, Germany Studied at the Bauhaus in Weimar. Worked as a silversmith in Leipzig in the thirties.

Jean Emile Puiforcat (1897–1945) Paris, France Trained in his father's workshop as a silversmith and with Louis Lejeune as a sculptor. Leading French silver designer in the twenties and thirties.

R

Waldemar Rämisch, Berlin, Germany Teacher at the Vereinigte Staatsschulen für freie und angewandte Kunst in Berlin-Charlottenburg.

Omar Ramsden (1873–1939) London, Great Britain Trained in Sheffield, together with Alwyn Carr. They formed a partnership in 1898, but after 1919 worked independently.

Julius Olaf Randahl (1880–1972) Chicago, Illinois, USA Born and trained in Sweden. Emigrated to the USA in 1901. After working for Tiffany and Gorham Mfg. Co., he went to Chicago. There he worked in the Kalo Shop and in 1911 opened his Randahl Shop. In 1957 the Randahl firm purchased the Cellini Shop, in 1969 Cellini Craft, and in 1965 Randahl's itself was sold to Reed & Barton.

Reed & Barton, Taunton, Massachusetts, USA Founded in 1824. Started to produce flat- and hollow-ware in sterling silver in 1889.

Piet Regenspurg (1894–1966) Enschede, the Netherlands Pupil of Frans Zwollo Sr at the Akademie voor Beeldende Kunst in The Hague. Founded his own workshop in 1922.

Olga Reynier (1884–1917) Munich, Germany Designer. Studied at the Debschitz-Schule in Munich.

Franz Rickert (b. 1904) Munich, Germany Trained with Adolf von Mayrhofer in Munich and studied at the Staatsschule für angewandte Kunst. Worked as a silversmith from 1926 and taught silversmithing at the Staatsschule für angewandte Kunst from 1935.

Ernst Riegel (1871–1939) Darmstadt, Cologne, Germany Trained with Fritz von Miller and worked from 1900 as a silversmith in Munich. Joined the artists' colony in Darmstadt in 1907. In 1912 became a professor at the Städtische Werkschule in Cologne and was from 1920 in charge of the goldsmithing workshop in the Institute for Religious Art in that city.

Richard Riemerschmid (1868–1957) Munich, Germany Architect, painter, designer. One of the founders of the Vereinigte Werkstätten für Kunst im Handwerk in Munich. His designs for flatware were executed by Bruckmann & Söhne in Heilbronn and Carl Weishaupt in Munich.

Ludwig Riffelmacher (b. 1896) Berlin, Germany Trained with Josef Pöhlmann in Nuremberg and studied at the Kunstgewerbeschule in that city. In 1923 he worked with Otto Stüber in Hamburg and in 1924 with Karl August Weiss in Pforzheim. From 1924 to 1946 he was director of the workshop of H.J. Wilm in Berlin.

Hildegard Risch (b. 1903) Halle, Cologne, Germany Studied from 1923 at the Kunsthandwerkerschule Burg Giebichenstein in Halle with Karl Müller. In 1927 she started a workshop in Halle with her friend Eva Elsässer. In 1928 she worked with Fritz Breuhaus in Düsseldorf. In the thirties she devoted herself to the production of jewelry.

Otto Rittweger (d. 1965) Designer, silversmith. Studied at the Bauhaus in Weimar and Dessau, and worked in Berlin.

Roberts & Belk Ltd, Sheffield, Great Britain Founded in 1809. Walter P. Belk, architect, was a silversmith and designer for the firm in the late twenties and thirties.

Rudolf Rochga, Munich, Germany Sculptor. Designed silver hollow-ware for Bruckmann & Söhne in Heilbronn c. 1902.

Johan Rohde (1856–1935) Copenhagen, Denmark Sculptor, architect, and painter. Produced the first silver designs for Georg Jensen in 1906. After 1913 he worked as a designer for the Sølvsmedie. He also designed silver for A. Dragsted.

Walle (Gustav Vlademar) Rosenberg (1891–1919) Helsinki, Finland Painter. Designed silver for Alm Oy in Porvoo.

Emmy Roth, Berlin, Germany and Voor-schoten, the Netherlands Trained with Anton Beumers in Düsseldorf. Worked as a silversmith in Berlin-Charlottenburg from 1916. Went to the Netherlands c. 1938 and then to the USA in 1940.

M.J. Rückert, Mainz, Germany Founded in 1838. Manufacturer of small silver objects and flatware. Executed designs by Peter Behrens, Hans Christiansen and Patriz Huber.

S

Eliel Saarinen (1873–1950) Helsinki, Finland and Bloomfield Hills, Michigan, USA Finnish architect. Emigrated to the USA in 1923. Designed buildings for the Cranbrook Foundation, Michigan, in 1925. His designs for silver were made partly by Arthur Nevill Kirk and Charles Price in the Cranbrook metal workshop and partly by the International Silver Co. of Meriden, Connecticut.

Sophie Sander, Vienna, Austria Goldsmith and enameler in Vienna. Taught enamelling at the Haarlemsche School voor Kunstnijverheid in the Netherlands in 1911 and 1912.

Gérard Sandoz (b. 1902) Paris, France Trained in his father's workshop as a jeweller and silversmith. Executed small enam-elled and lacquered objects and hollow-ware. After 1931 he turned to painting and film-making.

Georg Adam Scheid, Vienna, Austria Founded in 1862. Silversmith and jeweller famous for high-quality enamelling. Executed designs by Koloman Moser.

Frank Scheidecker, France French designer of metalwork and silver c. 1900–10. His silver was sold by H. Hébrard in Paris.

J. Schijfsma, Sneek, the Netherlands Executed flatware designs in the decorative and geometric style c. 1905.

Hermann Schmidhuber (b. 1878) Cologne, Germany Executed designs by Dagobert Peche in Zurich. Taught metalwork at the Werkschulen in Cologne from 1924. In 1931 opened his own workshop.

Friedrich Schmid-Riegel, Nuremberg, Germany Worked as a silversmith in the twenties and thirties.

Ernst Schmidt, Berlin, Germany Worked as a silversmith in the late twenties and thirties.

Fritz Schmoll von Eisenwerth (1883–1963) Munich, Germany Born in Vienna. Studied in Karlsruhe and Munich at the Debschitz-Schule. Designed silver for P. Bruckmann & Söhne in Heilbronn and M.T. Wetzlar in Munich. After 1920 worked as a sculptor.

Gertraud von Schnellenbühel (b. 1878) Munich, Weimar, Germany Trained in the metal workshop of the Debschitz-Schule in Munich. Worked in the workshop of Adalbert Kinzinger in Munich from 1911 and in the thirties worked in Weimar.

J. van Schouwen, Haarlem, The Hague, the Netherlands Trained in the metal workshop of the Haarlemsche School voor Kunstnijverheid with Frans Zwollo Sr and his successor A. Peddemors. Had a workshop in Haarlem 1916–26 and in The Hague 1932–5.

Wilhelm Schulze, Bremen, Germany Worked in Bremen in the twenties and thirties.

Cyril James Shiner (b. 1908) Birmingham, Great Britain Trained with Bernard Cuzner in Birmingham and studied at the Royal College of Art in London. Worked as a craftsman and teacher in Birmingham and designed hollow-ware for Wakely & Wheeler Ltd in London.

Shreve & Co., San Francisco, California, USA Jewelry shop opened in 1852. In 1904 the firm manufactured its first flatware.

Reginald (Rex) Silver (1879–1954) and Harry Silver (1882–1922) The Silver brothers were partners in the Silver Studio until 1916. The studio, founded by their father in 1880, provided designs for Liberty's 'Cymric' range until 1910. Rex managed the studio. Harry's designs for Liberty were influenced by Archibald Knox.

Edgar Simpson, London, Great Britain Silversmith and metalworker 1896–1910. His silver and jewelry show the influence of C.R. Ashbee.

Simpson, Hall, Miller & Company, Wallingford, Connecticut, USA Founded in 1866. In 1895 the firm began manufacturing sterling silverware. It became part of International Silver Co. in 1898, but continued to use its own makers' mark.

Johan Sirnes (1883–1966) Oslo, Norway Designer for David-Andersen 1914–27. Teacher at the Royal School of Arts and Crafts in Oslo from 1912.

Harald Slott-Møller (1864–1937) Copenhagen, Denmark Painter. Designed silver for A. Michelsen for the Exhibition in Paris in 1900.

Peer Smed (1878–1943) New York, New York, USA Silversmith. Trained in Denmark. Opened own workshop in New York and worked for Tiffany & Co. in the thirties.

Oskar Sørensen (b. 1898) Oslo, Norway Silversmith, designed for J. Tostrup. Teacher at the Royal School of Arts and Crafts in Oslo 1922–65.

Edward Spencer (1872–1938) London, Great Britain Succeeded Nelson Dawson as chief designer in the Artificers' Guild in 1903. He combined materials such as shagreen, ivory, mother-of-pearl and gourds with silver.

William Spratling, New Orleans, Louisiana, USA, and Taxco, Mexico Architect. Settled in Mexico in 1925 to revive the art of silversmithing. Incorporated original Aztec motifs in his designs.

Harold Stabler (1872–1945) London, Great Britain Studied at Kendal Art School, Cumbria. In 1898 director of metalwork at nearby Keswick School of Industrial Art. From 1906 teacher and a year later head of the art department of Sir John Cass Technical Institute in London. Opened his own workshop and designed silver for Adie Bros and Wakely & Wheeler.

Theodore B. Starr, New York, New York, USA Active between c. 1885 and 1924. Taken over by Reed & Barton.

Johannes Steltman (1891–1961) The Hague, the Netherlands Studied at the Königliche Preussische Zeichenakademie in Hanau. Opened a jewelry shop in 1917 and started production of hollow-ware a few years later, when the silversmith Robert Mack joined the jewellers.

Sterling Silver Mfg. Co., Providence, Rhode Island, USA Manufacturers of sterling flat and hollow-ware in Art Nouveau style.

Carl Stock (b. 1876) Heilbronn, Frankfurt, Germany Sculptor and designer. Trained with P. Bruckmann & Söhne in Heilbronn and from 1908 with the architect Eberhardt in Frankfurt.

Arthur J. Stone (1847–1938) Sheffield, Great Britain and Gardner, Massachusetts, USA Trained and worked in Sheffield. Went to the USA in 1884. Founded his workshop in Gardner in 1901. His craftsmen all signed their work.

Robert E. Stone (b. 1903) London, Great Britain Studied at the Central School of Arts and Crafts in London. Founded his workshop in London c. 1930.

Storck & Sinsheimer, Hanau, Germany Founded in 1874, manufactured hollow-ware in Art Nouveau style.

Paula Strauss, Germany Designed silver for P. Bruckmann & Söhne, Heilbronn, in the twenties and thirties.

Max Strobl, Munich, Germany Silversmith in Munich c. 1910. Possibly identical with A. Strobl, who executed designs for Ed. Wollenweber c. 1900.

Otto Stüber, Hamburg, Germany Trained with Fritz von Miller in Munich and worked for some years in Scandinavia. Founded a workshop in Hamburg with Christoph Kay in 1910.

Alexander Sturm, Vienna, Austria Firm founded in 1882. Executed silver designs of Josef Hoffmann c. 1902 and c. 1930 and of Antoinette Krasnik in 1902.

Hermann Südfeld & Co, Vienna, Austria Founded in 1835. Manufacturer of silver in the decorative and geometric style c. 1900–10.

Louis Süe (1875–1968) Paris, France Painter and architect. In 1919 set up with André Mare, the Compagnie des Arts Français. Designed silver for Orfèvrerie Christofle.

Suomen Kultaseppät Oy, Turku, Finland First Finnish silver-manufacturing firm.

Millicent Sutherland Founded the Duchess of Sutherland's Cripples Guild. The metalwork, made by young handicapped people, was sold in The Shop Beautiful.

T

M. Takkinen, St Petersburg (Leningrad) Russia Silversmith active in Russia in the second half of the nineteenth century.

Raymond Templier (1891–1968) Paris, France Studied at the École des Beaux Arts 1909–12 and worked in the family firm, founded in 1848. Designed jewelry and small enamelled objects.

Maison Tétard, Paris, France Founded in 1880. Designers were Valéry Bizouard and Tardy. The first designs by Jean Tétard were shown in 1930.

André Fernand Thesmar (1843–1912), Neuilly, France Experimented with different enamelling techniques and rediscovered *plique à jour* enamel.

Louis Comfort Tiffany (1848–1933) New York, New York In 1879 he founded Louis C. Tiffany and Company Associated Artists, which closed in 1885. He then formed the independent Tiffany Glass Company; the name was later changed to Tiffany Studios. Here were executed his designs for leading glass lamps and 'Favrile' glasses. The silver for his Studios was generally made by Tiffany & Co., the firm founded by Tiffany's father.

A. Tillander, St Petersburg (Leningrad), Russia and Helsinki, Finland Founded in St Petersburg in 1860. Executed silver in Art Nouveau style. Fled to Helsinki after the revolution of 1917 and founded a new firm.

G. Tomasek, Munich, Germany Silversmith active in Munich in the thirties.

J. Tostrup, Oslo, Norway Firm founded in 1832. Famous for their *plique à jour* and *champlevé* enamels. Manufacturers of flat and hollow-ware.

Étienne Tourrette, Paris, France Trained with the enameller Louis Houillon. Included gold *paillons* in his enamel.

Ernst Treusch, Leipzig, Germany Silversmith active in Leipzig in the late twenties and thirties.

Nicolaus Trübner (1849–1910) Heidelberg, Germany Executed several mounts for Daum glasses at the turn of the century.

Wolfgang Tümpel (1903–78) Halle, Cologne, Bielefeld, Germany Silversmith and designer. Studied at the Bauhaus in Dessau and the Burg Giebichenstein in Halle. Opened a workshop in Halle in 1927, moved to Cologne in 1930 and settled in Bielefeld in 1934.

U

Unger Bros, Newark, New Jersey, USA Founded in 1872. Important manufacturer of silver in the Art Nouveau style, designed by Philomen Dickinson.

Alfons Ungerer (1884–1961) Dresden, Berlin, Pforzheim, Germany Trained with Theodor Heiden in Munich. Studied at the Kunstgewerbeschulen in Pforzheim and Dresden. Opened a workshop in Berlin in 1910, and from 1918 taught at the Kunstgewerbeschule in Pforzheim.

V

Fleetwood C. Varley, Chipping Campden, Great Britain Enameller, member of the Guild of Handicraft. Later supplied W.H. Haseler's in Birmingham and Connell's in London with pictorial enamels for cigarette boxes, etc.

Thyra Veith, Denmark Silver hollow-ware c. 1910, influenced by Thorvald Bindesbøll.

Henry van de Velde (1863–1957) Brussels, Belgium and Weimar, Germany Painter, architect, and designer. One of the most influential and versatile artists between 1895 and 1940. His silver designs were executed by A. Debain, Koch & Bergfeld, Theodor Müller, and his pupil Albert Feinauer.

Vereinigte Silberwaren-Fabriken, Düsseldorf, Germany Founded in 1810. Manufacturer of silver flat- and hollow-ware.

Vereinigte Werkstätten für Kunst im Handwerk, Munich, Germany Founded in 1898. Advertised in 1903 as 'Workshop for chiselling and enamelling. Flatware. Sole representative for Riemerschmid flatware'.

E.L. Viëtor, Darmstadt, Germany Executed small silver objects designed by members of the artists' colony in Darmstadt: Johann Vincent Cissarz, Paul Haustein and Hans Christiansen.

Elias Voet (1868–1940) Haarlem, the Netherlands His own designs are always exquisitely engraved. He also executed designs by H.P. Berlage and Harm Ellens.

Heinrich Vogeler (1872–1942) Worpswede, Germany and Karaganda, Russia Painter. Designed silver for M.H. Wilkens & Söhne, Bremen-Hemelingen. Travelled to Moscow in 1923 and settled in Karaganda in 1932.

W

Wilhelm Wagenfeld (b. 1900) Weimar, Berlin, Germany Trained with Koch & Bergfeld in Bremen. Studied first at the Staatliche Zeichenakademie in Hanau, then at the Bauhaus in Weimar. From 1925 to 1929 assistant and in 1929–30 director of the metal workshop of the Staatliche Hochschule für Baukunst und Handwerk in Weimar. Professor at the Kunsthochschule in Berlin and worked as designer of glass and ceramics.

Otto Wagner (1841–1918) Vienna, Austria Architect, professor at the Academy in Vienna. Two of his pupils were Josef Hoffmann and Josef Olbrich. Designed silver for J.C. Klinkosch in 1902.

Wakeley & Wheeler, London, Great Britain Founded in 1791. Craftsmen in the twenties and thirties were F.S. Beck, W.E. King and the chaser B.J. Colson. Executed designs by Leslie Auld, R.M.Y. Gleadowe, Reginald Hill, Kenneth Mosley, Cyril Shiner, Harold Stabler and James Warwick.

Cecil Walker, London, Great Britain Designed silver for Mappin & Webb in the late twenties and thirties.

John Walker, Sheffield, Great Britain Silversmith. Also designed modern silver for Elkington & Co. Ltd in Birmingham in the late twenties and thirties.

J.J. Warnaar (1868–1960) Voorschoten, Haarlem, the Netherlands Trained with J.M. Van Kempen & Zn, Voorschoten in 1880 and worked as a designer in the firm until 1922, then as an engraver in Haarlem.

Karl Emanuel Martin ('Kem') Weber (b. 1889) Berlin, Germany and Los Angeles, California, USA Studied with Bruno Paul at the Vereinigte Staatsschulen für freie und angewandte Kunst, Berlin-Charlottenburg. Went to the USA in 1914. Opened a design studio in Hollywood in 1927.

Svend Weihrauch (b. 1899) Aarhus, Denmark Silversmith who worked for Frantz Hingelberg from 1928.

Carl Weishaupt, Munich, Germany Workshop founded in 1802. Executed flatware designs by Richard Riemerschmid.

Clara Barck Welles (1868–1965) Chicago, Illinois, USA Designer and founder of the Kalo Shop in 1900.

Theodor Wende (1883–1968) Berlin, Darmstadt, Pforzheim, Germany Studied at the Königliche Preussische Zeichenakademie in Hanau and the Vereinigte Staatsschulen für freie und angewandte Kunst, Berlin-Charlottenburg. Member of the artists' colony in Darmstadt from 1913. Appointed professor at the Badische Kunstgewerbeschule in Pforzheim in 1921.

M.T. Wetzlar, Munich, Germany Silversmith, worked in Munich from c. 1905. Workshop closed in the Second World War.

Erich Wichman (1890–1929) Utrecht, the Netherlands Sculptor and painter. Modelled objects for C.J. Begeer in Utrecht 1917–19.

Wiener Werkstätte, Vienna, Austria The Vienna Workshop was founded in 1903 and closed in 1932. Designers of silver were Carl Otto Czeschka, Josef Hoffmann, Koloman Moser, Dagobert Peche, Otto Prutscher and Eduard Josef Wimmer-Wisgrill. Silversmiths with a maker's monogram were Josef Berger, Adolf Erbrich, Augustin Grötzbach, Josef Hossfeld, Josef Husnik, Josef Czech, Karl Kallert, Alfred Mayer, Anton Pribit, Eugen Pflaumer, Karl Ponocny, J. Sedlicky and Josef Wagner.

M.H. Wilkens & Söhne, Bremen-Hemelingen, Germany Founded in 1810. At the turn of the century the firm was, with P. Bruckmann & Söhne in Heilbronn, the leading silver manufacturers in Germany. Designers were Peter Behrens, Albin Müller and Heinrich Vogeler. H. Bulling, A. Donant, C. Krauss and Karl Müller designed for the firm between 1910 and 1940.

Ferdinand Richard Wilm (1880–1971) Ber-

lin, Germany Studied at the Königliche Preussische Zeichenakademie in Hanau. From 1911 he worked in the family firm, founded in 1767. He promoted the use of sterling silver for handmade silver. In 1932 he founded the Gesellschaft für Goldschmiedekunst. In the twenties designs by his friend Peter Behrens were executed in his workshop.

Josef Wilm (1880–1924) Berlin, Germany Trained with his father in Dorfen and with Fritz von Miller in Munich. From 1909 he was a teacher in the metal workshop of the Vereinigte Staatsschulen für freie und angewandte Kunst, Berlin-Charlottenburg.

Henry Wilson (1864–1934) London, Borough Green, Great Britain Architect. Set up a metal workshop c. 1895. Taught metalwork and enamelling at the Royal College of Art from 1901.

Eduard Josef Wimmer-Wisgrill (1882–1961) Vienna, Austria Designer. Studied at the Akademie für angewandte Kunst in Vienna and became a professor in 1910. Designed silver for the Wiener Werkstätte.

Ludvig Wittmann (1877–1961) Munich, Germany and Oslo, Norway Worked with Theodor Heiden in Munich until 1910 and from 1910 to 1928 was a designer for David-Andersen in Oslo.

Karl Wojtech, Stockholm, Sweden Silversmith who exhibited in Paris in 1925.

Wolfers Frères, Brussels, Belgium Founded in 1812. Philippe Wolfers (1858–1929) trained with his father in Brussels and the enameller Louis Houillon in Paris, and became head of the family firm in 1890. He was succeeded by his sons the sculptor and lacquerer Marcel (1886–1976) and Lucien.

E. Wollenweber, Munich, Germany Workshop which executed designs by A. Strobl c. 1900 and Adelbert Niemeyer c. 1912. Closed in the Second World War.

Erna Wolter (1885–1973) Magdeburg, Germany Sculptor, silversmith. Studied at the Kunstgewerbeschule in Magdeburg. Opened a metal workshop in 1907.

Alois Wörle, Munich, Germany Silversmith in Munich in the twenties and thirties.

Würbel & Czokally, Vienna, Austria Founded in 1860 or 1862. Executed silver designed by Josef Hoffmann in 1902.

Württembergische Metallwarenfabrik (WMF), Geislingen, Germany Founded in 1853. Specialized in silverplated flat- and hollow-ware. Started manufacturing silverware c. 1928, some of it designed by F.A. Breuhaus.

Z

Erna Zarges-Dürr (b. 1907) Stuttgart, Germany Trained with P. Bruckmann &

Söhne, Heilbronn and studied at the Kunstgewerbeschule in Pforzheim. Worked with Ernst Treusch in Leipzig and H.J. Wilm in Berlin. Set up her own workshop in 1933, first in Heilbronn, then from 1936 to 1939 in Stuttgart.

Herbert Zeitner (b. 1900) Berlin, Germany Studied at the Königliche Preussische Zeichenakademie in Hanau. Opened a workshop in Berlin in 1924 and worked as a teacher at the Vereinigte Staatsschulen für freie und angewandte Kunst in Berlin-Charlottenburg.

Julius Zimpel (1896–1925) Vienna, Austria Studied at the Kunstgewerbeschule in Vienna. Designed silver for the Wiener Werkstätte.

Frans Zwollo Jr (b. 1896) Oosterbeek, the Netherlands trained with his father and opened his own workshop in 1931.

Frans Zwollo Sr (1872–1945) Amsterdam, The Hague, the Netherlands and Hagen, Germany Trained with Bonebakker in Amsterdam and Delheid in Brussels. The first metalwork teacher at the Haarlemsche School voor Kunstnijverheid 1897–1907. Director of the Hagener Silberschmiede 1910–14. Settled in the Hague and taught metalwork at the Haagsche Akademie voor Beeldende Kunst until 1932.

SILVERMARKS 1880-1940

Silver standards are different in every country. Moreover, every country uses its own hallmarking system to guarantee these legally required standards. Familiarity with such national control marks simplifies the identification of a piece of silver.

Silver objects usually have a maker's mark, generally formed from the initials, sometimes in combination with a symbol. As both individual silversmiths and large silver firms employing several craftsmen use a maker's mark, this mark does not necessarily indicate the particular maker. Besides, retailers, and sometimes designers, also use marks.

Date letters are used in Finland, Great Britain, the Netherlands and Sweden. In some countries, imported silver has to be reassayed and is then given an import mark.

AUSTRIA

In Austria silver made between 1872 and

1922 has four legally guaranteed standards of fineness: 0.950, 0.900, 0.800 and 0.750, indicated by a head of Diana facing right in an outline which varies with the quality. A letter in the standard mark indicates the assay office: A for Vienna, C for Prague, P for Budapest.

.950   900

800

750

Import mark from 1872 to 1901:

from 1902 to 1922:

Silver made after 1922 is marked by a head of a bird (a hoopoe) for 0.935, 0.900 and 0.835 in different outlines:

.935   900   .835

and a toucan's head for 0.800:

800

Import mark after 1922:

Makers' marks usually consist of initials in varying outlines.

BELGIUM
In Belgium it has been optional since 1868 to have silver assayed by the state.

DENMARK
Since 1893 the silver standard in Denmark has been at least 0.826.

Every piece of silver has to be marked with the maker's name and the standard mark in figures. If the maker wants the assay office to verify the standard, the mark of the assay master and a control mark, three towers with the year underneath, are added to the maker's mark.

Control mark:

Assay Masters:

S. Groth 1863–1904

C.F. Heise 1904–1932

J. Sigsgaard 1933–1960

FINLAND
Finland has three legally guaranteed standards, 813H, 875H and 916H:

The state mark is a crown in a heart-shaped shield:

The import mark is a crown in an oval shield:

All objects have a city mark, a maker's mark and a date letter: A4–Z4 = 1882–1905; A5–Z5 = 1906–1929; A6–Z6 = 1930–1952.

FRANCE
France has two legally guaranteed standards:

0.950 indicated by a head of Minerva facing right in an octagonal shield:

0.800 indicated by a head of Minerva facing right in a barrel-shaped shield:

Small objects assayed in Paris have a boar's head facing left:

Small objects assayed in other offices have a crab in a five-lobed shield:

Makers' marks on silver are formed by initials with a symbol, always in a lozenge.

Date letters are not used.

GERMANY
Silver made since 1888 has a standard of at least 0.800.

The state mark comprises a crown and crescent:

The standard is struck in figures: 800, 900 and sometimes 925.

There is a maker's or retailer's mark.

Date letters are not used.

As no special import mark is used, foreign makers' marks are found with the crown and crescent.

GREAT BRITAIN
Since 1544 the legally guaranteed standard has been 0.925, indicated by a lion passant:

All British silver has a maker's mark, a mark of origin and a date letter which varies between assay offices.

London

Year		Year		Year	
1880	E	1901	f	1922	g
1881	F	1902	g	1923	h
1882	G	1903	h	1924	i
1883	H	1904	i	1925	k
1884	I	1905	k	1926	l
1885	K	1906	l	1927	m
1886	L	1907	m	1928	n
1887	M	1908	n	1929	o
1888	N	1909	o	1930	p
1889	O	1910	P	1931	q
1890	P	1911	q	1932	r
1891	Q	1912	r	1933	s
1892	R	1913	s	1934	t
1893	S	1914	t	1935	u
1894	T	1915	u	1936	A
1895	U	1916	a	1937	B
1896	a	1917	b	1938	C
1897	b	1918	c	1939	D
1898	c	1919	d	1940	E
1899	d	1920	e		
1900	e	1921	f		

Birmingham

Year		Year		Year	
1880	f	1895	v	1910	l
1881	g	1896	m	1911	m
1882	h	1897	x	1912	n
1883	i	1898	y	1913	o
1884	k	1899	z	1914	p
1885	l	1900	a	1915	q
1886	m	1901	b	1916	r
1887	n	1902	c	1917	s
1888	o	1903	d	1918	t
1889	p	1904	e	1919	u
1890	q	1905	f	1920	v
1891	r	1906	g	1921	w
1892	s	1907	h	1922	x
1893	t	1908	i	1923	y
1894	u	1909	k	1924	z

1925	A	1931	G	1937	N
1926	B	1932	H	1938	O
1927	C	1933	J	1939	P
1928	D	1934	K	1940	Q
1929	E	1935	L		
1930	F	1936	M		

Sheffield

1880	N	1901	i	1922	e
1881	O	1902	k	1923	f
1882	P	1903	l	1924	g
1883	Q	1904	m	1925	h
1884	R	1905	n	1926	i
1885	S	1906	o	1927	k
1886	T	1907	p	1928	l
1887	U	1908	q	1929	m
1888	V	1909	r	1930	n
1889	W	1910	s	1931	o
1890	X	1911	t	1932	p
1891	Y	1912	u	1933	q
1892	Z	1913	v	1934	r
1893	a	1914	w	1935	s
1894	b	1915	x	1936	t
1895	c	1916	y	1937	u
1896	d	1917	z	1938	v
1897	e	1918	a	1939	w
1898	f	1919	b	1940	X
1899	g	1920	c		
1900	h	1921	d		

Before 1904 foreign plate was struck with an F and since 1904 with the following import marks:

London (1904–06)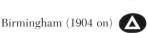

(1906 on)

Birmingham (1904 on)

Sheffield (1904–06)

(1906 on)

THE NETHERLANDS

Since 1814 the legally guaranteed standard for 0.934 has been indicated by a lion rampant:

and for 0.833 by a lion passant:

A head of Minerva facing left with a letter in the helmet indicates the particular assay office:

There is a date letter:

1885		1899		1913	D	1927	R
1886		1900		1914	E	1928	S
1887		1901		1915	F	1929	T
1888		1902		1916	G	1930	V
1889		1903		1917	H	1931	W
1890		1904		1918	I	1932	X
1891		1905		1919	J	1933	Y
1892		1906		1920	K	1934	Z
1893		1907		1921	L	1935	A
1894		1908		1922	M	1936	B
1895		1909		1923	N	1937	C
1896		1910	A	1924	O	1938	D
1897		1911	B	1925	P	1939	E
1898		1912	C	1926	Q	1940	F

and a maker's mark.

On small objects a Roman sword and a maker's mark are struck, but never a date letter:

Import mark used from 1893 to 1906:

and from 1906 onwards:

All makers' marks used between 1814 and 1980 (more than 13,000) are published.

NORWAY

There is no legal obligation to have silver assayed. However, officially assayed objects made since 1893 have a standard of at least 0.830.

The official guarantee mark is a crowned lion rampant:

All objects have a maker's mark and the silver quality in numerals ranging from 830S to 925S.

Date letters are not used.

RUSSIA

The legally guaranteed standards most frequently used in Russia were 84 zolotniks = 0.875, 88 zolotniks = 0.916 and 91 zolotniks = 0.974.

In 1896 the different city marks were replaced by a crowned woman's head as the indication of the standard.

From 1896 to 1908 the head faced left:

From 1908 to 1917 it faced right:

All objects have a maker's mark and the mark of an assay master.

SWEDEN

The legally guaranteed standard is at least 0.830.

All silver is marked with the state mark:

and a city mark.

There are a maker's mark and a date letter: M6–Z6 = 1890–1902, A7–Z7 = 1903–1926, A8–Z8 = 1927–1950.

UNITED STATES

There is no legally guaranteed standard or control, but makers' marks and a mark indicating the standard, usually Sterling = 0.925, are used.

MAKERS' MARKS

The marks reproduced here follow the conventionally accepted sequence: (1) letters in alphabetical order; left to right, top to bottom, (2) monograms, (3) human figures, (4) animals, (5) plants, (6) various, followed by (7) Russian names in Cyrillic lettering.

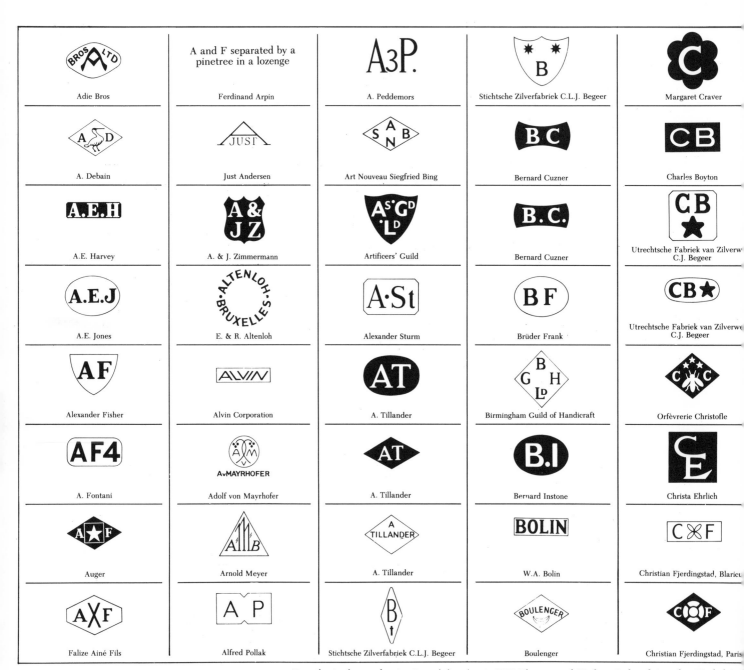

Adie Bros	Ferdinand Arpin	A. Peddemors	Stichtsche Zilverfabriek C.L.J. Begeer	Margaret Craver
A. Debain	Just Andersen	Art Nouveau Siegfried Bing	Bernard Cuzner	Charles Boyton
A.E. Harvey	A. & J. Zimmermann	Artificers' Guild	Bernard Cuzner	Utrechtsche Fabriek van Zilverw[...] C.J. Begeer
A.E. Jones	E. & R. Altenloh	Alexander Sturm	Brüder Frank	Utrechtsche Fabriek van Zilverw[...] C.J. Begeer
Alexander Fisher	Alvin Corporation	A. Tillander	Birmingham Guild of Handicraft	Orfèvrerie Christofle
A. Fontani	Adolf von Mayrhofer	A. Tillander	Bernard Instone	Christa Ehrlich
Auger	Arnold Meyer	A. Tillander	W.A. Bolin	Christian Fjerdingstad, Blaric[...]
Falize Aîné Fils	Alfred Pollak	Stichtsche Zilverfabriek C.L.J. Begeer	Boulenger	Christian Fjerdingstad, Paris

A and F separated by a pinetree in a lozenge

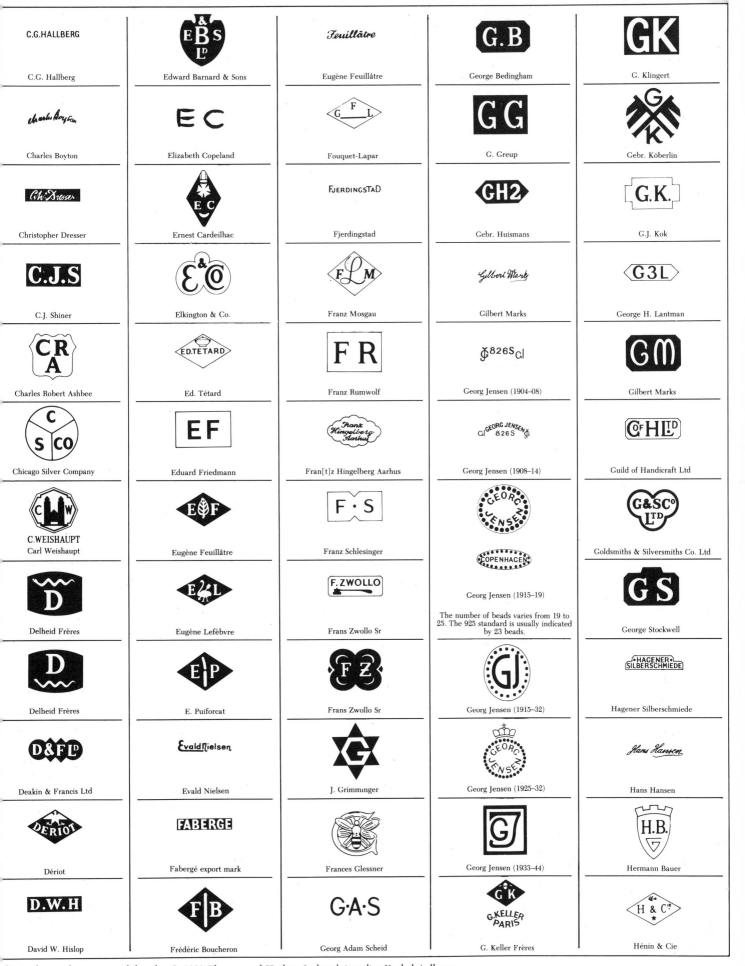

C.G. Hallberg	Edward Barnard & Sons	Eugène Feuillâtre	George Bedingham	G. Klingert
Charles Boyton	Elizabeth Copeland	Fouquet-Lapar	G. Greup	Gebr. Köberlin
Christopher Dresser	Ernest Cardeilhac	Fjerdingstad	Gebr. Huismans	G.J. Kok
C.J. Shiner	Elkington & Co.	Franz Mosgau	Gilbert Marks	George H. Lantman
Charles Robert Ashbee	Ed. Tétard	Franz Rumwolf	Georg Jensen (1904–08)	Gilbert Marks
Chicago Silver Company	Eduard Friedmann	Fran[t]z Hingelberg Aarhus	Georg Jensen (1908–14)	Guild of Handicraft Ltd
C.Weishaupt Carl Weishaupt	Eugène Feuillâtre	Franz Schlesinger	Georg Jensen (1915–19) The number of beads varies from 19 to 25. The 925 standard is usually indicated by 23 beads.	Goldsmiths & Silversmiths Co. Ltd
Delheid Frères	Eugène Lefèbvre	Frans Zwollo Sr		George Stockwell
Delheid Frères	E. Puiforcat	Frans Zwollo Sr	Georg Jensen (1915–32)	Hagener Silberschmiede
Deakin & Francis Ltd	Evald Nielsen	J. Grimminger	Georg Jensen (1925–32)	Hans Hansen
Dériot	Fabergé export mark	Frances Glessner	Georg Jensen (1933–44)	Hermann Bauer
David W. Hislop	Frédéric Boucheron	Georg Adam Scheid	G. Keller Frères	Hénin & Cie

HGM H.G. Murphy	**HZ 3** Fa. Hoeker & Zn	**J⤚K** Jan Kriege	STERLING HAND WROUGHT AT THE KALO SHOP Kalo Shop 1918–70	**L & Co** Liberty & Co.
HH Schoonh. Zilverfabr. H. Hooykaas	**I E M** Inger E. Møller	**JPC** John Paul Cooper	**KBS** Kaj Bojesens Sølvsmedie	**L G** Lucien Gaillard
H & H Hukin & Heath	**J** J.A. Jacobs	**JPC** Jacques & Pierre Cardeilhac	**KB** Van Kempen Begeer & Vos	**G L** G.L. Connell
H & H Hukin & Heath	Jarvie Robert Jarvie	**J·R** Johann Rothbauer	**KB** Van Kempen Begeer & Vos	LH Lucien Hirtz
H — L Lapparra	**J & C** Jones & Crompton	**JS₂** J. van Schouwen	**KK** Karl Karlsson	**LR** Louis Kuppenheim
HN Harald Nielsen	**JCK** J.C. Klinkosch	**J S** J. Schijfsma	K.Groß Karl Gross	LL & Cie with a royal crown in a lozenge L. Leroy
HS Hagener Silberschmiede	**J D** Jean Després	**JW & C⁰** James Walker & Co.	**K·M** Karl Motl	**L & L** Lagriffoul & Laval
·HS· Harold Stabler	JDesprés Jean Després	**J·W·D** J.W. Dixon	**L** Emil Lettré	**Lᵞ & C⁰** Liberty & Co. London (1898–190
H·S Henry Stradford	**J D** Jean Dunand	**JTH JHM** Heath & Middleton	Lebolt & Co.	**M** A. Michelsen
H·S Herman Südfeld	**J.E +** Jan Eisenloeffel	**JWH JTH** Hukin & Heath	LEBOLT HANDBEATEN Lebolt & Co.	**M** Marius Hammer
Henri Husson	**JEAN E. PUIFORCAT** Jean E. Puiforcat	HAND BEATEN AT KALO SHOPS PARKRIDGE STERLING Kalo Shop 1904–14	LALIQUE René Lalique	**M** C.M. Cohr
H W Henry Wilson	**JH3** Fa. Wed. Heuvelmans	HAND WROUGHT AT THE KALO SHOPS CHICAGO AND NEW YORK Kalo Shops 1914–18	**LB** L. Bosch	Martele 950-1000 FINE Gorham Martelé

Maison Eschwege	P. van Maaren	Siegfried Bing Art Nouveau	HAND MADE The Petterson Studios	William H. Haseler
Marshall Field & Co.	RAYMOND TEMPLIER Raymond Templier	Art Silver Shop	Zilverfabriek Voorschoten	WIENER WERK STÄTTE Wiener Werkstätte
Michelsen	Roberts & Belk	SHREVE SAN FRANCISCO STERLING Shreve, San Francisco	Vincent Carl Dubb	William Spratling
M. Takkinen.	Rissler & Carré	Arthur J. Stone	Gerritsen & Van Kempen	William T. Blackband
Mappin & Webb	Ravinet d'Enfert	Tétard Frères	Fa. J.M. van Kempen & Zn	W. Voet & Zn
Nelson Dawson	René Lalique	T. Hayes	Fa. J.M. van Kempen & Zn	Wakely & Wheeler
Napper & Davenport	RL with a royal crown in a lozenge R. Linzeler	Theodor Heinze	Fa. Wiskemann	Frans Zwollo Jr
Olier & Caron	Omar Ramsden & Alwyn Carr	TH·WENDE Theodor Wende	W.A.S. Benson	Amstelhoek
OD Oscar Dietrich	ROBERT ALTENLOH. Robert Altenloh	TH.MÜLLER DEPOSÉ Theodor Müller	Wilhelm Binder	August Haarstick
Peter Müller-Munk	Gebr. Reggers	TIFFANY&COMPY Tiffany & Co.	William Hutton & Sons	Albin Müller
Peer Smed	E. Schöpflich	Tiffany & Co.	Wolkenstein & Glückselig	As. Bonebakker & Zn
Société Parisienne d'Orfèvrerie	Fa. Stoffels & Co.	Tirbour	Walker & Hall	Hermann Bauer

H. Bernd	Forster & Graf	Dagobert Peche	W.P. Regenspurg	H.G. Murphy
Karl Johann Bauer	Franz Bolze	Otto Prutscher	Wiener Werkstätte	P. Bruckmann & Söhne
Peter Behrens	Henri Husson	Johan Rohde	E.J. Wimmer	Arts and Craftsshop Shreve Crump & Low
Emil Brackenhoff	Josef Hoffmann	Jacob Gross	E.J. Wimmer	Gebr. Friedländer
Christian Dell	Patriz Huber	Rossdeutscher & Reisig	Carl Otto Czeschka	Körner & Proll
Wilhelm Lucas von Cranach	J. Blinxma	Richard Riemerschmid	Vereinigte Silberwaren-Fabriken	Brüder Frank
Jan W. Eisenloeffel	Marga Jess	A. Ströbl	J.C. Klinkosch	Suomen Kultaseppä Oy
Erna Zarges-Dürr	Fa. L.W. van Kooten & Zn	J. Steltman	Gorham Mfg. Co.	Hugo Böhm
Eva Mascher-Elsässer	Lutz & Weiss	André Fernand Thesmar	Gebr. Deyhle	Alexander Sturm
Erna Wolter	Koloman Moser	Vereinigte Werkstätten	E.L. Viëtor	Wolfers Frères
Erik Magnussen	Harry Methorst	Fa. H.J. Wilm	Franz Bahner	Wolfers Frères
F. Hoogendijk	Josef Maria Olbrich	Philippe Wolfers	Baer & Deibele	Martin Mayer

Unauthorized reproduction is prohibited – © 1989 Thames and Hudson Ltd and Annelies Krekel-Aa

Georg Adam Scheid	Koch & Bergfeld	Hochschule für Handwerk und Baukunst	Simons Bro. & Co.	Fabergé Moscow
			К.ФАБЕРЖЕ	
Ed. Friedmann	M.H. Wilkens & Söhne	Robert Fischer	Fabergé St Petersburg	Ovchinnikov
			К.ФАБЕРЖЕ	БР.ГРАЧЕВЫ
Bremer Silberwarenfabrik	Kaj Bojesen	Henry van de Velde	Fabergé Moscow	Mikhail & Semen Grachev

BIBLIOGRAPHY

CATALOGUES

'Ambachts- en Nijverheidskunst' (International Exhibition, Brussels, 1910), Ned. Ver. voor Ambachts- en Nijverheidskunst, Amsterdam 1910.

'Amsterdamse School, Nederlandse Architectuur 1910–1930', Stedelijk Museum, Amsterdam, Amsterdam 1975.

'Art Nouveau in België', Europalia, Vereniging voor Tentoonstellingen, Brussels 1980/1981.

'Birmingham Gold and Silver 1773–1973', City Museum and Art Gallery, Birmingham, Birmingham 1973.

'Catalogue de la Section des Pays Bas à Paris 1925', Comité Gouvernemental, The Hague 1925.

'Christopher Dresser 1834–1904', Arkwright Arts Trust, Camden Arts Centre, London 1979.

'De Tijd Wisselt van Spoor, Nederland rond 1900' Singer Museum, Laren, Laren 1981.

Design in America, the Cranbrook Vision 1925–1950', Detroit Institute of Art/Metropolitan Museum of Art, Detroit/New York, N.Y. 1983/1984.

'Die Fouquet, 1860–1960, Schmuckkünstler in Paris', Museum Bellerive, Zurich 1984.

'Ein Document Deutscher Kunst – Darmstadt 1901–1976', Vols. 1–5, Eduard Röther Verlag, Darmstadt 1976.

'L'Art Hollandais à Paris 1925', The Hague 1925.

'Ori e Argenti dall'Ermitage', Villa Favorita, Lugano 1986.

'Peter Behrens in Nürnberg', Bayerisches Nationalmuseum, Munich 1980.

'Sieraad 1900–1972', De Zonnehof, Amersfoort Lemniscaat, Rotterdam 1972.

'Traum und Wirklichkeit, Wien 1870–1930', Museen der Stadt Wien, Vienna 1985.

Appuhn, H., 'Dänisches Silber des 20. Jahrhunderts' (introduction), Dänisches Museum für Kunst und Gewerbe, Dortmund 1972.

Bakels, A.C., 'Erich Wichman' (introduction), Stedelijk Museum Amsterdam, Amsterdam 1959/1960.

Barten, Dr Sigrid, 'Daum/Nancy, Glas des Art Nouveau und Art Deco' (introduction), Kunstgewerbemuseum und Museum Bellerive, Zurich 1986.

Bayer, Herbert, Gropius, Walter, and Gropius, Ise, 'Bauhaus 1919–1928', The Museum of Modern Art, New York, New York, N.Y. 1938/1975.

Begeer, Carel J.A., 'Holland, Sier- en Nijverheidskunst 1900–1926' (exhibition, Leipzig, 1927) Nederlandse Kamer van Koophandel voor Duitsland, The Hague 1927.

Begeer, S.A.C., and Molen, Dr J.R. ter, 'Mensen en Zilver, Bijna twee eeuwen werken voor Van Kempen en Begeer' (introduction), Van Kempen en Begeer, Zoetermeer 1975/1976.

Bott, Gerhard, 'Jugendstil, Kunsthandwerk um 1900' (collection catalogue), Eduard Röther Verlag, Darmstadt 1973.

Breuer, Robert, 'Deutschlands Raumkunst u. Kunstgewerbe a.d. Weltausstellung in Brüssel 1910' (introduction), Julius Hoffmann Verlag, Stuttgart 1910.

Brunhammer, Yvonne, 'Jean Dunand – Jean Goulden' (introduction), Galerie du Luxembourg, Paris 1973.

Burkom, F. van, and Mulder, H., 'Erich Wichman 1890–1929, tussen Idealisme en Rancune', Centraal Museum Utrecht, Utrecht 1983.

Cannon-Brooks, Peter, 'Omar Ramsden 1873–1939', City Museum and Art Gallery, Birmingham, Birmingham 1973.

Citroen, Karel A., 'Collectie Citroen', Gemeentemuseum Arnhem/Museum Boymans-van Beuningen, Arnhem/Rotterdam 1959.

Citroen, Karel A., 'Jugendstil, Sammlung Citroen', Museum Folkwang, Essen, Essen 1962.

Clark, Robert Judson, 'The Arts and Crafts Movement in America 1876–1916' (introduction), Princeton University, Princeton, N.J. 1972.

Daenens, L., and Krekel, A., 'Legaat N.F. Havermans 1909–1987, Zilver Nederland-België-Denemarken' (introduction), Museum voor Sierkunst, Ghent 1988.

Darling, Sharon S., 'Chicago Metalsmiths', Chicago Historical Society, Chicago 1977.

Dennis, Richard, and Jesse, John, 'Christopher Dresser 1834–1904', Richard Dennis/John Jesse/The Fine Arts Society, London 1972.

Felix, Zdenek (co-ordinator), 'Der Westdeutsche Impuls 1900–1914, Die Folkwang-Idee des Karl Ernst Osthaus', Karl Ernst Osthaus Museum, Hagen 1984.

Felix, Zdenek (co-ordinator), 'Der Westdeutsche Impuls 1900–1914, Margaretenhöhe, Das Schöne und die Ware', Museum Folkwang, Essen, Essen 1984.

Gysling-Billeter, Erika, 'Objekte des Jugendstils, aus dem Sammlung Kunstgewerbemuseums Zürich' (collection catalogue), Museum Bellerive/Bentelli Verlag, Zurich/Berne 1975.

Heilmann, Angela, 'Silber des Jugendstils', Stuck-Jugendstil-Verein, Munich 1979.

Heppe, Dr Karl Bernd, 'Der Goldschmied Conrad Anton Beumers 1837–1921' (introduction), Stadtmuseum der Landeshauptstadt Düsseldorf, Düsseldorf 1987.

Herzogenrath, W., and Kraus, S., 'Bauhaus Utopien, Arbeiten auf Papier' (introduction), Kölnischer Kunstverein/Edition Cantz, Cologne 1988.

Herzogenrath, W., Teuber, D., and Thiekotter, A., 'Der Westdeutsche Impuls 1900–1914, Deutsche Werkbund-Ausstellung Köln 1914', Kölnischer Kunstverein, Cologne 1984.

Hillier, Bevis, 'The World of Art Deco', Studio Vista, The Minneapolis Institute of Arts, Minneapolis, Minn. 1971.

Hughes, George Ravensworth, 'The Worshipful Company of Goldsmiths as Patrons of their Craft 1919–1953', The Worshipful Company of Goldsmiths, London 1965.

Huisken, Jacobine E., and Lammertse, Friso, 'Koninklijke Geschenken, traditie en vernieuwing rond de eeuwwisseling', Stichting Koninklijk Paleis te Amsterdam, Amsterdam 1988.

Jansen, Beatrice, 'Nederlands Zilver 1815–1960' (introduction), Haags Gemeentemuseum, The Hague 1960/1961.

Joppien, Rüdiger, 'Christopher Dresser, Ein Viktorianischer Designer 1834–1904' (introduction), Kunstgewerbemuseum der Stadt Köln, Cologne, 1981

Kras, Reyer, 'Industry & Design in the Netherlands 1850–1950', Stedelijk Museum, Amsterdam, Amsterdam 1985.

Krekel, A., and Blum, H., 'Modernes Niederländisches Silber 1895–1935', Kreismuseum Zons, West Germany 1982.

Krekel-Aalberse, A., and others, 'Klokken, Zilver en Sieraden uit de Nederlandse Art Nouveau en Art Deco' (introduction), Nederlands Goud- Zilver- en Klokkenmuseum, Utrecht 1976.

Krimmel, Bernd, 'Joseph M. Olbrich, 1867–1908' (Exhibition Mathildenhöhe Darmstadt), Darmstadt 1983.

Lightbown, R.W., 'Catalogue of Scandinavian and Baltic Silver' (collection catalogue), Victoria and Albert Museum, London 1975.

Löhr, Alfred, 'Bremer Silber, Von den Anfängen bis zum Jugendstil', Bremer Landesmuseum (Focke Museum), 1981/1982.

McCarthy, Fiona, and Nuttgens, Patrick, 'Eye for Industry' (introduction to 'The Renaissance in British Design'), Royal Society of Arts/Lund Humphries, London 1986.

McFadden, David Revere, 'Scandinavian Modern Design 1880–1980', Harry N. Abrams, Inc./Cooper-Hewitt Museum, New York, N.Y. 1983.

Molen, Dr J.R. ter, 'Frans Zwollo Sr en zijn Tijd' (introduction), Museum

Boymans-van Beuningen, Rotterdam 1982.

Nerdinger, Winifried, 'Richard Riemerschmid, Vom Jugendstil zum Werkbund, Werke und Dokumente' (introduction), Prestel Verlag, Munich 1982/1983.

Neuwirth, Waltraud, 'Joseph Hoffmann, Bestecke für die Wiener Werkstätte', privately published by Dr Waltraud Neuwirth, Vienna 1982.

Neuwirth, Waltraud, 'Wiener Werkstätte; Avantgarde, Art Deco, Industrial Design', privately published by Dr Waltraud Neuwirth, Vienna 1984.

Opstad, Lauritz, 'Norwegen, Bildweberei und Email von der Jahrhundertwende bis zur Gegenwart', Deutsch-Norwegische Gesellschaft, Münster 1982.

Petrasch, E., and Franzke, I., 'Jugendstil, eine Auswahl aus den Schausammlungen' (collection catalogue), Badisches Landesmuseum, Karlsruhe, Karlsruhe 1978.

Sänger, Reinhard, 'Bestecke des Jugendstils' (introduction), Deutsches Klingenmuseum/ Rheinland-Verlag, Solingen 1979.

Sänger, Reinhard, and Tietzel-Hellerforth, B., 'Jugendstil', Europalia, Vereniging voor Tentoonstellingen, Brussels 1977.

Sänger, Reinhard, 'Massenfabrikation in Silber' (exhibition 'Der Westdeutsche Impuls 1900–1914'), Museum Folkwang, Essen, Essen 1984.

Schmidt, Karl Eugen, 'XXVII Ausstellung der Vereinigung bildender Künstler Österreichs–Secession', Vereinigung bildender Künstler Österreichs, Vienna 1906.

Schümann, Carl-Wolfgang, 'Wilhelm Wagenfeld, Du Bauhaus à l'Industrie (French ed.). Kunstgewerbemuseum der Stadt Köln, Cologne 1973/1975.

Schwandt, Jörg, 'WMF, Glas. Keramik. Metall, 1925–1950', Kunstgewerbemuseum, Berlin, Berlin 1980.

Sekler, Eduard, 'Josef Hoffmann als Mensch, Künstler und Lehrer', Museum Bellerive, Zurich 1983.

Singelenberg, P., Bock, M., and Broos, K., 'H.P. Berlage, Bouwmeester 1856–1934', Haags Gemeentemuseum, The Hague 1975.

Spielmann, H., Barten, S., Bürcklin, H., and Heusinger, J. 'Die Jugendstil-Sammlung' (collection catalogue), Museum für Kunst und Gewerbe Hamburg, Hamburg 1979.

Spielmann, Heinz, 'Wolfgang Tümpel und seine Schüler, Goldschmiedekunst und Design', Museum für Kunst und Gewerbe Hamburg, Hamburg 1978.

Stöver, U., and Bredel, F., 'Die Ehrenringträger der Gesellschaft für Goldschmiedekunst', Deutsches Goldschmiedehaus Hanau, Hanau 1966.

Turner, Mark, 'The Silver Studio Collection, A London Design Studio 1880–1963' (introduction), Lund Humphries, London 1980.

Vergo, Peter, 'Vienna 1900, Vienna, Scotland and the European Avantgarde', National Museum of Antiquities of Scotland, Edinburgh 1983.

Wichmann, Siegfried, 'Jugendstil Floral Functional, in Deutschland und Österreich . . .', Bayerisches Nationalmuseum, Munich/Schuler Verlag, Herrsching 1984.

Wingler, H.M., Hahn, P., and Wolsdorff, C., 'Bauhaus Archiv/ Museum, Sammlungs-Katalog' (collection catalogue), Bauhaus Archiv/Mann, Berlin 1981.

BOOKS

Besteck-Buch, Besteckmarken-Verzeichnis, Stuttgart 1952 and 1967 edns.

Bulletin of the Decorative Arts Society 1890–1940, Brighton, Sussex 1975

Dictionnaire des Poinçons d'Orfèvrerie, Paris 1970.

Diebeners Geschäftshandbuch für das Edelmetall- und Uhrengewerbe, Leipzig 1922.

Jaarboek VANK, Rotterdam 1930.

Navnestempler Registreret hos Statens Kontrol med Aedle Metaller, Copenhagen 1976.

Verslag van de Nederlandsche Afdeeling (International Exhibition Turin 1902), The Hague 1902.

Anon. 125 Jahre Koch & Bergfeld, Bremen [1954].

Ahlers-Hestermann, Friedrich, Stilwende, Aufbruch der Jugend um 1900, Berlin 1956.

Amaya, Mario, Art Nouveau, London 1966/1985.

Andrén, Erik, Swedish Silver, New York, N.Y. 1950.

Ashbee, C.R., Modern English Silverwork (with essays by Alan Crawford and Shirley Bury), London 1909/1985.

Aslin, Elizabeth, The Aesthetic Movement, New York, N.Y. 1969.

Bainbridge, Henry Charles, Peter Carl Fabergé, London 1966.

Becker, Vivienne, Art Nouveau Jewelry, London 1985.

Begeer, Carel J.A., and Brinkgreve M.J., Een Eeuw Edelsmeedkunst 1835–1935. The Hague 1935.

Begeer, Carel J.A., Inleiding tot de Geschiedenis der Nederlandsche Edelsmeedkunst, 1919.

Blaauwen, A.L. den, and others, Art Nouveau, Jugendstil, Nieuwe Kunst, Amsterdam 1972.

Bonneville, Françoise de, Jean Puiforcat, Paris 1986.

Bouilhet, Henri, 150 Ans d'Orfèvrerie, Christofle, Silversmith since 1830, Paris 1981.

Bouilhet, Tony, L'orfèvrerie française au 20ème siècle, Paris 1941.

Bouillon, Jean-Paul, Journal de l'Art Nouveau 1870–1914, Geneva 1985.

Bradbury, Frederick, Bradbury's Book of Hallmarks, Sheffield 1927/1985.

Bradley, Ian, William Morris and his world, London 1978.

Brunhammer, Yvonne, Cinquantenaire de l'Exposition de 1925, Paris 1976/ 1977.

Buddensieg, T., and Rogge, H., Industriekultur, Peter Behrens und die AEG, 1907–1914, Berlin 1978.

Bury, Shirley, New light on the Liberty metalwork venture (Bulletin of the Decorative Arts Soc.), Brighton 1975.

Chalmers Johnson, Diana, American Art Nouveau, New York, N.Y. 1979.

Crisp Jones, A.K., The Silversmiths of Birmingham and their Marks 1750–1980, London 1981.

Culme, John, The Directory of Gold- and Silversmiths (Vol. I, II, The Biographies, The Marks), Woodbridge, Suffolk 1987.

Darling, Sharon S., Chicago Metalsmiths, Chicago 1977.

Diebener, Wilhelm (publisher), Adress- und Handbuch für das deutsche Goldschmiedegewerbe, Leipzig 1903.

Dresser, Christopher, Principles of Decorative Design, London 1973.

Duncan, Alistair, American Art Deco, London 1986.

Ellens, H., De Disch, Rotterdam 1926.

Farmer, J. David, 'Metalwork and Bookbinding' in Design in America, The Cranbrook Vision 1925/50, New York, N.Y. 1983/1984.

Fenz, Werner, Koloman Moser, Salzburg/Vienna 1984.

Gans, Dr L., Nieuwe Kunst, Utrecht 1966.

Garner, Philippe (ed.), Phaidon Encyclopedia of Decorative Arts 1890–1940, Oxford 1978/1982.

Gropius, Walter, The Theory and Organization of the Bauhaus, Weimar 1923.

Hammes, Ing. J., Goud · Zilver · Edelstenen, Amsterdam 1944.

Hillier, Bevis, Art Deco of the 20s and 30s, London 1968/1973.

Hiort, Esbjorn, Modern Danish Silver, Copenhagen 1954.

Honour, Hugh, Goldsmiths and Silversmiths, London/New York, N.Y. 1971.

Howarth, Thomas, Charles Rennie Mackintosh and the Modern Movement, London 1972.

Hughes, Graham, Modern Silver, London 1967.

Jones, Owen, The Grammar of Ornament, London 1856/1986.

Koch, Hofrat Dr Alex., Schmuck und Edelmetall-Arbeiten, Hanover (originally Darmstadt) 1906/1985.

Larner, Gerald and Celia, The Glasgow Style, Edinburgh 1979.

Leidelmeijer, Frans, and Cingel, Daan van der, Art Nouveau en Art Deco in Nederland, Amsterdam 1983.

Lenning, Henry F., The Art Nouveau, The Hague 1951.

Lesieutre, Alain, The Spirit and Splendour of Art Deco, London/New York, N.Y. 1974.

Madsen, Stephan Tschudi, Art Nouveau, Amsterdam (Dutch edn.) 1967.

Madsen, Stephan Tschudi, Sources of Art Nouveau, New York, N.Y. 1956/ 1975.

McClinton, Katharine Morrison, Collecting American 19th Century Silver, New York, N.Y. 1968.

Møller, Jørgen E.R., Georg Jensen, The Danish Silversmith, Copenhagen 1985.

Naylor, Gillian, The Arts and Crafts Movement, London 1971.

Naylor, Gillian, The Bauhaus

Reassessed, Sources and Design Theory, London 1985.

Neumann, Eckhard (publisher), Bauhaus und Bauhäusler, Erinnerungen und Bekenntnisse, Cologne 1985.

Neuwirth, Waltraud, Wiener Silberschmiede und ihre Punzen, Vienna 1976.

Neuwirth, Waltraud, Wiener Werkstätte, Die Schutzmarken, Vienna 1985.

Olbrich, Josef M., Ideen von Olbrich, Leipzig [1904].

Paulson, Paul L., Guide to Russian Silver Hallmarks, Foxhall 1976.

Pevsner, Nikolaus, Pioneers of Modern Design: From William Morris to Walter Gropius, Harmondsworth (Middlesex) 1936/1949/1974.

Powell, Nicholas, The Sacred Spring, The Arts in Vienna 1898–1918, London 1974.

Rainwater, Dorothy T., Encyclopedia of American Silver Manufacturers, New York, N.Y. 1975.

Rainwater, Dorothy T., Sterling Silver Holloware, Princeton, N.J. 1973.

Ramakers, Renny, Tussen Kunstnijverheid en Industriele Vormgeving, de N.B.K.I., Utrecht 1985.

Rheims, Maurice, L'Objet, 1900, Paris 1964.

Schmuzler, Robert, Art Nouveau, New York (originally Stuttgart) 1962.

Schweiger, Werner J., Wiener Werkstätte, Kunst und Handwerk 1903–1932, Vienna 1982.

Sluys, Corn. van der, Binnenhuiskunst, Amsterdam 1916.

Smith, John Boulton, The Golden Age of Finnish Art, Art Nouveau and the National Spirit, Helsinki 1975/1976.

Solodkov, Alexander von, Russian Gold- and Silverwork, New York, N.Y. 1981.

Tardy (publisher), Poinçons d'Argent (les poinçons de garantie internationaux pour l'argent), Paris 1971.

Tilbrook, A.J., The Designs of Archibald Knox for Liberty & Co., London 1976.

Velde, Henry van de, Geschichte meines Lebens, Munich 1962.

Vever, Henri, La Bijouterie française au XIXe siècle (Vol. III), Paris 1908.

Voet, Elias, Jr (re-edited by P.W. Voet), Nederlandse Goud- en Zilvermerken, The Hague 1963.

Waddell, Roberta, The Art Nouveau Style – in Jewelry, Metalwork . . .', New York, N.Y. 1977

Weisberg, Gabriel P., Art Nouveau Bing: Paris Style 1900, New York, N.Y. 1986.

Wilm, Frau, Ferdinand Richard Wilm, 11 Oktober 1930, Berlin 1930.

Wolfers, M., Philippe Wolfers, précurseur de l'art nouveau, Brussels 1965.

Zimmermann-Degen, Margret, Hans Christiansen, Leben und Werk eines Jugendstilkünstlers, Königstein im Taunus 1985.

INDEX